THE PENTAGON WATCHERS

The PENTAGON WATCHERS

Students Report on the National Security State

Edited by

LEONARD S. RODBERG

and

DEREK SHEARER

ANCHOR BOOKS

Doubleday & Company, Inc.
Garden City, New York

THE PENTAGON WATCHERS was published simultaneously in a hardcover edition by Doubleday & Company, Inc.

Printed in the United States of America

NOTES ON CONTRIBUTORS

ROBERT BOROSAGE is currently studying law at Yale.

MARCUS RASKIN is codirector of the Institute for Policy Studies, editor (with Bernard Fall) of *The Vietnam Reader,* and author of the forthcoming *Being and Doing.*

DEREK SHEARER, a graduate of Yale, was guest lecturer (spring 1970) at the University of Maryland and coordinated the summer investigation of the Pentagon; he is presently a free-lance journalist.

WILLIAM STIVERS graduated from Reed College in political science in June 1970 and plans to do graduate work in political science.

TOM KLEIN is a student at Columbia University.

DAVID SIMS is a graduate student in city planning at Harvard.

MARY McCARTHY graduated in June 1970 from Radcliffe and plans to do graduate study in law or journalism.

NANCY LIPTON is a graduate student in government at Harvard.

LEONARD RODBERG, former chief of science, policy research of the Arms Control and Disarmament Agency, is a fellow at the Institute for Policy Studies.

MARK KRAMER is a graduate student in physics at the University of Michigan.

SAM BAKER is a graduate student in economics at Harvard.

KERRY GRUSON, a graduate of Radcliffe, is a reporter on the *Raleigh News & Observer* (N.C.).

CONTENTS

III. ARMS AND INDUSTRY

APPENDIX

INTRODUCTION

THE papers in this book are based primarily on the research conducted by a group of students in the summer of 1969, under the sponsorship of the Institute for Policy Studies, in Washington, D.C. Other contributors, such as Marcus Raskin and Leonard Rodberg, served as advisers to the students in the course of their investigations. The idea for a student investigation of the national security establishment, especially the Pentagon, was suggested by the experience of the law students called "Nader's Raiders," who spent a summer looking closely at the Federal Trade Commission. The same summer that our investigation took place, Ralph Nader expanded his operation to encompass over a hundred students investigating a number of other federal agencies. The national security establishment itself has often used the summer study technique to examine a new weapons system or defense doctrine.

Early in the program, we recognized the dearth of critical research on the institutions that encompass the military-industrial complex. Academic scholars in the fields of political science and economics have tended to ignore the problems that America's huge defense establishment has created for the country. We found that a few investigative journalists and a handful of young researchers had done the pioneering work that was to serve as a basis for our project.

Our desire was not to discover individual instances of wrongdoing, but rather to attempt to understand the policies by which the defense establishment is operated. It is not difficult to see that America has become the new imperial power. Every day, the headlines about Southeast Asia drive the message home. What we wanted to elucidate was the workings of that imperial system.

Our method was to enter the world of the defense establishment by studying its own artifacts. The student investigators read military and defense-industry journals and studied the reports of defense research organizations. Interviews were conducted with officials in the Pentagon, the State Department, and the Washington offices of large defense contractors. No use was made of classified material. The sources consulted are open to newsmen and the public; however, they are little used other than by military contractors and military-oriented professional organizations.

For the safety of the country, the defense establishment must be opened to public scrutiny. Our study group was unable to find effective voices anywhere within the defense establishment urging a slowdown in the development of new, more-sophisticated weapons. The story of what happens to the few officials who try to rock the boat, as in the case of Air Force cost expert Ernest Fitzgerald, who was fired for doing his job too well, is now widely known. Similarly, there did not seem to be any individuals in an effective position to advocate alternative ways of achieving the goal of "national security," except through increased military spending. The defense establishment seems to have been designed to encourage only the growth and autonomy of the military machine.

It is our firm belief, after many conversations within the Pentagon and elsewhere in Washington, that the security classification system is being used not to prevent information from being revealed to potential enemies, but to insure control by the executive branch over national security policy and to prevent its revelation to the American people. Congress, supposedly consisting of the representatives of the people, has found, as it has tried to reassert some measure of control over national security policy, that the defense establishment is loath to make public any information that may cast doubt on the wisdom of defense programs and policies. (Witness the difficulty that Senator Symington's subcommittee on foreign commitments has had in obtaining release of its own hearings on Laos. The State Department censored the testimony so badly that Symington said it would be misleading to release the butchered version to the public.)

We make no claims that the summer project produced the definitive study on the workings and rationale of the defense establishment. It is, we hope, a beginning contribution. The work will be carried on by groups around the country, a number of which are listed in the appendix.

Appreciation is owed to the Institute for Policy Studies and its codirectors, Richard Barnet and Marcus Raskin, who agreed to sponsor the summer project; to the Businessmen's Educational Fund, for their financial support; to Mike Klare, of the North American Congress on Latin America, and Seymour Hersh, the well-known investigative reporter, both of whom advised the students; and to Judith Coburn, who helped recruit members of the project. For the final form and content of the book, we take responsibility.

LEONARD S. RODBERG
DEREK SHEARER

Washington, D.C.
March 9, 1970

I. STATE POWER

This volume is not intended as another attack on the military-industrial complex. America is not simply a victim of an insidious conspiracy emanating out of a single power bloc. It appears more accurate to say that America is becoming a National Security State, whose dominant ideology and institutions are focused upon the military establishment and its military solutions to national policy problems. The issues that have been in the headlines—the cost overruns on weapons systems, the extent of the chemical and biological arsenal, the worthless ABM system, the atrocities at My Lai—are not accidents or exceptions. They are part of the operation of a total system that was consciously organized during World War II, framed into law in the postwar era by the Truman administration, strengthened by the Eisenhower administration, and brought under centralized control during the Kennedy and Johnson periods.

The papers in this section describe the erosion, in the two decades of Cold War, of what citizens of a patriotic breed used to call the "American System." The checks and balances set out in the Constitution have been swept aside by the growth of a vast national security establishment and the increasing power of its associated large corporations. It should be clear that the issue is not how to control the military, but how to regain control of a state structure that has become a self-propelling juggernaut.

Robert Borosage describes how, in the immediate postwar era, all elements of American society were fitted into the National Security State: how the power of the executive increased as it assumed legislative functions in the defense sector; how Congressional scrutiny of the defense budget became perfunctory and approving; and how the Pentagon expanded its power and influence. Marcus Raskin's study, by an individual who served on the staff of the National Security Council in the early sixties, describes the transition of power from Eisenhower to Kennedy, and the consequences for the nation of the outlook that McNamara and others brought toward defense policy.

Institutional structures like the Pentagon, once enlarged, even for legitimate purposes, gain a momentum of their own. Derek Shearer's description of Pentagon propaganda shows how the Defense Department attempts to brainwash the public into accepting its actions both abroad and at home. Civilian policy makers have failed to curb such activities, because they support the Pentagon's view of the world and the role it has set for the military.

It is perhaps ironic that America, whose leaders claim that they have only responded to the world-wide challenge of totalitarian regimes in Russia and China, should increasingly resemble the repressive state that George Orwell depicted in *1984.* As in that work, the life of the state has become an end in itself, and as in Fascist Italy or Nazi Germany, the work of the state becomes the making of war. Such a direction is built into the structure of the growing National Security State.

THE MAKING OF THE NATIONAL SECURITY STATE

by Robert Borosage

FROM 1945 to 1950, the rationalization of the American postwar state took place. It is to those years that we must turn to understand the development of the ideological consensus and institutional arrangements that formed the basis for the modern American imperium. The governing mechanisms established after the Second World War constituted the National Security State, an independent system within the polity, which would control national security policies.

American postwar foreign and military policies were based upon an imperial conviction: that the United States should define the postwar order. This conviction, shared by virtually all the civilian leaders of the state, was derived from three primary sources.

First, as William Appleman Williams has demonstrated, a basic tenet of American foreign policy in this century has been the abiding belief that "America's domestic well-being depends upon sustained, ever-increasing economic expansion." This belief was particularly prevalent during and after the Second World War.

A major fear of the wartime leaders of the United States was the possibility of a postwar depression. It was clear that the hodgepodge of New Deal programs had failed to end the prewar depression, and that full production returned only with wartime mobilization. A return to peacetime conditions seemed to threaten a return to stagnation.

Both administration leaders and economists viewed the economic problem as one of excessive supply over demand. Additionally, it was clear that the United States was becoming increasingly dependent upon raw materials acquired abroad. Thus, the development of stable foreign markets for American goods, and stable foreign sources of raw materials, was viewed as essential for postwar prosperity.

This view was repeatedly expressed during the war. The best example of the administration's position was the famous statement made by Dean Acheson, then Assistant Secretary of State, before the Select Committee on Postwar Economic Policy and Planning, in 1944:

> It seems clear that we are in for a very bad time, so far as the economic and social position of the country is concerned. We cannot go through another ten years like the ten years at the end of the twenties and the beginning of the thirties without having the most far-reaching cconsequences upon our economic and social system. . . .
>
> . . . [W]e may say it is a problem of markets. . . . We have got to see that what the country produces is used and is sold under financial arrangements which make production possible. . . . You must look to foreign markets.
>
> The first theory that I want to bring out is that we need these markets for the output of the United States. If I am wrong about that, then all the argument falls by the wayside, but my contention is that we cannot have full employment and prosperity in the United States without foreign markets.

To insure domestic prosperity by establishing stable open markets abroad, it was necessary to shape the postwar order. Gabriel Kolko has detailed the maneuvers of the American leadership during the war to insure the country's postwar economic position. By 1945, the Truman administration assumed that, in Truman's words, the "United States would then take the lead in running the world in the way that the world ought to be run."

The second major source for the American imperial commitment was what Arthur Schlesinger, Jr., calls America's "liberal evangelism," that strong element of moral rectitude that has always accompanied American expansion. Each postwar President announced that it was the responsibility of the United States to preserve and extend freedom in the world. Equation of American expansion with the extension of freedom, belief in a *mission civilatrice,* added thrust to the American imperial conviction. That American leaders supported harsh dictatorships while serving the cause of "freedom" does not indicate that such claims were empty rhetoric. "The Anglo-Saxon," wrote Harold Nicolson, "is gifted with a limitless capacity for excluding his own practical requirements from the application of his idealistic theories." For American statesmen, the belief that what was beneficial for the United States was good for freedom, helped, in the long run, to sustain the often bloody course of postwar expansion.

These two themes, of economic expansion and missionary idealism, have imparted a forward thrust to American foreign policy throughout this century. The third source of postwar policies made the crucial difference; that was the emergence of the United States as the most powerful country in the world. As Ronald Steel has written,

> As a result of her participation in the war, America became not only a great world power, but the world power. Her fleets roamed all the seas, her military bases extended around the earth's periphery, her soldiers stood guard from Berlin to Okinawa, and her alliances spanned the earth.

"We were witnessing," wrote President Truman, "the transformation of the United States into a nation of unprecedented power."

The American victory in World War II, which had entailed the marshaling and deployment of massive force against enemies on three continents, engendered abiding belief in the efficacy of military power. As Truman addressed the Congress in his 1947 State of the Union message, "The power which the United States demonstrated during the war is the fact that underlies every phase of our relations with other countries." Emboldened by possession of the atomic bomb, the Truman administration considered military power to hold the key to enforcement of America's conception of the postwar world order. The United States was prepared, Truman announced in 1945, "to support a lasting peace, by force if necessary."

Belief in the necessity of power as a means to achieve ends led to the requirement of maintaining a clear superiority in military force. This mixing of means and ends characterized the postwar leadership of the United States.

In opposition to the American conception of a postwar world order, stood two forces: the Soviet Union, and the Communist and non-Communist Left. With Britain exhausted, France humiliated, and Germany shattered, the Soviet Union was the only European country to emerge from the war independent of American dominance. Although it acquiesced in Asia, the Soviet Union was unwilling to adhere to American dictates in Eastern Europe. There, as had been arranged with Churchill, the U.S.S.R. was consolidating a buffer zone of sympathetic governments. This action directly violated the American vision of the postwar European system. To an American leadership convinced of its right to define that order, the consolidation of a Soviet sphere of influence in Eastern Europe was most unwelcome.

The second opponent to the American postwar order was the spread of nationalist revolution throughout the world. In many countries, the Communist and non-Communist Left, inspired by the interruption of colonial or rightest rule, and armed and organized in wartime resistance activities, led movements against the returning colonial or conservative regimes. The civilian leaders of the Truman administration were opposed to the social and economic goals of the Left, as well as dismayed by the stridency of their claims. The American leadership equated peace with order, and order with stable capitalist regimes. The Left thus threatened the American guidelines for the postwar world in Europe, in the Middle East, and in Asia.

To rouse the American people to the sustained effort necessary to support American expansion, the leadership of the Truman administration propagated an anticommunist ideology. The American imperial thrust was presented to the populace as a defensive reaction to unjustified aggression. The official ideology was clear and logical. The Soviet Union, like Nazi Germany, was an expansionist, totalitarian state, bent on world hegemony. It was committing open aggression in Eastern Europe, and subversive aggression throughout the world through subservient Communist parties. To protect American interests and security, the United States, as the beleaguered champion of democratic government, must oppose the forces of aggression not only in Europe, but throughout the world. Our opponent was not merely the Soviet Union, but communism itself. If we successfully opposed the forward thrusts of communism, eventually the Soviet regime would moderate its designs, or be overthrown from within.

The ideology rested upon numerous myths. First was the identification of the Soviet regime with Nazi Germany. Although Stalin had demonstrated his barbarity in the prewar purges, the U.S.S.R. was not another Germany. It had been an underdeveloped country going through the excesses of modernization. After the war, it was far weaker than Hitler's Germany, both absolutely and in relation to American prowess. Russia had had twenty million men killed during World War II. Its population over eighteen had been decimated: almost 40 per cent of its adult males were dead. Moreover, from the end of the war until the proclamation of the Truman Doctrine, the Soviet Union had demobilized its armies, reducing them from eleven and one half million to less than three million men. The Soviet regime was far more restrained than Nazi Germany. Its expansionist designs extended only to the establishment of a defensive perimeter of sympathetic states; everywhere else, it acceded to American expansion.

The second myth was that the Kremlin masterminded the forces of revolution throughout the world. In addition to the non-Communist Left, many Communist parties were far more nationalist than Communist. In China, in Greece, and in Korea, Communist parties worked for national goals in the face of Soviet opposition or, at best, Soviet neutrality.

The third myth was the belief that military pressure would weaken the Soviet grasp on Eastern Europe and undermine the regime from within. It was only after the formation of NATO that the Soviet Union remobilized (even then it had difficulties because of manpower shortages). It was only after the enunciation of the Truman Doctrine that non-Communists were ejected from Eastern European governments, and Stalinization took place.

Moreover, the identification of the Soviet Union with communism and of communism with revolution placed the United States against the forces of revolution and change throughout the world. America became the *gendarmerie* of stability, a conservative imperial power consolidating and protecting a conservative world order.

The ideological statement of American policy was best summarized by the Truman Doctrine, promulgated in March 1947. Calling for Congressional approval of military aid to Greece and Turkey, of universal military training, and of a resumption of the draft, Truman elaborated the official world view:

> One way of life is based upon the will of the majority, and is distinguished by free institutions, representative government, free elections, guarantees of individual liberty, freedom of speech . . . , and freedom from political repression. . . .
>
> The second way of life is based upon the will of a minority forcibly imposed upon the majority. It relies upon terror and oppression, a controlled press and radio, fixed elections, and the suppression of personal freedoms.

The Truman Doctrine called for the United States to resist both internal and external aggression throughout the world. "I believe," said Truman, "that it must be the policy of the United States to support free people who are resisting attempted subjugation by armed minorities or by outside pressures."

Thus, American expansion was expressed in a call for a world order based upon a *Pax Americana.* As Truman wrote in his *Memoirs,* it was "the turning point in America's foreign policy, which now declared that wherever aggression, either direct or indirect, threatened the peace, the security of the United States was involved."

The American imperial commitment required the elaboration of new institutional arrangements and the molding of a new consensus. These new governing structures would form the basic framework for the National Security State, the substate governing the nation's foreign and military policies and related matters. This paper will not cover the economic institutions and programs that guided American economic expansion. It will attempt only to discuss the postwar institutional arrangements created in order to rationalize the state's military policies and create the new consensus underlying them.

National Security Act of 1947

Sen. Bridges: What you are talking about here today . . . is not unification . . . ; what you are talking about is . . . the integration of all of the forces of this country.

Sec. Forrestal: That is right, sir.

Sen. Bridges: In the face of the propaganda that has been circulated for this bill, do you think that the people as a whole understand [that] . . . ? . . .

Sec. Forrestal: . . . . . I doubt they do . . .

The basic institutional foundation for the National Security State was delineated by a single piece of legislation, the National Security Act of 1947. Its purpose, expressed in the preamble, was

to provide an integrated program for the future security of the United States; to provide for the establishment of integrated policies and procedures . . . relating to the national security. . . .

James Forrestal, then Secretary of the Navy, revealed the extent of this program in the Senate hearings on the bill:

This bill provides . . . for the co-ordination of the three armed services, but what is to me even more important . . . , it provides for the integration of foreign policy with national policy, of our civilian economy with military requirements; it provides for . . . continual advances in the field of research and applied science.

The act established the National Security Council and

the Central Intelligence Agency; it unified the services in the National Military Establishment, which also included the Joint Chiefs of Staff and industrial and research boards; and it co-ordinated industrial production and military research.

The bill grew out of discussions on unification of the armed services, which had begun during the war. As early as 1943, General Marshall had proposed unification of the War and Navy departments. The Select Committee on Postwar Military Policy held hearings on unification in the spring of 1944. The Joint Chiefs of Staff and the War and Navy departments each prepared reports on the feasibility of unification.

Initial attempts after the war to pass unification legislation were blocked by the opposition of the Navy and its supporters on the Hill. Led by Forrestal, the Navy resisted unification plans, fearing the loss of the Marines to the Army and Naval Air to the newly independent Air Force.

Forrestal was deeply concerned with the need "to link our diplomatic capabilities with the military capabilities. . . ." The Eberstadt Report, sponsored by the Navy Department, emphasized the need for "organizational ties" between the military and agencies concerned with foreign policy, industrial mobilization, and intelligence activities.

In order to gain Navy support, Truman guaranteed the department administrative independence and retention of its land and air arms. Moreover, as Truman related in his *Memoirs,* the President "endorsed the Navy's emphasis on the need for some means of more effectively meshing military planning with our foreign policy. . . . [I]t was clear to me that a national defense program involved not just reorganization of the armed forces, but actual coordination of the entire military, economic, and political aspects of security and defense." An Army-Navy agreement was effected, and the National Security Act was sent to and passed by Congress.

The National Security Act of 1947 created the institutional arrangements that would frame the governance of American postwar foreign and military policies. The rationalization of these institutions reflected what C. Wright Mills called the adoption of the "military definition of reality" by the civilian leadership. It was insured that military force would be an active element in the pursuit of foreign-policy aims. Civilian control was reaffirmed, but the civilians were militarized.

The National Security Act of 1947 legitimated wartime institutions and priorities for the peacetime state. This resulted in a drastic reordering of the state. In 1939, the Congress appropriated less than two billion dollars to the military. From 1946 to 1950, expenditures, at their postwar lows, would average over twelve billion dollars per year, ranging from a high of 14.3 billion in 1947 to a low of 10.96 billion in 1948. Military spending remained about one third of the federal budget during these years, and, according to Truman, ". . . in any analysis of the federal budget we must always keep in mind the fact that about ¾ths of our expenditures relate directly to war, the effects of war, or our efforts to prevent a future war. . . ." By 1949, the waste that was to characterize military spending was already apparent; the 1949 Hoover Report criticized the "continued disharmony and lack of unified planning . . . [and] the extravagance in military budgets and waste in military costs and spending."

Essentially, the bill was a codification for peacetime of *ad hoc* wartime arrangements. Admiral Nimitz noted that the function of the bill was

> to incorporate the lessons of the past war. It gives legal status to those co-ordinating and command agencies which were

found most effective to the conduct of global war. This is a forward-looking bill [sic].

Each of the institutions served a separate function; each was supplemented with additional working arrangements. *In toto,* they provided the foundation for the National Security State.

The National Security Council

The National Security Council was created to advise the President with "respect to the integration of domestic, foreign, and military policies relating to national security, so as to enable the military services and other departments . . . to cooperate more effectively. . . ." The statute designated as members the President, the Secretaries of State and Defense, and the three service secretaries. By 1949 amendments, the latter were dropped, and the Chairman of the Joint Chiefs of Staff began to meet regularly with the Council. The machinery of the Council was intended to be, and has been, quite flexible, the President calling on any individual he wishes to sit on the Council.

The Council provided, as Forrestal expressed it, "the formal legal co-ordination between the framers of foreign policy and the formulators of military policy." Such coordination, Forrestal explained, would lead to the "thorough integration of our foreign policy with our military policy. You are all familiar with the observation that military policy is but an extension of foreign policy."

Thus the basic purpose of the Council was to insure that military strength would be a basic and active component of postwar foreign policy. This purpose was reflected in a number of institutions that supplemented and served the Council. The planning board established under the Council to prepare data and papers had representatives from both the State and Defense departments. In 1949, pursuant to directives from the NSC, the Interdepartmental Steering Committee of Foreign Assistance Programs was established. It contained representatives from the departments of State and Defense, the Economic Cooperation Administration, and "others where appropriate." Its purpose was to co-ordinate the military and foreign-aid programs.

These co-ordinating structures at the top of the hierarchic order are but examples of a number of similar interdepartmental committees organized throughout the national security bureaucracy. The culminating expression of the belief that military and foreign policies were interrelated was the emphasis on "fusion" of outlook and function. Samuel Huntington has written that "the demand for fusion dominated civilian thinking on the administrative problems of civil-military relations in the postwar period." The politico-military officer, assimilating the perspectives of both the diplomat and the warrior, represented the postwar ideal.

The military was particularly responsive to calls for fusion. A Brookings Institution report noted that

> the Military Establishment has done a more effective job of developing military officers with substantial knowledge and skill in political and economic affairs than the foreign policy agencies have done in developing officials with expertise in military affairs. . . .

This response was reflected in the extraordinary influx of military men to civilian posts of importance in the immediate postwar years. Huntington has written that "military officers wielded far greater power in the United States during this period than they did in any other major country." In 1948, it was estimated that one hundred and forty-eight military men occupied important policy-making posts in the civilian government. The demand for fusion was also manifested in the formation of the National War College, which opened in September 1946 with one hundred high-ranking foreign service officers and military officers in attendance. The curriculum emphasized the interrelationship of political and military problems in international affairs. The three service war colleges also instituted new training courses in international politics and economics.

The National Security Council was intended to be the direct advisory council to the President. Under Truman, it was given major responsibility for the development of policy, and for the management of international crises. As such, it became a powerful subcabinet, divorced from the entire Cabinet in both size and function. In his memoirs, Dean Acheson, after lauding the performance of the National Security Council and minimizing the importance of Cabinet meetings, notes, "The Cabinet, despite its glamour, is not a major instrument of Government; the National Security Council, properly run, can and should be."

The Council, of course, met secretly, and never revealed its policy papers. Thus it served to remove consideration of vital issues from the Cabinet, the Congress, and the public. As Blair Bolles wrote, "Since the Council meets without publicity, the American people cannot challenge its thinking directly. Decisions which it makes are never attributed to it."

It was therefore of vital importance what views were represented on the Council. The predilections, interests, and outlooks of the men who sat on the Council had major influence over the course of the state. These men attempted to define broad policy outlines and attitudes for the national security bureaucracies. Numerous studies of the backgrounds of these advisers have been made. They demonstrate that, under each of the postwar Presidents, the men at the top of the national security bureaucracies were predominantly members of what C. Wright Mills has called the "power elite." Under Truman, for example, meeting with the National Security Council were Secretary of State Acheson, of Covington & Burling, a Washington law firm; Averell Harriman, of Brown Brothers, Harriman; James Forrestal, of Dillon, Read; and, of course, Generals George Marshall, Omar Bradley, and Walter Bedell Smith, director of the CIA.

According to Richard Barnet, twenty-two key posts in the State Department, ten in the Defense Department, and five other key national security positions in the Truman years were held by bankers. On a broader scale, Gabriel Kolko's study of 234 top foreign-policy positions revealed that 59.6 per cent were held by men from big business, investment houses, and major corporate law firms.

The leaders of the national security bureaucracy were thus men who identified American prosperity with their own fortunes. This assumption was not a petty one. Rather, it was a deeply ingrained notion that what was good for America was good for them, and that the increasing security and stature of both could only serve the best aims for all. They were deeply committed to American expansion and to the extension of the American system. Schooled in foreign policy during the war, dedicated to the consolidation and extension of a world order defined by the United States, they were convinced that military force was the primary element determining the success of a country's foreign policy. One could only negotiate from "positions of strength" (in which case, as Cora Bell has pointed out, one needn't negotiate at all); military superiority was therefore essential to peace and security. These were the views of the men who dominated the National Security Council.

The National Military Establishment

Title II of the National Security Act delineated the National Military Establishment, which formed the basis for the modern Defense Department. The Air Force was established as an equal branch of the armed forces, and the three services were placed under the direction of the new Secretary of Defense.

The Defense Secretary was designated the "principal assistant to the President in all matters relating to the national security." Directed to eliminate unnecessary duplication between the services, he assumed control of budget preparation. Initially, the position of the Secretary was quite weak; the service departments were guaranteed administrative independence, and the Secretary's staff was very limited. Each successive reorganization of the Military Establishment served to augment the powers of the Secretary. In 1949, the first of these transformed the Military Establishment into a single executive department, headed by the Secretary, with increased power over budgeting and expenditures and a vastly increased civilian staff.

As head of the Military Establishment, the Secretary was charged with responsibility for the strength of the armed services. His information concerning necessary strength levels and related cost estimates came from the three service departments. Each of the military branches campaigned for a greater share of total defense expenditures; each recommended an increase in the total defense budget, in the interest of national security.

Within the Establishment, the Secretary was thus judged on his effectiveness as a spokesman for increased military expenditures. He was, in a sense, a mediator between the President's office and the military. If, as in the case of Louis Johnson, who was Secretary of Defense during the retrenchment of 1948–49, the Secretary lost the respect of military leaders, his programs met great resistance within the Establishment. The position of Secretary of Defense was one of both great power and frustrating impotence. It is little wonder that the first two men to hold the position were both driven insane.

The Joint Chiefs of Staff

The expression of "professional military opinion" was institutionalized independent of the Secretary's control over the service departments. The 1947 Act established, for the first time in peacetime United States, the permanent Joint Chiefs of Staff. The JCS was provided with a permanent Joint Staff, the members of which were responsible to the Joint Chiefs rather than to their respective services. The Joint Staff was originally limited by law to one hundred officers, but grew to over one hundred and seventy before the law was amended to remove the one hundred-man limit.

The JCS were instructed to act as the "principal military advisers to the President and the Secretary of Defense." By law, the Joint Chiefs were provided with independent access to the President. The JCS were assigned responsibility for the preparation of strategic and logistical plans, the formulation of policies for the training and education of the members of the armed forces, and the establishment of unified field commands.

In the 1949 amendments to the National Security Act, a non-voting Chairman of the Joint Chiefs was established. Although not a formal member, the Chairman represented the views of the Chiefs on the National Security Council. Within the executive branch, the Chiefs provided a constant voice in favor of increased military expenditures, and served as a powerful opponent of spending cutbacks.

Their strength should not be overemphasized. In the immediate postwar period, the Chiefs were weakened by vicious disputes among the service branches over resource allocation and strategic doctrine. The Navy and the Air Force helped defeat the Army's pet Universal Military Training program; the Army and the Air Force torpedoed the Navy's supercarrier plans. Within the executive branch, the Chiefs had to be negotiated with over the size of the budget. After the budget figures were set, however, the Chiefs generally used their prestige to strengthen the President's independence from Congressional review. The Congress, faced with the consensus opinion of the military and the executive, was generally content to work within the general framework of the Administration's budget estimates.

The Central Intelligence Agency

The National Security Act of 1947 established the CIA, the peacetime extension of a wartime agency. During the Second World War, Colonel William "Wild Bill" Donovan had established the Office of Strategic Services to coordinate government intelligence activities and to perform espionage operations. After the war, Donovan's initial attempt to form a centralized intelligence service was blocked in the Pentagon. In October 1945, Truman transferred by executive order the research and intelligence functions of the OSS to the State Department. In January, due in part to resistance within the State Department, Truman reversed himself and established the Central Intelligence Group, under a National Intelligence Authority. The Group was directed to insure that "foreign intelligence activities be planned, developed, and coordinated." The

1947 Act replaced the Group with the Central Intelligence Agency, placed under the direction of the National Security Council.

According to the Act, the purpose of the CIA was to coordinate, correlate, and evaluate intelligence for the Council. In addition to the Agency, each branch of the service retained its intelligence force, and the State Department its intelligence office. The CIA was also intended to be an operating agency for clandestine activities. The 1947 Act provided that the Agency "shall perform . . . such additional services . . . as the National Security Council determines. . . ." The extent of the activities envisioned was perhaps best intimated by Allen Dulles in a memorandum he sent to the Senate hearings on the National Security Act:

> The prime objectives today are not solely strategic or military. . . . They are scientific. . . . They are political and social. We must deal with the problems of conflicting ideologies as democracy faces communism not only in the relations between Soviet Russia and the countries of the West, but *in the internal political conflicts within* the countries of Europe, Asia, and South America. (my emphasis)

In 1949, the Central Intelligence Act was passed, providing the legal basis for an unlimited range of secret activities. The Agency was empowered to transfer and receive funds from other government agencies. The amount and purpose of the funds were to remain secret, hidden in the recesses of the budget from both the public and the legislature. In order to protect intelligence sources, the Agency was exempted from any law requiring the publication or disclosure of the "organization, functions, names, official titles, salaries, or numbers of personnel employed by the Agency." Finally, all sums expended by the Agency for "objects of a confidential, extraordinary, or emergency nature" were to be accounted for "solely on the certificate of the Director."

The Agency was thereby established, as Dean Acheson warned Truman, in such a way that "neither he [the President], the National Security Council, nor anyone else would be in a position to know what it was doing or to control it." The members of the NSC were too harried by pressing duties in their own departments to oversee the operations of the CIA. An informal "Special Group" evolved, made up of the Director of the CIA, the Undersecretary of State for Political Affairs, and representatives from the military establishment. Since the CIA Director presided over the group, it seldom probed deeply into Agency activities. The budgetary provisions of the 1949 Act virtually eliminated Congressional control. The Armed Services and Appropriations committees of both houses established subcommittees on the CIA, but neither provided more than cursory review.

Senator Mike Mansfield has commented that "secrecy beclouds everything about the CIA–its cost, its efficiency, its successes, and its failures." Behind its veil of secrecy, the CIA undertook independent intelligence and espionage activities. From its inception, the Agency had its own agents in each of our missions abroad, reporting to Washington in a separate code. In 1950, the CIA provided undisclosed financing for the Center for International Studies at MIT. In 1951, Truman appointed Allen Dulles to head the "Plans Division," the operating arm of the Agency. In 1953–54, the CIA got its first tastes of success in toppling governments–in Iran and Guatemala. The CIA provided the executive branch with an undercover organization of unrevealed size and resources, operating without legislative control or public awareness.

Co-ordinating Boards

The National Security Act also established two co-ordinating boards under the direction of the Secretary of Defense. The Munitions Board, composed of a civilian Chairman and an Undersecretary or an Assistant Secretary from each of the three service departments, succeeded the Joint Army-Navy Munitions Board. Essentially, it served to co-ordinate and evaluate military procurement programs and to supervise the postwar stockpiling of critical raw materials.

The Research and Development Board, composed of a civilian Chairman and two representatives from each of the services, was established to co-ordinate military research and development. It succeeded, in part, the ORSD, the Office of Research and Scientific Development, which had co-ordinated the wartime research and development operations.

The two boards assisted in the development of postwar military procurement and research contracting. They were, in a sense, focal points for the elaboration of the industrial and scientific-educational estates that developed after the war. These will be discussed in more detail below; at this point, suffice it to say that the codification of the co-ordinating boards indicated the civilian areas that would be assimilated into the National Security State.

Although officially a civilian agency, the Atomic Energy Commission, established in 1946, was a major contributor to military research and development. Its relationship with the military was outlined by the legislation that created it. The history of the legislation featured a clash between civilian scientists, who sought government financing and civilian control, and the leaders of the service departments, who felt very strongly that the control of atomic development should be under their auspices.

The resulting legislation, a compromise between the two conceptions, provided a framework, in Truman's words, for "civilian direction which will serve military needs." The Commissioners of the AEC were to be appointed by the President, with the advice and consent of the Senate. Four divisions were established—a division of research, of production, of engineering, and of "military application," all under the supervision of a General Manager. The director of the last division was required to be a member of the armed forces. The act provided for coordination with industry and universities through the General Advisory Committee, consisting of nine civilian members appointed by the President.

Additionally, a Military Liaison Committee, with representatives from the services, was established to advise the Commission. In 1949 the Committee's mandate was broadened, and the AEC was directed to "advise and consult with the Committee on all atomic energy matters which the *Committee deems* to relate to military application." The Commission was further directed to "keep the Committee fully informed on all such matters before it." The Liaison Committee was thus empowered not only to decide which matters "relate" to military application, but also to review action on such matters. Moreover, the Committee was directed to appeal any Commission decision "if the Committee at any time concludes that any action, proposed action, or failure to act of the Commission . . . is adverse to the responsibilities of the Departments of War or Navy." The appeals were to be heard by the Secretary of Defense and, if necessary, the President.

The result of the structure was, naturally, an emphasis on serving military needs. Oppenheimer reported that the GAC concluded that the "principal job of the Commission was to provide atomic weapons, good atomic weapons, and many atomic weapons." In 1948, Truman emphasized the standards by which the Commission was judged, stating:

> Today we possess powerful atomic weapons. . . . [R]ecent tests have demonstrated that . . . our position . . . has been substantially improved. Such advances vindicate the faith of the American people in the principles of civilian control of atomic energy. . . .

The Contract Mechanism

In the postwar years, contracting with private business, universities, and research corporations was established as the predominant method of procuring weapons research, development, and production. Like the other institutional arrangements of the postwar security establishment, the prevalence of the contract procedure stemmed from wartime experiences.

The prodigious scale of the mobilization for World War II had required the organization of the nation's industrial and intellectual resources. Initially, proposals for the nationalization of the war effort–the militarization of industry and drafting of the necessary personnel–had been considered and rejected. The basic operating system adopted had been essentially one of enlisting industrial corporations and universities in the war effort under contractual arrangements. This wartime arrangement was continued in the postwar period, and the contract became the basic mechanism for postwar procurement.

The Military Establishment's contracting authority was delineated in the Armed Services Procurement Act of 1947. The Act authorized the services to contract with industries and universities by the general policy of advertising and bidding. If any one of sixteen exceptions applied, however, the contract could be negotiated. The exceptions included contracts for personal or professional services, for services rendered by a university, for experimental and research work, for technical equipment "to assure standardization," and for "supplies for which it is impracticable to secure competition." The act further stipulated that a contract could be placed with a corporation if the service secretary determined that it was in "the interest of national defense" that the manufacturer be made or kept available for military production.

The effect of these exceptions on the policy of open bidding was exposed by an exchange during the Senate hearings on the bill:

Sen. Byrd: This bill simply means that we are changing our policy from buying by advertising to a policy of buying by negotiations, provided the agency head certifies that it should be done, in the interest of the government.

Sec. Kinney: That is substantially correct, Senator . . . [but] . . . it is the intent that the bulk of these contracts should be let by advertising and competitive bidding.

Sen. Byrd: I have learned by long experience that you should not extend an authority unless you expect that authority to be exercised. . . .

From 1947 to 1949, 70.1 per cent of the total dollar value of military contracts was negotiated.

For major-weapons procurement, the Munitions Board, established by the National Security Act, attempted to co-ordinate the military procurement agencies and bureaus. From 1947 to 1950, expenditures for major-weapons procurement averaged about 2.5 billion dollars per year, excluding money spent on the feeding and clothing of troops and the operation and maintenance of military aircraft, much of which was also contracted.

The Munitions Board was also a major source of capital stock in the postwar years. During World War II, the federal government had financed the construction of over fifteen hundred manufacturing plants, worth 12.7 billion dollars. Many of these were sold by the military to industry at a fraction of their actual cost. At the end of fiscal 1949, the Secretary of Defense reported that eight hundred war plants worth over nine billion dollars were "owned and controlled by the military departments, reserved under the National Security Clause, or in the same use for which they were built." Thus, the military made certain that the plant capacity built during the war would remain oriented to military production. The capital stock that the military controlled was also available to defense contractors, who, on military procurement contracts, were paid at a lucrative profit rate for manufacturing weapons in military-owned and/or -leased plants.

The procurement agencies and the Munitions Board were supplemented in the postwar years by a spate of contracting agencies for research and development. Two organizational means were used to conduct postwar R&D: "in-house" research undertaken by military scientists,* and project contracting to universities, industries, and research corporations. The latter means predominated.

* "In-house" research is research carried out in military arsenals and laboratories, by scientists directly employed by the services. After the war, scientific personnel were scarce. The service branches attempted to acquire trained scientists by receiving Congressional authorization for the employment of scientific personnel at high rates of pay. The services also recruited German scientists who had acquired some expertise during World War II. The Navy was authorized to waive statutory prohibitions to payment of salaries to non-citizens for "those persons determined by the Secretary of the Navy to be necessary in order to obtain . . . special technical or scientific knowledge or experience. . . ." We forget so quickly the barbarity of the past war in order to prepare for the next.

Central co-ordination for R&D contracting was the responsibility of the Research and Development Board. It attempted to oversee the research financed by the service bureaus and agencies. In 1946, the Navy received Congressional approval for the Office of Naval Research, which both co-ordinated Naval research and carried on a large program in basic research itself. The other services followed, and the Office of Air Research and Army Research and Development were soon active.

Military research from 1947 to 1950 averaged over five hundred million dollars per year, exclusive of the AEC. In 1947, military expenditures on R&D were five hundred million dollars, with the rest of the government spending only one hundred twenty-five million dollars more. Additionally, the AEC was spending approximately three hundred forty million, almost all of it on military uses. Military R&D expenditures therefore accounted for over 85 per cent of all federal financing of research and development. In the services, 80 per cent of the expenditures were contracted out, with industry receiving ninety per cent and universities about 10 per cent.

In more-concrete terms, universities in 1949 received an estimated fifty-three million dollars in military research, with another eighty-one million coming from the AEC. The Office of Naval Research alone in the same year sponsored an estimated twelve hundred projects at over two hundred universities, with an annual expenditure of close to twenty million dollars, involving some three thousand scientists and twenty-five hundred graduate students.

In both procurement and R&D, the services became a major source of income in the postwar years. Possessing an increasing budget, these institutions began to distribute largess on a grand scale. Their beneficiaries grew increasingly dependent upon this distribution. As their dependence increased, their appetites sharpened, and they began to view the distribution as a right. To assure their continued livelihood, they formed into estates, creating stable relationships with the national security institutions.

The Industrial Estate

The manifold benefits of a symbiotic military-industrial relationship had been clearly demonstrated during the war. The wartime mobilization of industry had been directed by *ad hoc* agencies primarily staffed by "dollar-a-year" men—leaders of business, generally big business. Industry had profited greatly from this arrangement. Production and profits had soared. The government had financed extensive capital expansion. As the war drew to a close, the combination of military leaders and leading industrialists had delayed demobilization, to the benefit of both the military and big business.

In the postwar years, the close relationship continued. Both the military leadership and corporate executives desired strong ties. The former wanted to insure a continued source of weapons supply and development. The latter sought to protect their market position in the procurement process.

The civilian and military leadership quickly established advisory committees and boards to provide the basis for continued cooperation. In 1944, Forrestal founded the National Security Industrial Association to insure that "American business will stay close to the services." By the end of 1948, the Munitions Board was assisted by nineteen advisory committees comprising over four hundred leading industrialists. The Naval Research Advisory Committee, made up of fifteen leading scientists from major corporations and universities, exemplified the technical advisory committees that proliferated in the service agencies. By 1948, fifteen advisory committees to the Research and Development Board were in operation.

These advisory committees greatly influenced the contracting process. The 1947 Steelman Report noted that advisory committees

> are influential in awarding contracts commonly negotiated without competitive bidding. Since the outstanding scientists of the country are frequently associated with the largest industries and universities, institutions engaged in or attempting to secure contract work often have officers or employees who sit upon the program-planning and evaluative committees.

Advisory committees were the most visible means of integrating corporate and military goals, but not the most effective.

The basic method of integration was the development of interlocking managerial positions. The personnel traffic between the corporate and military administrative structures increased dramatically after the war. In the middle levels of the national security bureaucracy, defense apparatchiks (both civilian and military) found themselves, as H. L. Nieburg explained, "dealing with private corporate officials who often were their own former bosses and continue as companions to their present bosses. . . ."

The same interchangeability took place at the top of the bureaucracy, as defense industries began to offer lucrative positions to high-ranking officers upon retirement. The Hebert subcommittee in 1961 revealed that 261 generals and admirals and 485 retirees above the rank of colonel and Navy captain were employed by companies with 80 per cent of the contracts. The traffic went both ways, as key businessmen and their lawyers assumed major positions in the Defense Department, determining guidelines before their return to business. By 1959, the Air Force was to draw 46 per cent of its procurement personnel at supervisory levels from private-business backgrounds. Through these connections, corporations involved in major defense funding insured themselves a steady and continuous flow of military contracts.

In the procurement process, the company that received a research contract to develop the prototype for a given weapons system often was given sole-source, prime-contractor status for the weapon. The advantages gained in experience, know-how, and organization in the research stage gave the company a preferred position for the procurement contract. To capitalize on this tendency, companies that were, as the president of General Dynamics put it, "in the defense business to stay," organized sophisticated research laboratories and dominated the R&D contracting process. In 1947, the ten largest contractors held 65 per cent of the combined Army and Navy contracts outstanding.

As companies became increasingly dependent upon military contracts, industrial research laboratories took the initiative for the development of new weapons, or of sophisticated versions of old ones. By the mid-fifties, military procurement agencies were to receive hundreds of unsolicited plans for new weapons systems. The technology race gained its own momentum.

The relationship between the military and industry developed after the war was to have many effects. During the postwar years, corporations began to rely on the government to finance risk-free research and development. Since scientific manpower was limited, and military R&D contracts dominated federal research contracting, firms supplying the military began to stockpile scientific talent. The emphasis on military research, and the fierce recruitment of scientific talent by military-oriented firms, was to produce a neglect of research on civilian technology—such as transportation, health, urban housing, environmental control. As Philip Morrison, a physicist at Cornell, has noted, "We cannot tie science to the military and hope to see it act for peace, no matter how ingeniously we write the contracts."

With ever-increasing military procurement expenditures, major military contractors were to become like small governments, distributing wealth and power by subcontracting for components of a weapons system. Such subcontracting occasionally went through four or five layers before actual production. By the sixties, military expenditure was to support substantial portions of the total employment in several states, providing a base for consumer services and stores.

Additionally, military financing of research and procurement was to be used by three administrations to achieve a sort of backhanded planning. Contracts were signed to encourage expansion of a regional area, reduce unemployment in depressed areas, or merely to keep a given company going. These functions for military spending, a sort of crackpot Keynesianism, were inaugurated after the war. By 1948, for example, the report of the Secretary of Defense announced that "special measures were also taken to promote the President's program to stimulate industry in areas where unemployment exceeded 12% of the estimated labor force. The measures included the placement of military contracts in those areas wherever practicable." The quickest method of stimulating economic growth was to enlist greater sectors of the economy onto the military dole. When Kennedy entered the White House, he was to find that "of all major federal agencies, the Department of Defense was obviously best equipped to put money into circulation rapidly, with blueprints in hand and industrial contracts arranged."

The postwar integration of the military with industries produced an ardent and wealthy proponent of increased armaments. As John Kenneth Galbraith has written, "the industrial system helps win belief for the image of implacable conflict that justifies its need" (for military expenditures). Massive advertising, public education centers, formal lobbies, financial contributions to campaigns—all were to be marshaled to support the requisite image of impending threat.

As one noted commentator summarized, ". . . the increased flow of military expenditures into narrow areas of the economy tends to create a self-perpetuating coalition of vested interests. With vast public funds at hand, industries, geographical regions, labor unions, and the multitude of supporting enterprises band together with enormous manpower, facilities, and Washington contacts to maintain and expand their stake."

The Scientific and Educational Estate

During the war years, universities had been intimately tied in with the National Security State. The mobilization for World War II had attracted scientists and scholars to Washington, along with the industrialists. Universities had constructed laboratories for military research. The Manhattan Project had engaged thousands of university scientists. MIT had contracted to develop radar; Cal Tech, rockets. The University of Chicago had set up the first sustained nuclear reactions; the University of California had fabricated the first atomic bomb. Social scientists had been employed by the OSS in interdisciplinary studies of friend and foe.

These relationships were continued in the postwar years. The larger and wealthier institutions maintained large laboratory facilities, constructed and financed by military grants. In some cases, semiautonomous military research centers were established. In the social sciences, centers for international studies proliferated, most of them modeled after the Russian Institute at Columbia (financed by the Rockefeller Foundation) and the MIT Center for International Studies (financed in part by the CIA). The RAND Corporation became the prototype of the "think-tank" in 1948, when it became a non-profit corporation with strong ties to the Air Force.

The extent of the major universities' ties with the security bureaucracies had serious ramifications in the educational estate. The postwar shortage of scientists, combined with the frenetic recruitment by armaments industries, produced a large shortage in qualified science professors. The major universities, in order to attract skilled scientists, approved an increasing flow of military research contracts that would inflate salaries. Since R&D contracts to universities were even more concentrated than were those to industries, the smaller colleges fared poorly. In 1947, the Steelman Report decried the shift of scientists from smaller to larger schools, noting that

> the shift has recently been accelerated to a point where it threatens to cripple many institutions. Competent men and women are frequently getting as much as a forty percent increase in salary by leaving smaller institutions.

As a result of military contracts on campuses, a new glamour scientist was produced–one who spent his time advising and consulting in Washington, proposing and supervising research projects, and supplementing his salary by creating spin-off industries to market the patented products developed in his military research. The new glamour connected with research resulted in a decrease in time spent in the classroom. By 1960 the effect was quite serious, as Philip Abelson noted:

> A whole generation of able young faculty members [has developed] who never knew a time when affluence did not prevail. Thus it is hardly surprising that a few of them exhibit an

opportunism that startles their elders. They . . . regard the agencies that provide the research grants as their real sources of nourishment. . . . In their view, students are just impediments in the headlong search for more and better grants, fatter fees, higher salaries, and higher status. . . .

In the social sciences, the same trends were apparent. Professors spent much of their time searching for research grants, advising government agencies, and addressing pragmatic solutions to technical political problems. In 1950, the Congress for Cultural Freedom was founded by liberal anti-Communists, with funds from the CIA. The Congress and the associated American Committee for Cultural Freedom established the polemical staples of the next decades. According to Christopher Lasch, these included the declaration of "an end of ideology, the assertion that conventional political distinctions had become irrelevant in the face of the need for a united front against Bolshevism." Another was the necessity for intellectuals to choose between the Soviet Union and America, between communism and democracy. The forging of liberal anti-communism led to a decade of what C. Wright Mills called the "celebration of American politics," the uncritical support of American policies.

In the next two decades, the complicity of the intellectuals was to reach its apogee: Universities would contract to run AID programs abroad. Political scientists would combine with police-administration professors to train counterinsurgency police in Vietnam. Social scientists would elaborate deterrence doctrines, and play war games in Cold War strategy. Systems analysis, developed and popularized by RAND as "value-free analysis," would provide the rationale for an ever more insane armaments race. Intellectuals contracted with the national security bureaucracy in order to influence it; in the end, they only succeeded in rationalizing its processes. As Hans Morgenthau wrote, "The integrity and independence of the educational community has been impaired by the academic-political complex. . . . The educated community has in large measure become the handmaiden of the government, while maintaining the pretense of independence."

Surrounding all these endeavors was a shroud of secrecy, which shielded the discoveries, activities, and studies of the academicians from public view. By 1949, the AEC had 308,000 reports on hand, and only 10 per cent of them were declassified. Professor Don K. Price noted the "irony" of professors who engaged in defense activities. For many, "the main article of faith is academic freedom, which would clearly be extinguished by a Communist triumph. To prevent such a triumph, American scientists are now required to work in a complicated network of secret and confidential data, and to communicate on many subjects only with those who have been officially investigated and cleared."

More importantly, the whole notion of the scientific and intellectual enterprise–the search for understanding for the benefit of mankind–was rendered perverse. Scientists and engineers contracted to invent technology that increased both the capacity and the appetite of the state for dominance. Social scientists invented doctrines that rationalized the possession of nuclear stockpiles and the use of counterinsurgency technology. Little wonder that Albert Einstein would reflect about his career and conclude, "If I would be a young man again, and had to decide how to make my living, I would not try to become a scientist or scholar or teacher. I would rather choose to be a plumber or a peddler in the hope to find that modest degree of independence still available under present circumstances."

Perhaps the best example of the pervasive military influence was the National Science Foundation Act, passed in 1950. The call for a civilian institution that would finance basic research and supply fellowships to graduate students received the support of the administration, of scientists, and of the military, who felt, with Secretary of War Patterson, that "such a foundation could carry on the necessary research work in peacetime . . . with propriety."

The Foundation was charged with promoting basic research and education in the sciences, and was authorized to contract for research and give grants and fellowships to graduate students. In spite of the fact that the military programs for R&D were already well developed, the Foundation was also directed to "initiate and support . . . at the request of the Secretary of Defense, specific scientific research activities in connection to matters relating to the national defense. [sic]"

The NSF was permitted to contract with foreign nationals, but "only with the approval of the Secretary of State . . . consistent with the foreign policy objectives of the United States." Projects in the area of nuclear energy had to receive the prior approval of the AEC that they would not adversely affect the common defense. In conjunction with the Defense Department, the NSF was directed to maintain such security requirements as either it or the DOD deemed necessary. Each researcher was required to sign an "affadavit" that he did not believe in, teach, or support an organization that believes in the overthrow of the United States Government. An oath of allegiance was also required.

The National Science Foundation, established to promote basic scientific research and education, was forced to accept military direction for a portion of its grants, security classifications for some of its research, and loyalty oaths and affirmations for all its contractees. The priorities of the National Security State were etched by those omnipresent restrictions.

Secrecy, Loyalty, and Security

Of late years, the government is using its power as never before to pry into . . . lives and thoughts upon the slightest suspicion of less than complete trustworthiness. It demands not only probity, but unquestioning ideological loyalty.—Mr. Justice Jackson, dissenting in *Frazier* v. *U.S.*, 335 U.S. 497, 515

The logic of the ideology demanded concern with internal subversion in the United States. The portrait of communism emphasized its reliance upon stealth and chicanery to overthrow governments. Communist parties and fronts and "fellow travelers" were the equivalent of Hitler's "fifth column" movements. The revelations of the Canadian espionage ring in June 1946 provided a basis for the fears of subversion.

The second tenet of the postwar ideology, belief in the value of American power, postulated the ability and right of the United States to define the postwar order. The continued revolutionary surge throughout the world, culminating in the loss of China, could only be accounted for as an American failure. The logic of the ideology would lead its less sophisticated adherents to seek out subversives as accountable for that failure. The House Un-American Activities Committee, made permanent after the war, immediately began a series of hearings on subversives in America.

The search for subversives led to the requirement of loyalty in government employment. Loyalty refers to a state of mind, connotating the sentiment of devotion. A requirement of loyalty can be interpreted as either an absence of disloyalty or the presence of positive allegiance. The loyalty program developed after the war generally demanded the latter.

As we have seen, a characteristic of the National Security State was its pervasive secrecy. The postwar institutionalization of secrecy entailed the maintenance of classification systems. Secrecy demands not only classification systems, but control over the persons who deal with secrets. Secrecy thus necessitates security. Security standards measure the trustworthiness of persons with access to sensitive positions. The postwar mania for protecting scientific, strategic, and policy secrets led to a stringent security program.

Conceptually, loyalty and security are distinguishable. The postwar programs for loyalty and security checks were, in some cases, enacted separately. In operation, however, the distinction faded. Reviews of an individual's trustworthiness considered both his loyalty and his stability, character, and personal habits (garrulousness, etc.). Loyalty checks reviewed his beliefs, associations, background, and, inevitably, his character, personal mannerisms, and stability. Thus, although the security standards were presumably limited to those with access to classified data, they were soon applied to everyone subsumed under either program.

In the Truman administration, the first step taken to insure security and loyalty came at the Cabinet level. In September 1946, having first cleared the speech with President Truman, Henry Wallace delivered a public address criticizing American foreign policy. It was his theme that American intransigence–its continued testing of atomic weapons, its continued production of long-range bombers, its exclusion of the U.S.S.R. from the Far East, its repeated imprecations about conditions in Eastern Europe–could only be viewed by the Soviet Union as threatening in the extreme. He suggested that it was both possible and necessary to reach a *détente* with the

U.S.S.R. The speech produced an uproar in the Administration; Secretary of State Byrnes and his assistant Acheson immediately complained to Truman that Wallace was undermining their policies and confusing foreigners. After privately rebuking Wallace, Truman was finally convinced to dismiss him.

The significance of the dismissal was not merely in the context of the exodus of liberal New Dealers from the Truman administration (the exclusion of Morgenthau, Ickes, and Wallace provides an interesting guide for the shift in administration attitudes toward the Soviet Union and Germany). Rather, it indicated the new requirement of public unanimity on the tenets of the new ideology. In announcing Wallace's dismissal, Truman declared,

> No change in our foreign policy is contemplated. No member of the executive branch of the government will make any public statement as to foreign policy which is in conflict with our established foreign policy. Any public statement on foreign policy shall be cleared with the Department of State. . . .

Following this incident, the requirements of loyalty and security were tightened throughout the federal bureaucracy. The government, of course, already had extensive loyalty and security procedures. In 1939, the Hatch Act had forbidden federal employment to members of a party or organization that "advocates" the overthrow of "our constitutional form of government" by force or violence. In 1941, the provisions of the act had been appended to all appropriation bills, and its measures extended to personal advocacy. In 1940, the Navy and War departments had been declared sensitive agencies, and had gained the power of summary removal of any employee if necessary to "the demands of national security." In 1946, this authority had been extended to the State Department. But with the HUAC hearings titillating the nation and his own administration trumpeting the danger of Communist subversion, Truman felt compelled to respond to the demands of his own ideology and revamp the government's loyalty and security programs.

In November 1946, following the Congressional elections, Truman established a temporary committee to investigate the loyalty program. Its report concluded that the employment of "disloyal or subversive persons presents more than a speculative threat to our system of government," although the committee admitted it could not state how far-reaching that threat was.

On the basis of the Committee's recommendations, Truman issued Executive Order 9835 in March 1947, prescribing new procedures for a federal employees' loyalty program. It required a loyalty investigation for every person entering the civilian employment of any federal agency or department. The investigation was to be directed by the Civil Service Commission. For each applicant, it was directed to check the files of the FBI, the Civil Service Commission, any other government investigative service (Army, Navy, Air Force, CIA, State Department, and AEC), local law-enforcement agencies, records of schools and colleges, former employers, references furnished by the applicant, and any other appropriate sources. The Commission was further directed to establish a "central master index" on everyone investigated since 1939.

If any of these sources revealed derogatory information, a full field investigation was to ensue. The executive order proscribed six categories of behavior: Three related to sabotage, espionage, treason, or advocacy thereof. The fourth forbade disclosure of confidential information; the fifth, action in the service of interests of another government; the sixth, "membership in, affiliation with, or sympathetic association with any foreign or domestic organization, association, movement, group, or combination of persons, designated by the Attorney General as totalitarian, Fascist, Communist or subversive." For an organization placed upon the list, there was no appeal or hearing. For a person who had associated with the organization prior to the publication of the list, the law was classically ex post facto. In 1947 the Attorney General's list included eighty-two organizations; by 1950 the total number was 197, including 132 listed as Communist or Communist-front groups.

If dismissed or refused employment, the individual had a right to an administrative appeal to a central loyalty board. The standard for dismissal or refusal of employment was that "on all the evidence available, reasonable grounds exist for belief that the person involved is disloyal." In 1951, this was altered to "reasonable *doubt* as to the *loyalty* of the persons involved."

The direct effect of the program was extensive. In 1953, the Civil Service Commission announced that, under the Loyalty Order alone, it had checked 4,756,705 persons. Of these, 1.7 million were employees incumbent in 1947; the rest, of applications for employment since that year. The FBI had undertaken over 26,000 investigative reports; there were 12,859 interrogations and over 4000 hearings. Of the 26,236 persons investigated, 16,503 were eventually cleared, 506 were removed, and over 6000 resigned or withdrew their applications. Most of the cases concerned association with black-listed organizations. The first chairman of the Loyalty Review Board stated:

> Not one single case or evidence directing towards a case of espionage has been disclosed in the record. . . . I say it is an extraordinary thing that not one single syllable of evidence has been found by the FBI . . . indicating that a particular case involves a question of espionage.

These figures do not include dismissals for security reasons, which, as Ralph S. Brown of Yale Law School has estimated, may have reached "twice as many" as those for loyalty. The federal security program was derived from wartime legislation. In 1942, the Army, Navy, and Coast Guard were granted the right of summary dismissal "warranted by the demands of national security." In 1946 the McCarran Rider appended similar provisions to the appropriations bill of the State Department. The CIA Director was accorded the authority in 1947 to terminate the employment of any employee if he deemed it "necessary or advisable in the interests of the United States."

In 1950, P.L. 733 superseded these bills. It extended summary suspension rights to the heads of State, Commerce, Justice, Defense, the three services, the AEC, the National Advisory Committee for Aeronautics, the Treasury, and the National Security Resources Board. Within thirty days after suspension, the employee could submit affadavits and statements to the relevant official. After a review, the agency head could, if he deemed it necessary, terminate the employment of the individual.

The federal security regulations extended beyond federal employees into the civilian work force. The AEC Act of 1946 provided that "no arrangement . . . shall be issued unless the person with whom the arrangement is made agrees in writing not to permit any individual to have access to restricted data until the Federal Bureau of Investigation shall . . . report . . . on the character, associations, and loyalty of such individual." Professor Brown reports that, in one instance at least, the AEC required a clearance on an employee who was situated so that he could "see a secret building." Similar restrictions were also applied to military R&D and procurement contracts.

In 1950, Truman issued an executive order under the authority of the Magnuson Act, declaring the security of the United States to be endangered "by reason of subversive activity." The order prescribed regulations for safeguarding American vessels, harbors, ports, and waterfront facilities. It empowered the Coast Guard to initiate a program designed to bar any person from seagoing employment or access to restricted areas unless "the Commandant is satisfied that the character and habits of life of the applicant are such as to authorize the belief that [his] presence . . . would not be inimical to the security of the United States."

The Administration's loyalty and security program was but one aspect of the postwar move against the Left. In 1948, the Administration began prosecuting Communists under the long-dormant Smith Act. Each action by the Administration only increased the fervor of the Right. The Taft-Hartley Act, passed over Truman's veto, required the leaders of unions to sign an oath that no leaders of the union were Communist. According to contemporary ACLU reports, the failure of court tests against the anti-Communist oath section "stimulated some unions to clean their houses of political infiltration." The union leadership was under great pressure to move to the right. In 1949, ten unions, representing one million members, were expelled from the CIO for not adhering to its new anti-Communist foreign-policy positions. In 1948, the AEC directed General Electric not to recognize the United Electrical Workers as representative of workers at atomic energy installations.

The mania spread through the country. In 1947, HUAC unleashed its attack against Hollywood, followed by the Bentley-Chambers revelations and the resulting Hiss scandal. Throughout the country, local governments, universities, public school systems, corporations, private clubs, and professional licensing boards began to require loyalty oaths. Ralph Brown estimates that by 1953 over 13.5 million people, one out of five in the total work force, were liable to some kind of loyalty procedure. All this was but the seedbed for McCarthyism.

In form and effect, the loyalty and security programs

instituted a period of purge in America. The loyalty program set out to eliminate, in Truman's words, "potential subversives," as Stalin had classified "kulaks" as the enemy. The loyalty program possessed none of the protections inherent in the rule of law. The program proscribed a state of mind—"disloyalty." The evidence deemed relevant to the establishment of this "crime" was vague and ill-defined. The operation of the program was based upon secret informants. The evidence that informants supplied was placed in the hands of the judges. The accused was given a list of the charges against him, but the identity of the informant was seldom revealed. The standard of proof—"a reasonable grounds for belief in the disloyalty of the accused"—travestied any concept of a presumption of innocence. As Eleanor Bontecou observed,

> Reasonable doubt is a phrase of art which in other fields of the law has gradually acquired concrete meaning. . . . It is still undefined in the loyalty program, where it is applied against instead of in favor of the accused person.

The accused thus bore the burden of proving his innocence, against a vague and ill-defined charge, made by informants who were not revealed, based upon information in the hands of the judges.

As a result, it quickly went out of control. Enemies could attack each other through the program. Those who had faint memories of radical flirtations proved their loyalty by constant vigil against any sign of "subversion." Subversion soon became identified with unorthodoxy and originality, commodities in scarce supply in any bureaucracy. In time, Senator William Fulbright has written, "the censorship of ideas . . . no longer needs to be imposed; it is internalized." Thus the postwar programs, which helped prepare the foundation for the McCarthy excesses, reflected the demand for ideological orthodoxy in the postwar period.

Additionally, the loyalty and security programs exemplified the basic psychology of the leaders of the national security bureaucracies. The will to control created the demand for acquiescence or agreement. Dissent was equated with disloyalty, radicalism with communism. The CIA was established to spy on people abroad; the FBI and related loyalty and security agencies were to spy on people at home. At home and abroad, the National Security State found it more and more necessary to keep tabs on millions of people.

Institutionalized Propaganda

The formation of the National Security State was justified by the new ideology. To protect its prerogatives and privileges, the American public had to be informed of the new credo. After World War II, the populace was essentially isolationist. Much to the dismay of Truman, Forrestal, Harriman, and the military leaders, the demand for demobilization and return to peacetime conditions rose to clamorous heights at the end of the war: Soldiers rioted to protest a slowdown in the rate of demobilization; labor unions struck for long-deferred wage demands; mothers mailed pair upon pair of baby shoes to Congress calling for the return of long-awaited fathers. The war was over; it was time for peace.

To reverse this tide of opinion, it was necessary, in Vandenberg's revealing phrase, "to scare the hell out of the country." Led by Acheson and Forrestal, the leaders of the postwar state viewed the public and Congress as objects to be manipulated in pursuit of their goals. They treated both cynically, injecting periodic doses of anti-communism in order to gain support for their foreign and military policies.

Acheson described the process by which this was accomplished, in his memoirs. Referring to his speaking tour in 1950, he noted that, in addressing the public,

> Qualification must give way to simplicity of statement, variety and nuance to bluntness, almost brutality in carrying home a point. . . . [P]oints to be understandable had to be clear. If we made our points *clearer than the truth,* we . . . could hardly do otherwise. . . .

In order to convince the American people of the necessity for a new international position, "our analysis of the threat combined the ideology of Communist doctrine and the power of the Russian state into an aggressive expansionist drive," which, according to Acheson, "it would take more than bare hands and a desire for peace to turn back. . . ."

Combined with lurid appraisals of the Communist threat was an emphasis on the necessity for American power. Secretary of War Patterson declared, "The peace of the world depends upon the presence of power in this nation." The role of the United States, announced Secretary of the Navy Sullivan, was "to guarantee peace through restrained strength."

The leaders of the Truman administration orchestrated the transfusions of anti-communism and militarism to correspond with their program needs. *US News & World Report* commented in 1948,

> President Truman is somewhat disturbed by the way the idea of imminent war with Russia hangs on in the country even after the official line has changed from war scares to more emphasis upon the prospect for peace. . . .
>
> War scares, encouraged by high officials only a few weeks ago, so alarmed the . . . US public that top planners now are

having to struggle hard to keep Congress from pouring more money into national defense than the Joint Chiefs of Staff regard as wise or necessary. It is proving more difficult to turn off than to turn on a war psychology.

By such tactics, the leaders of the state not only justified its new course, but helped instill the paranoia that was to lead to the McCarthy witch hunts. Acheson himself was to feel the lash of the fury he had nurtured.

Publicity for the National Security State was also institutionalized in the postwar period. The Voice of America was established to spread the American message abroad; the Military Establishment geared itself to tell the story at home. In 1949, the Office of Public Information was established in the Pentagon. Advising it was the Public Relations Advisory Council, made up of the heads of each of the service branches. The Office of Public Information was divided into ten branches, including a press department, a radio and television department, and a speakers and appearances branch. By 1950, public relations and information received a budget of 9.6 million dollars. In that year, Senator Homer Ferguson revealed that over twenty-seven hundred publicity personnel worked in the Department of Defense. In the Navy alone, 844 civilian and military personnel worked full time on publicity.

The best example of postwar organization for propaganda was provided by the Army. The War Department Public Relations Division was charged with over-all coordination of public matters. In 1946, an Army directive encouraged "the writing of articles . . . engaging in public and private discussion by officers and enlisted men . . . on topics of military or professional interest . . . in support of the military policy of the United States or in the interest of national defense. . . ." Commanders at all levels, in each unit and base, were directed to oversee public relations services within their jurisdictions to insure that the American public was informed of the purpose and activities of the Army, as well as its place in the American community. The directive required the appointment of a public relations officer to the staff of each post, camp, or station, and to the staffs of regiments, air force groups, and equivalent units of higher commands.

The military engaged in numerous different publicity activities. The Pentagon controlled news releases, sponsored radio and TV programs, assisted in the production of civilian films, produced and directed its own movies, organized a centralized speech bureau, sent officers to speak at high schools across the land. In 1946, the Army was the third largest advertiser in America. As a result, a pleased colonel related, ". . . magazines are very cooperative in [publishing] military stories. The newspapers and the radio, particularly, give a great deal of public service space and time."

The services used this propaganda to build respect for the armed forces, to promote favorable legislation, and to disseminate the ideology upon which increased armaments spending rested. A House committee headed by Representative Forrest Harness in 1948 concluded that the War Department was guilty of "using government funds in an improper manner for propaganda activities. . . ."

The encroachment of the military extended far beyond advertising activities. In 1946, the War Department ordered the reactivation of advanced ROTC in 129 universities. By 1953, more than 147,000 students received Army ROTC training, and units existed in 246 colleges and universities and 262 high schools. The Navy instituted its famed Holloway Plan in 1946. High school students competed for Navy scholarships with paid full tuition and certain allowances for four years of college. Upon graduation, the student was obligated for a minimum of three years' active duty. In 1951, fourteen hundred NROTC regulars graduated from participating schools.

In 1948, the peacetime draft was initiated by legislation that provided that every male citizen between the ages of nineteen and twenty-six was liable for training and service in the armed forces of the United States. For the first time, the power of the state to conscript the young in peacetime was established. At another level, the War Department, through the National Board for the Promotion of Rifle Practice, began selling obsolete equipment to the populace, including Enfield and Springfield rifles. As Major General Milton A. Reckord explained:

> One of the really great services rendered to the citizenry of the Nation by the National Board of Promotion of Rifle Practice is that of the sale of obsolete War Department property . . . to civilians. . . .

Thus, the National Security State was organized not merely to collect secret information and to spy on the populace, but to propagate its version of reality. Both the pronouncements of national leaders and the institutionalized propaganda of the military sought to spread the new truth to the population. The state enlisted the young through ROTC and the draft, affecting both the collegian and the dropout, the middle and the lower classes. Its power to saturate the public media, to control the information that the public would receive about its operations, and to influence the basic perceptions of the population, gave it immense power and license. The state monopolized the "marketplace of ideas."

Behemoth: the New State

With these brief sketches of postwar developments in mind, an attempt at assessing the form of the National

Security State, which developed from 1945 to 1950, can be made.

Within the branches of government, a realignment of power took place. The executive pre-empted many of the legislative functions. In the area of national security, the executive became sovereign; the legislature, except for its powerful committee heads, who are satraps of the security bureaucracies, was rendered impotent.

Thus by 1950 the President possessed the power to procure, disperse, and use atomic weaponry without Congressional approval. The decision to develop the hydrogen bomb was made in the executive branch of the government. By executive agreements and official pronouncements such as the Truman Doctrine, the President claimed the power to commit the nation abroad, without recourse to the treaty-approval functions of the Senate. On the basis of these commitments, the President controlled the dispersal of military bases and armaments throughout the world. Finally, the President assumed the power to take the nation to war without Congressional approval or declaration. In 1949, Truman dispatched troops to Korea; the Congress was presented with a *fait accompli*. In explanation, Secretary of State Acheson calmly told an irate Senate committee:

> the President [has] the authority to use the Armed Forces in carrying out the broad foreign policy of the United States and implementing treaties. . . . It is equally clear that *this authority may not be interfered with by the Congress* in the exercise of powers which it has under the Constitution. (my emphasis)

The Congressional power over the budget was also attenuated. In interventionist, bureaucratic governments, large portions of the budget are fixed costs—to pay off past debts, past commitments, continuing programs, permanent functions, and the permanent bureaucracy. These portions are removed from the legislative domain. In postwar America, in addition to fixed costs, the executive, because of the complexity involved and the increased reliance on fiscal controls for economic stability, took over the function of devising the budget. Budget estimates were derived from the demands of numerous areas of the bureaucracy, evaluated, rationalized, and then presented to the Congress. As Warner Schilling discovered in analyzing the budget process in fiscal 1949, the Congress made its decisions in ignorance, accepting the Administration's basic framework, having neither the time, the expertise, nor the interest to do otherwise.

The operations and the budget of the national security institutions were particularly immune from Congressional review and control. The size and complexity of the national security institutions insulated them from investigations. Moreover, the largess that the military dispensed was a powerful political force, and many Congressmen came from areas or states dependent upon military industry and bases. The wall of secrecy around the operations of the national security agencies left Congress dependent upon the "expert"–with special access to classified information. The Congressional investigative role was also limited: executive privilege could be claimed to support a refusal to reveal information to the Congress. The Congress was forced to rely on information supplied by the bureaucrats it was attempting to control.

The public's influence on the shaping of foreign and military policy was limited. Dependent upon information provided by the executive, and the dissemination of it by the media, public opinion tended to follow policy formulation, not to guide it. James Rosenau found that the opinion leaders in foreign policy tended to be the same persons who were the decision makers with the government.

Huntington reached a similar conclusion concerning military and defense policy.

As the national security institutions expanded, whole sections of the populace became involved in their activities. The involvement tended to create a consensus about basic assumptions and outlooks. The lower classes were enlisted through the draft directly, or through the labor unions. The unions, bureaucratized and centralized, purged of radical elements, became a pillar of the National Security State, accepting relative prosperity in trade for political docility. As military spending increased, more and more workers were involved in the production of military products. As the state became more involved in the economy, a strike took on the appearance of a move against the state, and its utility as a weapon for political and economic change diminished.

The middle classes were employed in the giant interlocked hierarchies of the National Security State and the industrial estate. Large portions of the country became dependent upon military expenditures, either directly or from profits generated by the purchases by troops garrisoned throughout the nation, or by employees of defense contractors. The intelligentsia, first harried by the purge, then seduced by the trappings of power and by opportunity for influence, surrendered their critical independence to the state. Influence and academic fame became dependent upon acceptance of basic assumptions and perceptions. Academicians were employed to rationalize and justify the actions of the security bureaucracies. Political scientists developed "value-neutral" systems analysis, and engaged in deterrence studies, in "pacification" planning, in "nation building." Scientists and social scientists who accepted the lure of grants and access surrendered the basic essentials for intellectual freedom: they worked shrouded in secrecy, bound by loyalty oaths, separated from other colleagues by blacklists.

Power within the state came to rest in the institutions concerned with national security and headed by the President. The President acquired great formal powers, yet he did not control the state. He was limited by the advice and information given him by his advisers. He was bound by past commitments that were difficult to ignore. He was increasingly fenced in by the pervasive belief in the ideology that his predecessors had helped to instill. His license was limited by the bureaucratic inertia of the state. Bureaucratic habit and routine drastically attenuated the ability of the President to make basic policy changes.

The top officials of the national security institutions attempted to use the bureaucracy to manage the empire. But initiative was often taken from their hands. The interlocking military-industrial management hierarchies produced a constant flow of technological improvements in weaponry. An independent pressure for bigger and better armaments resulted, leading toward a greater expenditure of resources and a larger accretion of power. The perspective of the top officials was dependent upon the information and the evaluations given them by the intelligence agencies in State, Defense, and the CIA. These agencies were staffed by bureaucrats of ideological orthodoxy, which was the result of the purge and perpetuated by the recruitment process. Deeply enmeshed in the affairs of foreign countries, agents in these countries could instigate crises and initiate the involvement of the state. The routinization of spying and intrusion brought a constant pressure for intervention and control. The increasingly diverse capabilities of the military created a constant pressure for military or paramilitary involvement. Violence became the common means of policing the empire.

In this decade, however, contradictions have begun to appear in the state. The existence of a whole class of people who were excluded from the economic system, the presence of widespread poverty, hunger, and racism, have created a coalition at odds with the exaltation of American politics. An oppressive and prolonged imperialistic war in Vietnam has revealed the barbarity of institutionalized violence. The ideology of anti-communism has grown increasingly removed from reality, and therefore much more difficult for the educated young to accept. The frustrating protest against the war and against poverty and racism has revealed the institutionalized strength of the National Security State.

Moreover, in response to the spreading dissent, the leaders of the national security bureaucracies have resorted to the means they believe most effective–violence. Thus, the nature of the state is exposed: it makes war upon the edges of the empire and at home; it spies against other peoples and its own; it colonizes foreign states and domestic ones.

These revelations contain the beginnings of the struggle against the aggrandizement of the National Security State. Its dismantling will not be easy. Given the increased use of violence at home as well as abroad, the words of the Senate Foreign Relations Committee take on added meaning:

> Already possessing vast power over the country's foreign relations, the executive, by acquiring the authority to commit the country to war, now exercises something approaching absolute power over the life or death of every living American–to say nothing of millions of other people all over the world. . . . The concentration . . . of virtually unlimited authority over matters of war and peace has all but removed the limits to executive power in the most important single area of our national life. Until they are restored, the American people will be threatened with tyranny or disaster.

NOTES

Rewarding sources on the roots of America's postwar foreign policy include:

Richard J. Barnet, *Intervention and Revolution* (New American Library 1968)

Gabriel Kolko, *The Roots of American Foreign Policy* (Beacon Press 1969)

Gar Alperovitz, *Atomic Diplomacy: Hiroshima and Potsdam* (Random House-Vintage 1967)

Herbert Schiller, "The Use of American Power in the Post-Colonial World," *The Massachusetts Review*, Autumn 1968

Ronald Steel, *Pax Americana* (Viking 1967)

The series of books written and/or edited by David Horowitz, *Free World Colossus* (Hill and Wang 1965); *Containment and Revolution* (Beacon Press 1967); *Corporations and the Cold War* (Monthly Review Press 1970)

And, of course, William Appleman Williams, *The Tragedy of American Diplomacy* (Dell 1959)

The Williams quote is from *Tragedy*, p. 11

Acheson's testimony is contained in the Hearings on Post-War Economic Policy and Planning, Select Sub-Committee on Post-War Economic Policy and Planning, House, 78th Cong., 2d Sess., 1944

Kolko's study is *The Politics of War* (Random House 1968)

Truman's quote is found in Williams, *Tragedy*, p. 240

Schlesinger's comment is taken from his primer on Vietnam: Schlesinger, *The Bitter Heritage*, p. 131. The book's best contribution is the quote Schlesinger takes from Schumpeter: "Created by wars that required it, the [military] machine now created the wars it required."

Steel's quote is from his *Pax Americana*, p. 4

The Truman quote is from Harry S Truman, *Memoirs, II, Years of Trial and Hope* (Doubleday 1955) p. 2

Truman's address from which the quote on the power of the United States is taken may be found in *Public Papers of the Presidents* 1946 (Government Printing Office [GPO] 1962) p. 42

The address that occasioned the quote connecting peace and force (a common theme among the leaders of the Truman administration) was taken from *Documents of American Foreign Relations, Vol. VIII 1946,* p. 3

An assessment of postwar Soviet strength may be found in Isaac Deutscher, "Myths of the Cold War," in *Containment and Revolution,* David Horowitz, ed.

For the speech enunciating the Truman Doctrine, *Public Papers of the Presidents, Harry S Truman,* 1947, pp. 178–79

National Security Act of 1947

The most complete account of the postwar unification of the services is provided by Demetrios Carley, *The Politics of Military Unification* (Columbia University Press 1966)

The lead exchange between Forrestal and Bridges is found in the hearings on the bill: Senate Committee on Armed Services, *Hearings National Military Establishment,* 80th Cong., 2d Sess., p. 28

For a full copy of the bill: 61 Stat 495

The Forrestal quote on the extent of the program envisioned is from p. 28 of the hearings

Forrestal's concern with the interrelationship of foreign and military policies is related in J. V. Forrestal, *The Forrestal Diaries,* Walter Millis, ed. (Viking 1951) p. 239

Truman's adoption of Forrestal's program is described in his *Memoirs,* Vol. II

Nimitz's "forward-looking" quote is from the hearings, p. 129

The National Security Council

The 1949 amendments to the National Security Act: 63 Stat 578

Forrestal quote is from the Senate hearings, p. 25

Huntington's treatment of the demand for fusion is found in Samuel Huntington, *The Common Defense* (Columbia University Press 1961)

A good account of the postwar reforms in military education is contained in John W. Maseland and Laurence Radway, *Soldiers and Scholars, Military Education and National Policy* (Princeton University Press 1957)

The quote from the Brookings study is from Senate Committee on Foreign Relations, *The Formulation and Administration of United States Foreign Policy,* Study by Brookings Institution, No. 9 (GPO 1960) p. 87

Acheson's quote is from the second volume of his memoirs: Dean Acheson, *Present at the Creation* (W. W. Norton & Co. 1969) p. 736

The quote on Security Council secrecy is from Blair Bolles, *The Military Establishment of the United States,* Foreign Policy Reports XXV, No. 8 (Foreign Policy Association 1949) p. 10

For information concerning studies of the backgrounds of the leaders of the national security bureaucracies, see: G. William Domhoff, "Who Made American Foreign Policy 1945–1963," in *Corporations and the Cold War* (Monthly Review Press 1969)
Richard J. Barnet, *The Economy of Death* (Atheneum 1969) pp. 86–101
Gabriel Kolko, *Roots,* supra

Cora Bell's brilliant dissection of this aspect of Acheson's foreign policy: Cora Bell, *Negotiation from Strength* (Alfred A. Knopf 1963)

The National Military Establishment

For general studies of the postwar military, see: Clark R. Mollenhoff, *The Pentagon* (Putnam 1967); John M. Swomley, *The Military Establishment* (Beacon Press 1964); Fred J. Cook, *The Warfare State* (Macmillan 1962); and Tristram Coffin, *The Armed Society* (Pelican 1964)

The first two Secretaries were James V. Forrestal, who jumped through a window (after his retirement from the position), and Louis Johnson, of whom Acheson was to say, ". . . evidence accumulated to convince me that Louis Johnson was mentally ill." Although by itself no proof, since Acheson tended to consider all who disagreed with his viewpoint as somewhat unbalanced, Johnson later underwent surgery for brain damage

The Joint Chiefs of Staff

For differing views on the influence of the JCS, see Kolko, *Roots,* pp. 37–43. He believes they had little or no influence, and that the concept of a "military ethic" is a myth. Mills, *Power Elite,* pp. 292–96 and passim, emphasizes the postwar influence of the military, and the dominance of the military perspective

The Central Intelligence Agency

For general treatments of the CIA, see: Henry Howe Ransom, *Central Intelligence and National Security* (Harvard University Press 1958); and David Wise and Thomas B. Ross, *The Invisible Government* (Random House 1964)

The Dulles memorandum is printed in the Senate hearings on the National Security Act, p. 526

The 1949 Act, "Act to Provide for the Administration of the CIA," 63 Stat 208

The Acheson quote is from *Present,* p. 214

The Mansfield quote and a good review of the issues is provided in Young Hum Kim, *The Central Intelligence Agency: Problems of Secrecy in a Democracy* (Heath 1968)

Co-ordinating Boards

Budgetary figures are collected from the annual and semiannual reports of the Secretary of Defense to the Congress. See particularly Department of Defense, *Semi-annual Report of the Secretary of Defense,* Jan. 1–June 30, 1950 (GPO 1950)

Truman's quote on the budget is from "Statement of the President on Review of the Budget," *Public Papers of the Presidents, Harry S Truman 1947* (GPO 1962)

The Hoover quote is from Report of the Commission on Organization of the Executive Branch of the Government to the Congress, on the *National Security Organization in the Federal Government,* House Document 86, 81st Cong., 1st Sess., 1949

NSC-68 is crucial to the understanding of postwar policy. It was initiated and pushed inside the State Department. The chairman of the interdepartmental committee that wrote the document was Paul Nitze, who was impressed with the need for military power from his work on the Strategic Bombing Survey. Nitze pushed for a new defense outlook that would result in expenditures between thirty-five and fifty billion per year. The JCS were at the time hoping for an increase to about twenty-three billion, but were pleased to acquiesce to civilian enthusiasm. Acheson considers NSC-68 to be central to postwar policy; see Acheson, *Present,* pp. 371–82

For a full, detailed description of the preparation of NSC-68, see

Paul Hammond, "USC-68, Prologue to Rearmament," in *Strategy, Politics, and Defense Budgets,* Warner Schilling, ed. (Col. Univ. Press 1962)

The Contract Mechanism

The quote on the enlistment of industry and universities is from Don K. Price, *The Scientific Estate* (Oxford Univ. Press 1965) p. 37

The Armed Services Procurement Act of 1947 is found: 62 Stat 21 (1947)

The exchange between Byrd and Kinney is from Senate Committee on Armed Services, *Hearings, Armed Services Procurement Act 1947,* 80th Cong., 1st Sess. (GPO 1947)

The figure on negotiated contracts is from Mollenhoff, *The Pentagon,* p. 128

The figures and accounts of Munitions Board activities are also from the reports of the Secretary of Defense to the Congress

For *note, the authorization for scientific personnel, see 61 Stat 715 (1947) and 62 Stat 604 (1948). For authorization for employment of non-citizens, see P.L. 307, 60 (1946)

The best history of the provisions and operation of the AEC is by Richard G. Hewlett and Oscar E. Anderson, Jr., *A History of the United States Atomic Energy Commission* (Penn. State Univ. Press 1962)

The quote on the leaders of the service departments' feeling strongly about retaining control over atomic weapons is from Truman, *Memoirs II,* p. 3

The amendment to the AEC Act is 63 Stat 762 (1949)

Oppenheimer is quoted in H. L. Nieburg, *In the Name of Science* (Quadrangle 1966) p. 138

Truman's comment was on the Fourth Semiannual Report of the AEC in 1948, quoted in *Documents on American Foreign Policy* (1948) p. 262

The source for figures on R&D spending is the Steelman Report: President's Scientific Research Board, *Science and Public Policy II,* pp. 3 ff.

The Industrial Estate

The wartime relationship between the military and leading industrialists is described in Bruce Catton, *The War Lords of Washington* (Harcourt, Brace 1948)

See also Bureau of the Budget, *The United States at War* (GPO 1947)

A brief description of the activities of the National Security Industrial Assoc. is provided in Barnet, *Economy of Death,* pp. 104 ff.

Munitions Board advisory committees are discussed in Department of Defense, *Second Report of the Secretary of Defense,* Appendix B, Report Munitions Board, Fiscal 1948–49 (GPO 1950) p. 116. The report noted that "United States industry is found generally receptive and anxious to cooperate with the military forces."

Steelman Report on advisory committees from *Science and Public Policy III,* p. 180

Nieburg, *In the Name of Science,* p. 188

House Committee on Armed Services, Subcommittee Special Investigations, *Hearings, Sole Source Procurement, Part I,* 87th Cong., 1st Sess. (GPO 1961)

The Morrison quote is from Daniel S. Greenberg, *The Politics of Pure Science* (New American Library 1968) p. 136

The quote on measures taken to stimulate industry is from *Semi-Annual Report, Secretary of Defense* (1949) p. 10

Kennedy's discovery is noted by Seymour Melman, "Who Decides Technology," *Columbia Forum,* Winter 1968, p. 13

The Galbraith quote is from John Kenneth Galbraith, *The New Industrial State* (Houghton Mifflin 1967) p. 328

Summary provided by Nieburg, *In the Name of Science,* p. 193

The Scientific and Educational Estate

For a general documentation of contemporary military-university relationships, see Michael Klare, comp., *The University-Military Complex* (NACLA 1969)

A history of the controversial RAND Corporation is provided by Bruce Smith, *The RAND Corporation* (Harvard University Press 1966) But Smith's book must be read in conjunction with the review by Philip Green. Philip Green, "Science, Government, and the Case of RAND, A Singular Pluralism," *World Politics,* July 1968

The Steelman Report quote is from *Science and Public Policy,* IV, p. 20

Abelson's quote is from Philip Abelson, "A Critique of Federal Support of Research," *Science and Policy Issues,* Paul J. Piccard, ed. (Peacock 1969)

For the forging of liberal anti-communism and the story of the Congress for Cultural Freedom, see Christopher Lasch, *The Agony of the American Left* (Alfred A. Knopf 1969) pp. 61–114. The quote is from p. 64

Morgenthau is quoted from Hans Morgenthau, "Government Has Compromised the Integrity of the Educational Establishment," in *The CIA: Problems of Secrecy,* pp. 62–63

Price's quote is from Price, *The Scientific Estate*

Einstein is quoted in Nieburg, *In the Name of Science,* p. 155

Patterson's quote on the National Science Foundation is from House Committee on Interstate and Foreign Commerce, *Hearings on the National Science Foundation,* 80th Cong., 1st Sess., 1947, p. 28

Secrecy, Loyalty, and Security

The Wallace incident is related in Truman's *Memoirs I,* pp. 355 ff. Wallace, it should be noted, was replaced by Averell Harriman as Secretary of Commerce

Truman's statement at the time of the Wallace dismissal is taken from *Department of State Bulletin* 1946, p. 571

The statute denoting the Navy, Army, and Coast Guard sensitive agencies: 56 Stat 1053 (1942)

The extension of the provisions to the State Department: 60 Stat 453 (1946)

The Loyalty Committee report's quote is from *The Report of the President's Temporary Committee on Employee Loyalty* (GPO 1947) p. 21

Executive Order 9835 prescribing the new loyalty procedures may be found in 12 Fed. Reg. 1935

The best histories of the loyalty program in its early years are: Alan Barth, *Loyalty of Free Men* (Viking Press 1951); Eleanor Bontecou, *The Federal Loyalty-Security Program* (Cornell Univ.

Press 1953); and Ralph Sharpe Brown, *Loyalty and Security* (Yale, 1958)

The 1951 amendment of the standard was contained in Executive Order 10241, 16 Fed. Reg. 3690

The figures are from Brown, *Loyalty and Security,* pp. 54–55

The quote of the chairman is taken from the Senate Committee on Foreign Relations, *Hearings on State Department Employee Loyalty Investigation,* 81st Cong., 2d Sess., 1950, Pt. I, p. 409

The 1942 and 1946 security acts are cited above. The CIA authorization is found at 61 Stat 498 (1947)

P.L. 733 is found at 64 Stat 476 (1950)

The example of the extremes that security clearances reached is from Brown, *Loyalty and Security,* p. 62

Truman's 1950 Executive Order is E.O. 10173, 15 Fed. Reg. 7007

The ACLU comment on the CIO and other union purges: ACLU, *Our Uncertain Liberties,* 1947–48 Report (ACLU 1948) p. 7

For a detailed and very sympathetic account of the CIO and the 1949 incident, see Max M. Kampelman, *Communist Party and the CIO* (Praeger 1957)

The AEC-United Electrical Workers incident is related in Brown, *Loyalty and Security,* p. 77

Truman's statement that the loyalty program was intended to eliminate subversives is from Bontecou, p. 32

The comment on reasonable doubt is also from Bontecou, p. 70

For Fulbright's comment on bureaucratic orthodoxy, see William Fulbright, *The Arrogance of Power* (Random House-Vintage 1966) p. 29

Institutionalized Propaganda

Acheson's statements are taken from Acheson, *Present at the Creation,* p. 375. For a good review of his Memoirs, see Ronald Steel, "Commissar of the Cold War," *New York Review of Books,* Feb. 12, 1970, p. 15

The statements of the service secretaries are cited in John M. Swomley, *Press Agents of the Pentagon* (National Council Against Conscription, 1953) p. 36

The quote from *US News & World Report* is also from Swomley, p. 38

For the organization and Congressional investigation of postwar military publicity, see Swomley's pamphlet

The Army directives that contained the instructions on publicity are found in 11 Fed. Reg. 1768 (1946) and 11 Fed. Reg. 10910 (1946)

The colonel's comment on the cooperation of the media is from Swomley, p. 28

The figures on ROTC are cited in Masland and Radway, *Soldiers,* p. 251

The Selective Service Act of 1948: 62 Stat 604

Reckord's amusing quote is from House Subcommittee of Committee on Appropriations, *Hearings Military Establishment Appropriations Bill 1948,* 80th Cong., 1st Sess., 1948, p. 151

Behemoth

The title, of course, comes from Franz Neumann's classic study of Nazi Germany, *Behemoth* (Harper & Row 1944)

Acheson is quoted from his testimony at hearings held by the Senate Committee on Foreign Relations. It is cited in Merle J. Pusey, *The Way We Go to War* (Houghton Mifflin 1969) p. 9

The Congressional relationship to the military budget in 1950 is explored by Warner R. Schilling, "The Politics of National Defense: Fiscal 1950," in *Strategy . . . ,* Warner Schilling, ed.

Rosenau directs his attention to public influence on foreign policy in James Rosenau, *Public Opinion and Foreign Policy* (Random House 1961) p. 60 and passim

For the same point on military policy, see Huntington, *The Common Defense,* p. 235

The conclusory quote is taken from the Foreign Relations Committee's report on "National Commitments," cited in Pusey, *The Way . . . ,* p. 4

THE KENNEDY HAWKS ASSUME POWER FROM THE EISENHOWER VULTURES

by Marcus G. Raskin

WHILE a Senator, John Kennedy "exposed" the fact that there were only ninety-nine people in the whole government of President Eisenhower working on disarmament. Yet, eighteen months later, the Deputy Special Counsel to President Kennedy noted that there were still less than a hundred people, and he asked the head of the Disarmament Agency "to find" more people working on disarmament even if it included secretaries, so that there would be an appearance of greater action in that direction. Where was most of the action at the beginning of the Kennedy administration? It was in military affairs. And this "action" transformed American society.

Almost immediately after the presidential election, in 1960, Jack Kennedy offered the position of Secretary of Defense to Robert Strange McNamara, an industrial manager. Within one decade, two Secretaries had gone mad in the pyramid on the banks of the Potomac, James Forrestal and, according to Dean Acheson, Louis Johnson. Before offering the defense portfolio to manager McNamara, a Ford Motor Company employee who had served briefly as its president, Kennedy offered the post to Robert Lovett, a man who from the First World War "grew" with the aviation industry, investment banking, and the national security establishment, as Secretary of War for Air, Undersecretary of State, and then Deputy Secretary of Defense under George Marshall. But Lovett declined the Defense portfolio under Kennedy for health reasons.

President-elect Kennedy, ever mindful of his responsibilities as the chief minister of a coalition government, offered Republican Lovett the secretaryships of Treasury and State. He refused these "responsibilities" as well. It was said at the time that this investor in American national security on Wall Street and in Washington refused the three portfolios because he wanted all three of them, and that he intended to operate them from his roll-top partner's desk in Brown Brothers, Harriman. But surely that story was not to be taken seriously. The likelihood was that the war-making power of a Defense Department Secretary could cause one to be overwhelmed into madness; and Lovett did not want to take the chance. What was needed instead was a man who could systematize nuclear weapons, thermonuclear weapons, napalm, millions of men, rifles, chemical weapons, pencils, missiles, promotions, counterforce, aircraft carriers, anthrax virus, and counterinsurgency into organizational rationality. Robert McNamara seemed a natural for the job, having once been a professor at the Harvard Business School. However, it would be a disservice to Robert McNamara if we argued that he had no conscious ideology save that of the technology of organization. He burned with that quiet flame of the committed anti-Communist. After having told a Senate Committee how he had become familiar with the evils of communism as a Ford Motor Company executive, he said:

> There is no true historical parallel to the drive of Soviet Communist imperialism to colonize the world. This is not the first time that ambitious dictators have sought to dominate the globe. But none has ever been so well organized, has possessed so many instruments of destruction, or has been so

adept at disguising ignoble motives and objectives with noble phrases and noble words.

Furthermore, there is a totality in Soviet aggression which can be matched only by turning to ancient history, when warring tribes sought not merely conquest but the total obliteration of the enemy.

Soviet communism does not seek the physical obliteration of a conquered people, although it would not hesitate to do so, in my opinion, if this would serve its ends. But it does seek the total obliteration of their customs, their social structure, their political structure, their religion, and their freedoms. Everything and everybody must be remolded according to a blueprint laid down by Lenin and altered only for the purposes of ruthless efficiency by Stalin and the present-day leaders.

There is nothing too sacred–friendship, integrity, church, or family–that it escapes the attention of the Soviet Commissar or the Communist bureaucrat.

Soviet communism seeks to wipe out the cherished traditions and institutions of the free world with the same fanaticism that once impelled winning armies to burn villages and sow the fields with salt so they would not again become productive.

To this primitive concept of total obliteration, the Communists have brought the resources of modern technology and science. The combination is formidable. Twentieth century knowledge, when robbed of any moral restraints, is the most dangerous force ever let loose in the world. And the entire literature of Soviet communism can be searched without turning up the faintest trace of moral restraint.

If the free world should lose to communism, the loss would be total, final, and irrevocable. The citadel of freedom must be preserved because there is no road back, no road back to freedom for anyone if the citadel is lost. . . .

I cite this material because I want you to know the spirit in which I believe the education program of our Defense Establishment should be conducted. The threat is clear and it is immediate. Our fighting men should know the positive values of the freedoms which the Nation is calling them to defend, and they should know the nature of Soviet communism, which seeks to take them away.

When he took over the position of Secretary of Defense from Thomas Gates, McNamara appointed over one hundred twenty task forces to look into the various programs of the Department. Early in his stewardship, the Department of Defense was a hotbed of intellectual activity, where hard-core fantasists were given their chance at statecraft. Whereas a generation earlier the fantastic-minded might have gone to Hollywood to seek their fortunes in writing movies, in the early sixties many *from* California —and particularly the RAND Corporation—came to the Department of Defense. There they hawked their studies, created war games, and wrote scenarios that led to comprehensive defense policy and institutional changes. McNamara informed the House Appropriations Subcommittee on Defense that he "personally reviewed the results in detail in order to have the benefit of their advice and counsel." McNamara went on to tell the committee, ". . . we have examined all of the principal alternatives and have selected that combination of programs which we believe will give the Nation a fully adequate defense at the least cost, in the light of the threat as we view it today." He believed this view, although several years later he pointed out to the House Committee on Armed Services, ". . . we are, in effect, attempting to anticipate production and deployment decisions which our opponents, themselves, have *not* made." (emphasis added)

The strategic choices that the Kennedy administration made in its early days set the framework for a generation of defense planning. Weapons systems need at least five years of planning, development, and programming; and each weapons system brings with it a whole social, economic, and political support system. Even if the particular weapons system is changed or diminished, the "support" system remains to continue the martial spirit and bring in new weapons. The decisions made to build up the armed forces and develop key new weapons systems, produce them, and deploy them, were generated by internal government, bureaucratic, and corporate pressures. The dynamic needed to justify our offensive military posture was a crisis-oriented foreign policy which served as the pretext for a huge expansion of American military forces. The consequences of this policy were known at the time. It did not escape attention that the Kennedy/McNamara "combination of programs" would lead to a fantastic increase in the military-social system, the nuclear arms race, and war fighting, as well as America's intervention capability. The President had stated in his special defense budget message to Congress on March 28, 1961, "Our defense posture must be both flexible and determined. Any potential aggressor contemplating an attack on any part of the free world with any kind of weapons, conventional or nuclear, must know that our response will be suitable, selective, swift, and effective. . . . Our weapons systems must be usable in a manner permitting deliberation and discrimination as to timing, scope, and targets, in response to civilian authority, and our defenses must be secure against prolonged reattack as well as a surprise first attack."

Not only the civilian defense strategists were busy. The Joint Chiefs were asked by McNamara to establish a working group "to study the requirements for U.S. general-purpose forces to meet a number of possible non-nuclear combat situations in various overseas *potential trouble spots.*" Parallel studies were conducted in each of the services. Sixteen different situations were studied in Europe, the Middle East, Southeast Asia, and Northeast Asia for the purpose of determining requirements of a global policy. This study, undertaken by Lieutenant General J. W. Parker and Vice Admiral H. D. Riley, was a supplement to those studies conducted by civilians in the Secretary of Defense staff who studied thermonuclear war. Such plans had a powerful effect on the size, character, and matériel of the Department of Defense. After two years it resulted in:

A 100-percent increase in the number of nuclear weapons available in the strategic alert forces.

A 45-percent increase in the number of combat-ready Army divisions.

A one-third increase in the number of tactical fighter squadrons.

A 60-percent increase in the tactical nuclear forces deployed in Western Europe.

A 75-percent increase in airlift capability.

A 100-percent increase in general ship construction and conversion.

A sixfold increase in counterinsurgency forces.

As a result of these improvements, the American policy makers, according to McNamara, were prepared to undertake a

demonstrated willingness to risk using these forces in defense of our vital interests. Here are some examples:

The callup of about 150,000 reservists and the deployment of 40,000 additional men to Europe in the summer of 1961.

The confrontation of Khrushchev on the issue of Soviet offensive missiles in Cuba in October of 1962.

The dispatch of 16,000 U.S. military personnel to South Vietnam to assist that country with logistics and training support in combating the Vietcong insurrection.

The prompt response of the United States in sending Army and Marine Corps units to Thailand in May 1962, when it appeared that the Communists might overrun Laos.

. . . continuing efforts to assist other free nations in defending their sovereignty and in building a better future for their people. Our military and economic aid to such nations, particularly those on the periphery of the Communist bloc, has given them a more desirable alternative to communism and has made them less vulnerable to Communist penetration and subversion.

The United States intended under Kennedy to develop a war-fighting capability on all levels of violence from thermonuclear war to counterinsurgency. For the policy makers it was a heady time, in which strategy became a toy of war and men sat in "situation" rooms in the State Department, the White House, and the CIA, planning and manipulating the destinies of unsuspecting millions. The military and the civilian war planners designed strategies and weapons for every option and situation they could conceive. Their tools were violence and threat, and their ideology was the Roman notion of domination. If the question of justice was considered, it was the justice of Thrasymachus, wherein justice followed the decisions of the strong.

War and Threat

The use of threat and violence as tools of national policy required the ability to escalate the level of violence if the armed forces or the planners seemed to be losing at the particular level initially chosen by the war planners. The logic of such a strategy of escalation pressed the national security apparatus to prepare for a first-strike capability against the Soviet Union. Most Kennedy strategists and military planners believed in two theories in 1961: the willingness to escalate from any particular level of violence to a higher one, and the idea that the American people must be prepared to fight and intervene in other people's problems for the good of others and for the needs of the American state. It was believed that unless the American legions would fight in place *A*, they would have to fight in place *B* under less "advantageous" conditions. As Secretary McNamara said, "Readiness and mobility can greatly reduce requirements for general purpose forces. This is simply the principle of getting there first with the most, before the situation deteriorates and greater forces are required to recover lost ground."

A military build-up was consciously sought in order to back up the grandiose plans of the policy makers, who wished to have at their command every option no matter how unlikely its use might be. Looking back over his first years as Secretary of Defense, Secretary McNamara was particularly proud of "the substantial build-up in our military strength during the last three years, both for general and for limited war." He had early reported to Congress that a war fighting capability and counterforce were central to his theory. The instruments of violence were morally neutral and were to be applied whenever and however necessary. As McNamara pointed out, "We are implementing processes at all levels of authority to insure that our response can be graded by degree, by geographic and political area, and by target type, as would be appropriate to the type and extent of an enemy attack."

War was a natural extension of bureaucratic decision making. It was the life of the state–purposive, rational, and not wasteful. Weapons were not for show; they were for use–unless threat proved to be enough. This view represented a significant change from the policies of the Eisenhower administration, which saw threat value in the brandishing of nuclear weapons but did not envision fighting wars with them. Indeed, there were no war options under the Eisenhower administration once nuclear weapons were introduced against the Soviet Union. (The war plans of Eisenhower's administration were described by

Herman Kahn as a wargasm.) While Dulles talked like a brinksman, his military policies did not match his words. The great change in switching over to the Kennedy national security theory was that policy makers thought that nuclear weapons could be used as an instrument of war fighting. Thermonuclear war was no longer "unthinkable" as Eisenhower had said, or mad.

When Kennedy became President, he was told by strategists that nuclear weapons were a rational option, and unless he was prepared to use them, the NATO alliance and dreams of Atlantic community would be shattered. He was told that strategies for limited and full counterforce were absolutely essential for the Grand Design in Europe and Asia. With these strategies, he was told by his advisers, he could decide how many weapons he wanted to use, when, and where. The Kennedy fantasists believed that nuclear bombing or brushfire war or B-52 bombing or missile attacks could be "surgical." Much time was spent by the savants in the Kennedy administration talking about such "surgical" methods. The foreign policy now specifically stated the need to defend every place in the world that the leadership said needed either defending, attacking, engaging, or dominating. It was essential that budgetary constraints be dropped at the Defense Department. "Arbitrary" ceilings on defense expenditures were removed by Kennedy and McNamara. The new policy was to "recommend the size of Military Establishment and the type of Military Establishment that we believe is required to protect our national security, without regard to arbitrary budget ceilings."

The idea of active dominance was a central theme in the presidential campaign of 1960. Following its presidential nominee's lead, the Democratic Party appealed to the sense of American insecurity, which required that America as a state have "purpose" and be first in everything, whether making weapons or widgets.

Kennedy argued that United States prestige, power, and military arsenal were slipping. This view reflected the position taken by technocrats and manufacturers who were taking over the operations of major American corporate interests, and who were on the frontiers of new American industry such as electronics and missiles. The impetus for the loss-of-prestige argument was first presented during 1956–57 at hearings on air power and missile preparedness held by Senator Stuart Symington. Those hearings concluded that the Eisenhower military policies had failed to maintain a pre-eminent lead over the Russians in military matters. The claim that there was a bomber gap and then a missile gap was a political challenge by the Democratic Party to the middle-western, middle-class big businessmen who controlled the policy of the Eisenhower administration in the White House. Men like George Humphrey and Charles Wilson were unimpressed with preparedness arguments or even challenges within the Republican party to war-option mongers such as Nelson Rockefeller, who proposed to Eisenhower military policies similar to those that were put in practice a few years later by President Kennedy. The predominant thread of the national security establishment groups that attached themselves to the Rockefeller brothers' reports and the Kennedy presidential aspirations was that technique, technology, expertise, and risk taking for war were crucial in maintaining American dominance in the world arena.

The winner mentality of President Kennedy co-opted the Rockefeller position. Playing on the Soviet Sputnik success of 1957, Kennedy repeated over and over how America had to get moving again; that it did not have to *fall behind*—words that strike terror in the hearts of Americans—but could maintain dominance in all things. So, in 1960, large segments of the "educated" middle class believed in missiles, huge military expenditures, and adventures, as manifestations of America as Number One.

The Eisenhower administration, somewhat less pretentious, saw military budgets in different terms. After the Korean War ended, allocations to the Department of Defense were viewed by the Eisenhower Cabinet in two ways —one, as an economic pump primer, and the other, as a political pay-off to departmental agencies that wielded great power in the country and in Congress, so that they would not challenge civilian authority. The Budget and Treasury, with the President's approval, allocated a lump sum that the services could fight over and split among themselves. Thus, the pay-off had particular limits.

Eisenhower tried to limit military power by arguing for balancing the budget, a slogan that means business-class control over governmental bureaucratic expenditures, whether defense or otherwise. The powers within the Democratic party during the Kennedy period denied this view. Reflecting bureaucratic and technocratic expertise, they could not believe that money expended on the military should not be immediately translated into political power and pre-eminence in the world.

The Country Gets a New Strategic Theory

At the end of the Eisenhower administration, strategists from the RAND Corporation and Harvard, such as Herman Kahn and Thomas Schelling, urged the idea of making military power relevant to political bargaining. In their mind, there was an inherent illogic in having nuclear weapons and not making them advantageous to political bargaining. From their views and those of General Parrish in the Air Force, the strategy of counterforce was developed. Such nuclear-war theoreticians as William Kaufman (presently at the Brookings Institution), Henry Rowen (now director of the RAND Corporation), and Charles Hitch (the comptroller of the Department of Defense and later president of the University of California) helped to refine the counterforce war-fighting strategy. The war-fighting counterforce policy was first presented as a relevant instrument for political bargaining in the crisis over Berlin. In the spring of 1961, the Soviets were continuing to press, as they had done since 1950, to reinstate four-power control over Berlin. The cold war in Europe was centered around Germany, with the United States trying to integrate West Germany into a mythical Atlantic community, the Soviets wishing to have a neutral Germany not committed to an alliance. The restatement of this policy by Khrushchev caused the President to respond that he was a Berliner and that the United States was prepared to "defend" Berlin or NATO by initiating the use of nuclear weapons.

After discussions with Khrushchev in Vienna, Kennedy returned to the United States, called up the reserves, hurried studies of a first-strike attack on the Soviet Union, and otherwise responded in a way that showed the grit of President Kennedy with our lives. The counterforce strategy was an important instrument in this diplomatic battle. With President Kennedy's defense message of March 1961, the handwriting was on the wall for a counterforce strategy. Much was made of the idea of command and control. While this notion was billed publicly as a way to insure against accidental war, it was in fact an instrument for war fighting, so that policy makers would think that they could fight thermonuclear wars and control them. The hard-core counterforce planners believed in and advocated the need to be in the position of staging a pre-emptive strike on the Soviet Union, and some thinkers even advanced the idea of city swapping, or the "diffident" use of nuclear weapons. As a purely strategic matter, counterforce received its greatest impetus from those who saw that the ICBM could be suddenly launched, and that the speed and size of the attacking vehicle all make the task of detecting, tracking, and destroying the incoming warhead a technical problem of unparalleled difficulty. Needless to say, the superior force which had surprise on its side could, or so it was said, inflict enough damage on the other side through a disarming attack of its military bomber and missile installations, to make it unlikely that the Soviets could destroy the United States.

In situations such as Berlin, where it was decreed by the American leadership that America's vital interests were involved, this meant that the United States would have to be ready to perform a first-strike counterforce attack on the Soviet Union. Members of the White House staff such as Spurgeon Keeny and Jerome Wiesner carried the burden of the argument that no matter how many missiles the United States had, it would never have enough to carry out more than a deterrence-only strategy, because the Soviets would always have enough missiles left to destroy the urban industrial land space of the United States. Yet, by the spring of 1962, it appeared that the foreign policy of the United States, with its involvements in Vietnam, Laos, Berlin, and Cuba, was making the counterforce strategy more palatable.

The most explicit statement of this strategy came in a speech to the graduating class of the University of Michigan by the Secretary of Defense. In this speech, McNamara specifically advocated counterforce as the only viable American nuclear policy on the ultimate level of violence. From outside the policy-making circle but still very much within the nation's elite groups, scientists took an ad in the New York *Times* deploring the Secretary's speech and its implications of an unlimited arms race which might lead to pre-emptive war. But there was support for McNamara's position in the Congress. Senator Margaret Chase Smith, a spartan governess and senior member of the Senate Armed Services Committee, supported the "lonely" secretary, as she described him, and urged the President to come out in support of the Secretary, who had gone out on a limb for an unlimited arms race with maximum (though unattainable) options.

One recommendation of Senator Symington's preparedness subcommittee was that the United States improve its intelligence estimates of the Soviet Union. Yet it was clear, even by the early spring of 1961, that the presumed missile gap did not favor the Soviet Union, but the United States. This fact did not change the number of missiles recommended by the militarized civilians operating the Department of Defense.

In a committee hearing, Secretary McNamara was asked by Congressman Gerald Ford how seriously the Defense Department leadership took intelligence estimates. "But if we had a 25 per cent downgrade in the Soviet Union ICBM threat in the next several months, would that have a substantial impact on their total destructive force as far as we are concerned?" McNamara answered Ford's comment by observing that such estimates did have "impact but not very much" on the missile programs that the Department of Defense would submit to the Congress. McNamara later commented that, had the planners known then what they did later about Soviet plans in 1961, he would not have proposed such a massive ICBM build-up. There is very little in the record of 1961 to suggest that intelligence estimates played any but the most marginal role in our attempt to build a counterforce strategy. From intelligence reports, McNamara knew that the Soviets were not ahead of the United States in strategic missiles in early 1961. Such estimates were used only to rationalize policy or to report new "threats," not to change the basic ideology of war fighting on either the thermonuclear or limited-war level.

The tragic aspect of the McNamara and early Kennedy

administration advisers was their belief that technical answers could be found, so that thermonuclear war could be fought surgically and precisely. The Cuban missile crisis was thought to prove the viability of counterforce, that American missile strength had frightened the Russians into retreat. Critics of the Kennedy period suggest, instead, that Khrushchev had put missiles into Cuba in the first place in response to America's build-up of a first-strike capability.

The counterforce strategy has been a hard one to put down. It continues to live in the Pentagon and in the choices made for present-day weapons systems. During the McNamara period, the self-deception of the counterforce strategy was that it could limit damage in a thermonuclear war. Beneath this mask was the hard reality that policy makers wanted to use thermonuclear weapons for war fighting. McNamara, Paul Nitze, and others had hoped to interest the Soviets in the thermonuclear game of counterforce war fighting, but the Soviets continued to point out that they were not rich enough to aim at military targets. They repeatedly said in disarmament talks that they could "afford" only a deterrent strategy. They had only enough missiles to destroy the urban-industrial land space of the United States, and they would do this if a first strike were launched against them.

The notion of building a "flexible capability," as it was called, meant that the United States wanted the option of striking at a variety of targets, both city and military. The massive strike forces that the United States had in the early sixties–six hundred and fifty manned bombers on fifteen-minute alert, over two hundred operational Atlas, Titan, and Minuteman missiles, 144 Polaris missiles, with the prospect of far greater numbers of these missiles–required the planners to find more-exquisite ways of using such weaponry than an all-out thermonuclear holocaust.

The Soviet Union did not have, nor does it presently

have, enough missiles to destroy the military targets of the United States. Thus, in any nuclear conflict it always risks destruction of its cities, but the United States then and now continues to live with the illusion of war fighting at the highest level of violence. Such habits of mind, which attempt to create problem-solving options for insoluble problems, allowed the Kennedy leadership to believe that they would be able to undertake a counterforce strategy, and simultaneously to get the Russians to accept the idea of limited thermonuclear war, in which the United States would control the escalation because it possessed enough hardware to go to the highest level. This fantasy came to be accepted also for the less-than-general war level and guided the thinking of Army planners in counterinsurgency and brush-fire war. The next step up in the violence category was tactical nuclear war.

While Eisenhower attempted to argue the unthinkableness of nuclear war, strategists such as Henry Kissinger, as well as the Rockefeller brothers, men who have long had the public interest in their private hearts, attempted to find a way wherein tactical nuclear weapons could be used, and limited nuclear wars could be fought. The idea of a limited tactical nuclear war had much currency in fashionable intellectual circles during the late fifties, until various war games showed that the countries who were hosts to tactical nuclear weapons would, for all practical purposes, have been destroyed. What the great powers referred to as tactical nuclear war—war on someone else's land—was general war to the country upon which the warriors fought. War games run in the late nineteen fifties, such as Operation Carte Blanche, showed that Europe would be destroyed in any tactical nuclear war. Such defense experts as Sir Solly Zuckerman exploded the myth of a controlled tactical nuclear war and presented that evidence in 1961 to the White House staff, but this did not deter the Kennedy build-up of tactical nuclear weapons—options, of course, had to be maintained.

The Civil Defense Madness

With the counterforce strategy came the notion of civil defense to protect American cities and larger numbers of SAC planes on airborne-alert status. Both were to create a new martial spirit in the country and the bureaucracy. If there were civil defense, then as a Stanford Research Institute report said, "will-stiffening" could be performed on the American people, and American policy rulers could be that much tougher at the bargaining table. In effect, America would merely have to advertise, and never bargain.

A favorite thought of the time, never put into practice, was the idea of population evacuation. Cities would be evacuated to show the enemy that we were invulnerable to his deterrent, which was aimed at our cities. Once we were able to "take out" enough Soviet missile and bomber bases, with nuclear weapons left over to destroy the Soviet population, the United States would be able to enforce its will at the bargaining table. If the bargainers from the other side did not go along, then the United States could destroy the "enemy," and our people could survive.

The issue of Civil Defense was a political one as well for the President in the early months of his administration. Nelson Rockefeller was the Chairman of the panel on civil defense for the Governors Conference in 1961. He had worked hard, with advisers Edward Teller and Henry Kissinger, to initiate a shelter program in the state of New York. When he went to India, he attempted to convince Nehru of the importance of building civil-defense shelters for his people in India. Rockefeller at that time was an important political figure nationally who, it was feared, would challenge Kennedy in 1964. President Kennedy ordered his Special Assistant for National Security Affairs McGeorge Bundy, to put his staff to work on the civil-defense issue. The person put in charge of this effort, Carl Kaysen, wrote, with me, a study of the civil defense program which concluded that it would not work and so recommended to the President. However, the Special Counsel to the President, Theodore Sorenson, pressed for the program for political reasons, and it was devised by the Department of Defense and Carl Kaysen.

The Department of Defense received primary operating responsibility for civil defense from the Office of Civil Defense Mobilization. The Army hesitantly took the program, making clear that it was not giving up its primary mission as war fighters. The Army leadership feared that they would be reduced to a police operation, to fight off the rats and protect those with shelters from those who did not have them.

One view of those, like Kaysen, who were opposed to the program, was that it might be "insurance" but could never be more than that. The fear of the insurers was that civil defense would be seen as a "will-stiffener," causing the Russians to believe that America was preparing for a first strike. McGeorge Bundy, who might have been able to stop the program in the first rather than in a later stage, did not comprehend its consequences quickly enough to act with the kind of dispatch and force that might have stopped it. A program was put together, meant by the White House as insurance.

As some within the government, specifically Adam Yarmolinsky and then Steuart Pittman, saw their positions tied to civil defense, they presented a more comprehensive view of it through the Department of Defense.

By July of 1961, civil defense was becoming part of the American deterrent arsenal. In the White House, national security advisers had lost interest and responsibility for it. The new Assistant Secretary for Civil Defense, Steuart Pittman, said before the Senate Armed Services Committee that civil defense needed to be "a priority military assignment."

The program itself was absurd. It provided for protection only from fallout, not fire and blast. The public itself was to buy its own middle-class shelters, although the 207.9 million dollars requested in new funds was to provide a national program for identification and marking of community shelter spaces in existing buildings. Secretary McNamara also requested that a program be developed for the construction of shelters in new federal buildings. "This last program should also serve as an incentive for State and local governments and as a model for their buildings, schools, and offices." The federal government was going to make the conditions for nuclear war, and then the rest of the country would have to try to protect itself.

McNamara then went on to say, ". . . in order to make shelters usable, they must be equipped with the minimum essentials for survival during a 1-to-2 week period. Based on careful studies and tests, we regard the minimum essentials for survival to be five days' rations at 25-30 cents per person per day—an austerity ration with a long shelf life; 2 weeks' water supply at 1.5 cents per day per person; first-aid kits; sanitary supplies; tools to remove debris; and perhaps most important, radiation meter kits." Of course, studies showed that, even two hundred miles downwind, a person would imbibe enough radioactivity to guarantee his death if he came out of his shelter after the 15th to 20th day. Studies by scientists at the AEC showed that the only survivors would be the rats.

Politically, the most extraordinary example of bad judgment was a recommendation of the Department of Defense that President Kennedy go on television and state to the American people that everyone should have a defense shelter. He was to sign a letter to every family in the United States, and each family was to receive a civil-defense booklet, first prepared by the Time-Life people and later rewritten. This bit of statecraft madness was stopped by members of the White House staff. In Congress the program was given to Albert Thomas, who was opposed to it, and its active life ended while people from New Jersey, Washington, and Arizona debated how they were going to keep out their neighbors who did not have shelters.

The Army's New Opportunity

In 1953, the incoming Eisenhower administration brought with it a new view of how to manage national security and defense affairs. The so called New Look meant reliance on air power, and specifically structuring our defense posture so that the United States could never again involve itself in a war like Korea. What the military and the planners might have seen as limited, the people and the politicians saw as exhausting. Consequently, the Eisenhower policy favored a reduction of U.S. forces deployed overseas. Army forces would be kept small lest we be tempted to use them to fight another Korea by conventional means. The partisans of the New Look were convinced that the United States should never again make that mistake, and set about reducing Army forces to make it physically impossible even if our future leaders might be so inclined. This theory was of course predicated on the idea that if the United States did not have certain arms and armaments *in being,* it could not use them. The opposing view advocated sufficient arms to allow the leadership a wide range of options.

It is worth while to pause a moment on this debate. The Eisenhower administration was very concerned about budgeting and civilian control over the military. As General Maxwell Taylor describes it, when he was considered for Army Chief of Staff, then-Secretary of Defense Wilson told him that he expected obedience from the military and if Taylor had any reservations about such loyalty it would be better if he did not take the job. General Taylor averred that he could be obedient, since he had thirty-seven years' training in the art of obedience. Wilson then sent Taylor to see Eisenhower, his World War II commander. Eisenhower was also concerned about civilian control and, according to Taylor's account, spent most of that interview talking about the importance of civilian control. This was a period in which the President and his civilian advisers did not want any back talk from the military. They did not want another General MacArthur on their hands. Generals were expected to watch carefully their p's and q's, deferring to the civilians and to budgetary requirements as laid out by the Department of the Treasury, headed by George Humphrey, a buccaneer capitalist whose low esteem of the military was famous. Humphrey had been the head of Mark Hanna Mining, and the Treasury was not much more difficult to operate than international business investment and exploration. His replacement, Robert Anderson, came from Texas, where he had managed the King Ranch. These gentlemen were agreed on the importance of limiting military operations and of control as instruments of a business class that believed in balanced budgets for their own sake and as a dual instrument to control the military and hold down government spending and bureaucratic control which might challenge business power.

The generals who sought highest command chafed under this view of governing. They wanted wars to fight, men to use, interests to protect, and action. Maxwell Taylor, the author of the idea that less-than-nuclear wars should be fought to protect American interests, endeavored to press his point of view during the Eisenhower administration. He found few receptive ears until the last years of that administration, when he succeeded in convincing the Navy and Marines that if they ever wanted to fight wars again, they would have to have flexible responses, because when "push came to shove," as the saying went, the civilians would not authorize the use of nuclear weapons. There were those in the government and outside of it who believed Dulles and Eisenhower were secret softies. These men, it was said, were hiding under brinksman talk and paper alliances, but they were unable to match their talk and alliances with military force. Forward thinkers in the military field, such as General Taylor, Bernard Brodie, and B. H. Liddell-Hart agreed that the policy of mutual deterrence should give way to limited conventional wars of a smaller scale. Taylor made the argument that the U.S. military forces were muscle-bound, unable to respond, because the United States had adopted an all-or-nothing stance. Our threats to destroy the world, he said, were not credible. Indeed, had not Eisenhower once said that thermonuclear war was unthinkable?

On Taylor's mind lay the incident at Dien Bien Phu, where the flower of Western civilization, French colonialism, was lost to the Vietnamese. The spring of 1954 was a sad time in American policy-making circles. The CIA and military assistance were not enough to save the French in Indochina. Debates ran heavy about American military intervention to save the French chestnuts, as one American senator put it, or to feed on the dying carcass of French colonialism. The decision was to stage a series of air strikes in Indochina called Operation Vulture. This view was presented to Eisenhower, who had many of the characteristics of General Kutuzov in *War and Peace*. He told the advocates of Operation Vulture that, if they could get support from leading members of Congress and the allies, he would agree to the operation. There was no chance of that happening.

General Taylor was disappointed. He saw the American failure to intervene in Dien Bien Phu in two ways. One was a failure of nerve and leadership. And the other was a failure to have the fighting equipment and armed forces necessary for intervention and engagement with the Huns of Vietnam. Taylor agreed with General Ridgeway's position that bombing intervention would not work. As Taylor points out, we were unprepared to intervene. "During these deliberations and hesitations, the need was apparent for ready military forces with conventional weapons to cope with this kind of limited war situation. Unfortunately, such forces did not then exist in sufficient strength or in proper position to offer any hope of success. In May, Dien Bien Phu fell, and in the following July in Geneva, Indo-China was partitioned between Communism and Freedom at the 17th parallel [sic]. This event was the first, but not the last failure of the New Look *to keep the peace on our terms.*" (emphasis added)

General Taylor was not interested in respite from war, which he viewed as a continuous activity of the state. The Korean adventure was part of the over-all struggle for Southeast Asia between its inhabitants and the West. He wanted to press ahead. His own views on American intervention in Vietnam from 1961 on were directly related to his belief that the American rulers had not fulfilled their "responsibilities" at Dien Bien Phu. Members of the Eisenhower administration did not accept war fighting in their doctrine. On the other hand, Taylor did not believe that the covert activities of the CIA were enough to police the Third World. His view contradicted that of the brothers Dulles, who argued that the United States did not have to intervene militarily in various parts of the world. It would be able to dominate, through covert means, that is, through the CIA, and through threats of massive nuclear retaliation. The day-to-day activity of American involvement in the world would be through the CIA, which would both spy, and control through payoffs, bribes, and blackmail—the ancient methods of rulers. What the CIA could not do, it was assumed that various forms of foreign aid could accomplish. Eisenhower's Chief of Staff in World War II, Walter Bedell Smith, had been in charge of the CIA from 1950, where for three years he had worked at the task of defining the mission and the organizational structure necessary to carry out overt and covert activities. The formal institutionalization of the CIA's operation as the central arm of American foreign policy was "telegraphed" by Smith's shift from head of the CIA to Undersecretary of State in 1953.

"Wild Bill" Donovan, who had set up the Office of Strategic Services during the Second World War, was chosen by President Eisenhower in 1953 as ambassador to Thailand. His responsibility in that position was to set up a Southeast Asian spy control network in this area. At first he thought it necessary to undertake this task as a personal representative of the President—without diplomatic status. However, he was assured that such activities could be carried out directly through the Secretary and the Undersecretary of State.

The ascendancy of the CIA through the Dulles brothers and Smith during the Eisenhower period had the internal effect within the American national security bureaucracy of playing down the active use of the Army for purposes of war fighting. The United States had gone through a difficult Korean "limited" war engagement, which threatened the internal power balances between civilians and the military within the national security system. Furthermore, the Republican party itself had come to power specifically denying the policies of military engagement and intervention, and pressing the need to end the military war in Korea.

By the late 1950s, some of the Army general officers became concerned that war fighting, as in Korea, would no longer occur. Consequently, Army budgets would be constantly cut except for those portions earmarked for assistance in building the militaries of other countries, and, within the national security bureaucracy, the CIA would grow. The major *active* use of the armed forces during the Eisenhower administration was that of commanding the Seventh Fleet to evacuate seventeen thousand civilians and twenty-five thousand troops from the Ta Chen islands, which the mainland Chinese then occupied; and the U.S. intervention in Lebanon with fifteen thousand American troops, which were withdrawn within three and a half months.

The strongest advocates of a war-fighting capability, such as General Maxwell Taylor, thought they saw the power of the CIA growing as the Army's power decreased. General Taylor's development of the limited-war strategy enabled the Army officers to assert an *active* mission for the Army in the face of the CIA involvement and extensive paramilitary covert activities. The chance to control the CIA and to effect a decrease in its power occurred as a result of the Cuban adventure of April 1961, which was planned and executed by the CIA. After its failure, the President assigned the task of analyzing the Cuban failure and reallocating the power of engagement and intervention within the government to General Taylor and Robert Kennedy. Needless to say, General Taylor was not an "independent spokesman," since his bill of goods was the importance of fighting limited wars. So, while the Eisenhower administration threatened total nuclear destruction and simultaneously used the CIA as its chosen instrument of intervention, the Kennedy administration attempted to reallocate power within the national security bureaucracy, favoring continuous military engagement and a ready war-fighting capability.

In 1959, General Taylor believed that the United States had to "deter general war, to deter *or win* local war, and finally to cope with a general war if deterrence fails." Taylor pointed out in an article, which the Department of Defense refused to clear, that his program of defense would be costly. *"Without making a specific estimate, one may be sure that the total bill will exceed any peacetime budget in United States history."* (emphasis added) But in exchange for this bill, we would, he thought, be able to deter general war and win local war quickly. General Taylor was appointed by President Kennedy as his chief military adviser.*

Taylor's views were not unknown, so the President was not buying a pig in a poke. He wanted to increase American military power across the board. Not only was it necessary to be able to fight general wars through a counterforce strategy, it was also necessary to be able to fight local wars. It was expected that the U. S. Army would be prepared to fight guerrilla wars, limited wars, and general wars *simultaneously*. By 1961, General Taylor was in a position to rectify the American error at Dien Bien Phu. He was sent by the President with Walt Rostow, a deputy special assistant to the President, to Vietnam. They worked out a local war plan to save the South Vietnamese from a fate worse than death. In his first time before a Congressional committee with his own program, McNamara called for adding 230 million dollars to the limited-war budget. Secretary McNamara pointed out that the new planning of

* A little anecdote of some importance should be told. When Taylor was appointed military adviser to the President in the early summer of 1961, his offices were on the same floor as those of the National Security Council Staff—the third floor of the Executive Office Building. When he moved in, he immediately put guards around his office and those of his staff. This symbolic victory over the Bundy staff necessitated a retaliation. The Bundy staff got guards for its offices so that one had to go through guards in order to get to their staff as well. But now there were guards on that floor within one hundred feet of each other. An arms-control agreement was called, and guard desks were now put in front of the elevators to cover both staffs.

his group recognized the possibility that the armed forces would have to fight limited wars in different places at the same time: "My statement specifically states that the ability to respond promptly to limited aggression in more than one place at the same time is one of my objectives."

McNamara's view was held also by the new Secretary of the Army, Elvis Stahr, who later became the president of the University of Indiana. In his opening statement to the House Subcommittee on Defense Appropriations, Stahr gave the congressmen a lesson in international politics and diplomacy. He pointed out that there were "trouble spots in all parts of the globe—and the threats to freedom and survival that grimly and persistently stalk this planet are facts whose haunting reality weighs upon you. One simple truth is crystal clear: We must be prepared to deal swiftly and effectively with military adventures directed against any part of the free world. If we are not so prepared, those adventures will multiply and spread." The strategy of flexible response and brush-fire war was the Kennedy answer. On the Congressional subcommittees dealing with defense, there was wide agreement with this point of view. Congressman Dan Flood of Pennsylvania told McNamara, ". . . sound military planning will indicate that in your limited war the enemy is not going to be convenient and let you have one at Laos and stop; you are going to have a half dozen boils in a half dozen places."

If there was "trouble" in a certain part of the world, the United States was the fire department that would put out the fire with its hoses. If necessary, it would drown the area in the blood of its sons and the blood of the people in the brush fire.

According to Stahr, we also needed to "*strengthen our special forces*. The numbers of Allied indigenous forces in the fields of counterintelligence, civil affairs, and psychological warfare—all of which are essential to complete success in such-type operations—can be stepped up." If what was required was drowning the people in propaganda, spying, and American-style administration, so be it. We were moving again.

The Army's role in the Kennedy administration was to include fighting guerrilla brush-fire wars in the Third World, and mopping up after a thermonuclear war. The Army would have to maintain its position as a winner even *after* a nuclear exchange. Said Stahr, "Our Army must have the capability in general war to meet and defeat aggressor forces in the wake of the damage caused by nuclear exchanges. They must then be prepared to exercise direct, full-time, and comprehensive control over the land, the resources, and the peoples of the aggressor." Translated, this meant that the United States would have to occupy the Soviet Union after a nuclear war.

What was going on in the heads of the planners? In a convoluted way, the Stahr statement represented the unshackling of the Army from the leg irons of the massive retaliation strategy practiced by Eisenhower and Admiral Arthur Radford, Chairman of JCS. Radford did not believe in conventional war with the Soviet Union. Indeed, he did not believe in conventional war with anyone. Consequently, when as the Chairman of the Joint Chiefs of Staff he ruled that there could be no conventional wars and that all wars thenceforth needed nuclear weapons, the possibility of building up the Army as a force to fight conventional wars was virtually non-existent. Under Eisenhower, the cuts in budget of the Army were substantial. The Eisenhower Army budget went from $17,054,000,000 in 1953 to a low of $9,002,000,000 in 1956. The last Eisenhower Army budget was $10,293,000,000, in 1960. While cuts in the Army budget were made, Radford was unsuccessful in his attempts to change the so-called "forward strategy" of the United States. The Army's limited role in the nineteen fifties, as a "trip wire" in Europe in case of Soviet attack, or as the mop-up contingent after a nuclear war in the wake of massive retaliation, hardly seemed tenable to the professional soldier. Massive retaliation, it seemed, was a cover for not being willing to fight.

For the army, it was a welcome change from the Eisenhower days when President Kennedy asked for a call-up of the reserves in his June speech of 1961, to threaten the Soviet Union or, as was stated then, to show our will and determination in defending American allies and interests. A year later, in September of 1962, the President again asked for a call-up of 150,000 combat-ready reserves over the objection of conservative and right-wing Republicans. The arguments made by Bruce Alger, a right-wing congressman from Texas on the House floor against the call-up of 150,000 reservists was that this was a phony political gesture. "As I see it, it is a terrible mistake to call up 150,000 reservists, upset 150,000 families, and places of employment. This is no answer to world neighbors or our citizens for our lack of foreign policy."

In the same debate, Melvin Laird, later to become Secretary of Defense, also objected to the calling up of the reserves, as did Congressman Gerald Ford, who pointed out that eleven days before the debate McNamara had stated that "the potential need for a call-up of reserve forces to meet the military requirements similar to those imposed upon us a year ago, has been considerably reduced. Our conventional capability has been greatly enhanced during that period by the addition of five Army combat divisions, bringing our total to sixteen."

However, Ford suggested—outhawking McNamara—"if you really want to make Mr. Khrushchev believe that we mean business, then we ought to give to our President the full authority to recall up to one million men, excluding those who recently served. *This would give the President a real stick to shake in the face of Mr. Khrushchev.*" These men were cannon fodder in the hands of leadership, and the Department of Defense saw armies specifically in these technocratic terms—as instruments of power for the powerful.

The Navy Polices the World

With the Kennedy administration, there came the new Golden Age of Defense for the Navy as well. During the Eisenhower administration the Navy had been squeezed downward. Navy men complained that their ships were getting older and that age and disuse were setting into their arsenal. The total number of warships had dropped from 973 at the end of 1956 to 812 at the end of fiscal year 1960. The number of personnel in the Navy also fell during this four-year period, from 663,223 to 619,000.

The original Navy estimate for the 1962 period under a budget projected by the Eisenhower administration was 1.6 billion dollars less than the estimates put forward by the Navy once the Democrats came to power and transformed the imperial purpose. The Navy found itself gaining in the bureaucratic struggle for moneys by using two tactics. It could adopt massive retaliation strategy, which meant that Polaris missiles were needed to destroy the cities of our enemy. And it could simultaneously accept the flexible response strategy, since the Navy was essential in fighting wars around the world.

The Senate had long favored the Navy. As Senator Stennis said to Admiral Anderson at his nomination hearing as Chief of Naval Operations, "I feel like the U. S. Navy, to a great degree the world's policeman, and a mighty good one, represents the very best traditions of the armed services as well as of our great country."

During the Eisenhower administration, the Navy was the prime mover in a massive retaliation strategy, or, as it was described then, a city-busting strategy. The Polaris was the invulnerable deterrent. Yet, while the Polaris submarines were important as a deterrent, the central organizational problem for the Navy was that the Navy's activity as the world's policeman would disappear unless a different military and diplomatic strategy were pursued by the National Security managers. Because of the need for an expanded role for the Navy, it supported a new view of geopolitics, which required that the Navy be able to involve itself in many little wars simultaneously.

Admiral McCain, at the beginning of the Kennedy administration Commander of Amphibious Group 2 and now Commander in Chief, Pacific, noted to the House Defense Appropriations Subcommittee that "the spread of communism throughout the world may be likened to the cancerous growth in the human body where one does not know which vital organ will be attacked next." Consequently, said the Admiral, ". . . we must be prepared to move to any spot in a dozen different directions in order to be in a position to 'nip in the bud' any possible trouble in its inception."

President Kennedy in his first State of the Union address had said, "in all these areas of crisis the tide of events has been running out and time has not been our friend." All over, according to the Kennedy analysis, the American empire was on the run from the communists or their friends. American policies were unsubtle, failing to use military and related power against insurgencies in a way which would stem the tide of communism. The Navy view was that the Russians could be stopped if the United States could dominate the world's waterways. By playing down its city-busting policy in favor of the flexible-response policy, the Navy, like the other branches of the armed forces, wanted to participate in all levels of war fighting. As Admiral McCain put it, "We have just passed through an era wherein massive retaliation has been the governing philosophy. Because of the possibility of mutual annihilation, the policy of graduated deterrence is now in the ascendancy. Seaborne striking forces, because of their unique characteristics, are the ideal instrument for the execution of this policy. These ships have a capability of engaging in everything from a nuclear exchange, to a conventional war, to a mere demonstration of force."

According to Navy strategists, there was a "new sea frontier." Up to the time of the Korean War, the United States was "directly concerned with only about one ninth of the earth's land mass. Today, this has expanded to where we may be called upon to commit our Armed Forces any place along one third of the earth's land mass." Needless to say, such a view of imperial responsibility demanded a Navy to equal such ambition. But beyond the size of the Navy needed to carry out this worldwide policy, it was necessary to accept the idea that since there was a mutual standoff on the thermonuclear level, the United States needed to be able to enforce its will on other levels of violence.

The United States, it seemed, would spend vast sums of money, train men, and fabricate resources for imperial purposes that would give American policy rulers instruments of violence "in all shapes and sizes," as McGeorge Bundy so aptly put it. Because of American wealth and technological strength, it would be impossible for other nations to match the United States in its ability to mobilize for war, *remain* mobilized for it, and fight *permanent* war. The Kennedy version of the National Security State was predicated on a stable but growing corporate and military structure. The State would use the young people by challenging and channeling them into accepting and prosecuting the imperial purpose. The Peace Corps was one part of a mission of national purpose and sacrifice that the children of the middle class would be able to identify with and carry out. The working class and the subproletariat blacks would be drafted and mobilized for war. The children of these classes had their tasks to perform and their roles to play. This version of the National Security State played itself out in the bloody quagmire of Southeast Asia and the crumbling cities of the United States.

NOTES

Much of the material in this paper is based on personal observations of the author, while a member of the Kennedy administration, and on the material presented by officials of that Administration in Congressional hearings during the early 1960s.

Secretary of Defense McNamara's description of the Communist threat appears in *Hearings* on Sen. Res. 191 *Before the Senate Armed Services Committee,* Sept. 6 and 7, 1961. His later listing of the enhanced military capabilities the United States had achieved under his stewardship appears in *Hearings Before the Committee on Armed Services of the House of Representatives on Sunday Legislation Affecting the Naval and Military Establishments,* 1964, p. 6899.

The Secretary's explanation of the need for rapid deployment appears in HASC 1963, p. 430. His discussion of civil defense appears in SASC 1962.

General Maxwell Taylor's views on the need for a flexible-response policy are fully laid out in his book *The Uncertain Trumpet* (Harper & Row, 1969).

The Congressional debate on the Kennedy call-up of reserves appears in the *Congressional Record,* 1962, pp. 20501 ff.

THE PENTAGON PROPAGANDA MACHINE

by Derek Shearer

IN EARLY DECEMBER 1969, Senator J. William Fulbright in four consecutive speeches on the Senate floor offered a detailed picture of the public relations activities of the military establishment. The information unearthed by Fulbright's staff, while it might have startled a few members of Congress, was really nothing new: a Pentagon propaganda machine has been in operation for over two decades with the knowledge and support of America's civilian policy makers in the State Department and the White House. In fact, it is the civilian Cold Warriors who have laid down the fundamental tenets of anti-communism and fostered an atmosphere in which the public relations Newspeak of the military has thrived.

It was Dean Acheson, a graduate of Yale and Harvard Law School, and a member of the prestigious law firm of Covington & Burling, who agreed with Senator Vandenburg that the American people and Congress had to be "scared" into supporting the Truman Doctrine, which proclaimed America's willingness to intervene anywhere in the world. And it was James Forrestal, an investment banker from Wall Street, who as Secretary of Defense told the first graduating class of the Armed Forces Information School in 1948 that "part of your task is to make people realize that the Army, Navy, and Air Force are not external creations, but come from and are a part of the people. It is your responsibility to make citizens aware of their responsibility to the services."

Under Eisenhower, Secretary of State Dulles, with generous help from Senator Joseph McCarthy, continued to encourage anti-Communist hysteria in the American public. The liberals of the Kennedy administration—men such as Walt Rostow, Dean Rusk, Robert McNamara, and McGeorge Bundy—were no different; they, too, taught the people to see the world in Cold War terms. Under the Kennedy and Johnson administrations the funds allotted for military public relations increased tenfold, reaching $27,953,000 by 1969 (and the figure, based only on information made available by the Pentagon, is a conservative one). This money pays for a multitude of programs, which include film making, speakers' bureaus, traveling art shows, civilian "orientation" tours, and numerous publications, all aimed at convincing the American public that the road to true national security lies in more-sophisticated weapons systems, a worldwide counterrevolutionary military force, and patriotism that supports any and all military adventures in the name of anti-communism.

As Michael Parenti states in his excellent study *The Anti-Communist Impulse* (Random House, 1969), ". . . it was not the military that manufactured anti-communism, but anti-communism that built the military state." The liberal policy makers initially set the anti-Communist tone, and the military followed their logic. If the world is threatened by international communism, then naturally the United States must maintain an overwhelming military force to combat the threat—and it is important to convince the American people of this necessity in order to win funds and support from Congress. Having greatly expanded its power and influence in American society, in the process of stemming the Communist tide in the world, the military establishment now "maximizes the conditions that gave it rise"; it has become an institutional force in its own right.

What follows is a description of a number of military relations programs and the lengths to which the Pentagon will go to propagandize the public in order to maintain its privileged power position in American society.

Located on the second floor of the Pentagon is the Office of the Assistant Secretary of Defense for Public Affairs (OASDPA). With a budget in the fiscal year 1969 of $3,697,000 and a combined military and civilian staff of two hundred, OASDPA is responsible for the formulation of public-affairs policy guidelines for the services, and over-all co-ordination of Department of Defense public relations. A special office of seven people is responsible for co-ordinating Southeast Asia public-affairs activity and briefing the Washington press on the Vietnam War. Within the Pentagon, each service has its own budget and maintains its own information office. OASDPA and the three services, plus the Marines, operate three branch information offices–in New York, Chicago, and Los Angeles.

The joint-service Defense Information School (DINFOS), located at Fort Benjamin Harrison, outside of Indianapolis, trains military information officers, photographers, journalists, and radio and TV broadcasters. The school was created in July 1964, when Secretary of Defense Robert McNamara merged the Army and Navy information schools into a single institution. Enrollment rose steadily: when the school opened in 1964 there were eight hundred fifty students; during fiscal year 1968, DINFOS trained more than two thousand information experts. In addition to learning basic writing and broadcasting skills, students, according to *The Airman,* official magazine of the Air Force, "are taught how to identify the various opinion-making bodies and pressure groups likely to be found in a typical civilian community."

Upon taking office, Secretary of Defense Melvin Laird issued a policy statement to all information offices that "propaganda has no place in the Department of Defense public information programs." The distinction between information and propaganda is lost on military public-relations men. As an information officer in the Air Force explained, "We all knew Laird didn't mean what he said. He had to say that for the press and Congress, but we still go on with our job. We're in the image-making business. That's what we do."

Flicks

Creating the proper image necessitates a judicious use of all media, particularly motion pictures and television. The Motion Picture Branch of OASDPA provides support to movie-making companies whose films "will be in the interests of the Department of Defense."

In late 1968, the Navy and the Department of Defense agreed to cooperate with Twentieth Century-Fox on a film called *Tora, Tora, Tora* (the name derived from the code signal radioed back to tell Japanese commanders the attack on Pearl Harbor was a success). The Navy provided one of its own aircraft carriers, the 33,000-ton Yorktown, to play the role of a Japanese carrier. U. S. Navy pilots flew planes simulating Japanese bombers. All together, eight Navy ships were involved in the film making, including three destroyers. The support came at a time when the future of the aircraft carrier was being debated in Congress.

Representative John M. Murphy (D-NY) criticized the Navy's low-cost loan of the ships, and informed the public that a Navy crewman had been injured while cooperating with Twentieth Century-Fox. Responding to this criticism, movie mogul Darryl Zanuck took full-page ads in the

New York *Times* and the Washington *Post* stressing the public-service nature of *Tora, Tora, Tora,* which would remind the public to be ever vigilant against sneak attack.

In June 1969, Congressman Benjamin Rosenthal (D-NY) revealed the extent of the help that the Army had provided to actor John Wayne and his company, BATJAC, in the filming of *The Green Berets.* Rosenthal angrily stated that "the glorified portrayal of the Vietnam War, which is the heart of this film, raises serious questions about the Defense Department's role in using tax funds for direct propaganda purposes. . . . This alliance of Hollywood and the Pentagon seems to have brought out the worst in both institutions."

A report of the Comptroller General's office (requested by Rosenthal) revealed that the amount charged BATJAC for use of facilities at Fort Benning, Georgia, while filming *The Green Berets* did not accurately reflect the cost for troop support and used equipment. Rosenthal inquired as to what other films in past years had received Defense Department help. The Deputy Assistant Secretary of Defense for Public Affairs replied that all files on the subject over two years old had been destroyed.

The Los Angeles Public Affairs Office, located in the heart of screenland, is actively involved in promoting the military with Hollywood. The official "mission" book of the Air Force information office in Los Angeles states that the office must "maintain close contact with Screen Writers Guild to stimulate interest in using USAF environment in conjunction with proposed film stories, and generate and submit story ideas and outlines to story editors and producers of network entertainment TV series."

This office arranges for technical advisers to TV shows that deal with the Air Force. For example, an Air Force project officer was assigned to the ABC-TV series "12 O'Clock High," the story of B-17 pilots in the Eighth Air Force during World War II. It is the policy of the

Air Force to refuse aid to TV shows that do not meet with Air Force approval. One such show was "I Dream of Jeannie." While the Air Force would not appoint an official adviser to the series, the information office wanted to watch the show. "We didn't approve the show, of course," explained an officer in the Los Angeles office, "but we wanted to have some say in the production. Unofficial, you understand. So we sent over a couple of officers in uniform, medals and all, to observe. After they had been around for a few days, naturally the crew asked for some technical advice, and our men provided it. We wanted the show to portray the Air Force as accurately as possible."

The military is, of course, willing to help Hollywood when it is in its interest to do so, but to assure that the military "story" is given to the public "as accurately as possible," the Pentagon and the services find it advantageous to produce their own motion picture and TV films.

The Department of Defense operated five camera teams in Vietnam in 1968, under the direct supervision of MACV (Military Assistance Command–Vietnam). The film teams were approved in November 1965 by Deputy Secretary Cyrus Vance and activated in April 1966. A release from the Public Affairs office in the Pentagon explains, ". . . the purpose is to document, for release to national television, the feature aspects of the military participation in Southeast Asia often ignored or bypassed by national media film crews because of the pressure of hard news events. They are not in competition with the civilian media. Rather, they supplement the coverage by major networks. The high usage of the material produced by these teams is indicative of the effectiveness of their efforts."

One hundred eighteen films were produced by these units in 1968. Topics included the humane treatment of Vietcong prisoners, and activities of Thai medical forces near Kanchanaburi, Thailand, 125 miles northeast of Bangkok.

The Department of Defense has also produced over the years films of a more general, ideological nature. Some of the films listed in a catalog distributed by the OASDPA available for public showing include: *A Free People*—Folk music sung by Gordon MacRae, the New Christy Minstrels, and Peter, Paul, and Mary, accompany the scenes of this film telling the story of America and the American way of life from colonial times to the present. *The Line Is Drawn*—This story of Captain James P. Spruill, USA, who was killed while on duty in Vietnam, is based on his letters home. It covers his experiences in Vietnam and his view of the issues at stake there. *The Road to the Well*—James Cagney narrates this documentary on modern communism. The film traces the events that brought communism to power in Russia and other countries. *Third Challenge: Unconventional Warfare*—Insurgency and America's capability to counter it are examined closely in this film, which also touches on our capability of waging nuclear and conventional warfare. *Freedom and You*—An American citizen suddenly finds his town taken over by Communists in this dramatic feature film, narrated by Jack Webb, and is jolted into a full realization of the importance of his civic responsibilities.

In *Third Challenge,* which lasts forty-five minutes and was shot in color, we see a fictional Third World country threatened by guerrillas. The leader of the insurgents is dressed in a Nazi-like uniform; his number two man looks remarkably like Che. Trouble mounts in the country, the insurgency grows, then the United States enters the scene. The loyal government troops of the country are trained in counter-guerrilla measures by the United States and therefore wipe out the rebels' stronghold. The guerrilla leader escapes out to sea in a small boat to foment revolution in some other country (which is why the United States must be ever vigilant).

The hero of *Freedom and You* skips his union meetings for bowling. His wife reproves him, but he makes light of her. He goes to bed and (in his nightmare) wakes in the morning to find that his town has "gone Communist." At breakfast, his eldest daughter announces that she is leaving home to join a work brigade. The next day is Sunday and he tries to take the younger children to church, only to find that the church has been turned into a Peoples' Museum. He stares dumfounded at exhibits of ancient telephones and airplanes, which list Russians as the inventors. "Hey, Americans discovered these," he shouts and commences breaking apart the displays. He is arrested, and tried; his wife and children testify against him. Just as a pistol is being placed to his head, the nightmare ends and he awakens "to a full realization of the importance of his civic responsibilities."

Each of the services has its own film-making program. The headquarters for Army films is the Signal Corps Photographic Center, in Long Island City, New York. Here is located one of the largest motion picture studios in the East, built at a cost of $10 million, and purchased from Paramount Pictures by the Army in 1942.

A branch of the Signal Corps, the Special Photographic Office, was established during the Johnson administration to aid in propagandizing in the Cold War. According to Army Regulation 108-5, this office was established to work overseas "for the purpose of obtaining filmed documentation of U. S. Army activities in the cold war with a primary emphasis on counterinsurgency." A team is on duty in Korea, and in the third quarter of 1969 it shot 32,112 feet of motion picture film, and 1344 still photos, including color 16-mm. footage of the Republic of Korea Armed Forces Day ceremonies; bridges, roads, and rail lines throughout Korea, and the "Focus Retina" joint airlift exercise with U.S. and Korean forces.

The Big Picture is the Army's program that produces thirty-minute color films at a cost of almost a million a year for television. Fifty-five segments were produced in the latest two-year period and shown on overseas American Forces Television and in the United States on 313 commercial and fifty-three educational stations. Seventeen of the fifty-five segments dealt with Vietnam. These films, which are given free to stations, include titles such as *The Bridge*—in which John Daly hosts a visit to the Army Chaplains' School at Fort Hamilton, New York; *When the Chips are Down*—on the National Guard, with Bob Hope using his light touch to narrate this Big Picture presentation showing the training and readiness of the citizen soldiers; and *Shotgun Rider*—a description of this one reads: "The Shotgun Rider, protecting the stagecoach, blasted a colorful trail through the pages of American history. Today he still plays a colorful role, for the war in Vietnam has put the shotgun rider back in business. Not aboard a stagecoach, but in a helicopter. His weapon is no longer a shotgun, but a machine gun. His mission, however, is the same—to protect the interest of a free people as he stretches from his helicopter firing at enemy targets."

The Navy produces a similar series entitled "Victory at Sea." In 1968, the Navy made forty-nine news-film releases for TV, and fifty-five one-minute TV "news featurettes." Two of the films on the dangerous effects of drugs, *A Trip to Where* and *LSD,* the Navy estimates, have been seen by seventy-five million people. The Navy also distributes a film called *Stay in School and Graduate.* Other Navy films are narrated by Hollywood stars such as Jack Webb, Glenn Ford, and Henry Fonda. Not to be outdone by the likes of *Shotgun Rider,* the Navy has produced a twenty-eight-minute color film, *Eye of the*

Dragon—"The story of the American Navy advisers to Vietnamese junk forces, told in a panoramic style using a montage of sequences, native music, and the Kipling theme of 'East is East and West is West.'"

All three services record radio tapes which are made available to commercial stations. The Air Force appears to be the most imaginative: it produces *Pro Sports Report*—a weekly, five-minute radio sports feature containing Air Force spot announcements (distributed to one hundred fifty major-market commercial stations); and *Serenade in Blue*—a weekly thirty-minute radio feature starring the Air Force band, broadcast by approximately four thousand commercial and Armed Forces stations.

The Air Force produced 148 films and thirty-six TV film clips in 1968. The Air Force film *Trip*—which depicts a "bad trip," was shown to participants at a White House-sponsored governors' conference in December 1969, followed by Art Linkletter's lecture on how LSD killed his daughter. A recent Air Force film entitled *Operation Pathfinder Exercise* deals with American forces in Spain. A description reads: "Depicts largest airborne training exercise in Europe. Demonstrates USAF, U. S. Army, and Spanish troops in hypothetical combat situation. Pictures Morón, Spain, center of activity, where men, equipment, and supplies are dropped in enemy territory. Portrays paratroopers in mass assault to secure airfield. Shows effective tactical air power with proud forces marching before commanders. Depicts bullfight and reception given by Spanish people in honor of participants."

When Senator Fulbright read this blurb on the floor of the Senate in early December 1969, Senator Gore of Tennessee inquired, "I do not quite get how closing a movie with a bullfight will get more money out of Congress. That might be the purpose, but how does it operate?" Fulbright replied that he couldn't justify the program and that "the purpose of my comments is to show that they are not justified in the public interest, nor are they justified by, or even relevant to, the security of the United States."

Another 1968 addition to the Air Force film club is *The Other Side of the World,* which "documents civic action programs conducted in Thailand's rural areas by Air Force's 606th Air Commando Squadron. Shows operation of medical and dental clinics and construction of sanitation facilities. . . ." Senator Fulbright noted that, until seeing the film, he had not known that the United States was engaged in pacification-type activities in Thailand, and suggested that the Foreign Relations Committee "might learn more about the American presence around the world in watching Department of Defense movies than it does in briefings by executive-branch officers."

The Grand Tour

TV and movies are only one way the military uses to "inform" the general public. For the more-influential citizens, the military prefers the personal touch—a first-hand visit to the Pentagon or various military installations. Since 1948, the Department of Defense has held an annual series of Joint Orientation Conferences, in which "a group of approximately seventy business, industrial, and professional men are invited to visit representative military installations during this eight-day travelling conference."

Bennett Cerf described his reaction to such a conference in an article, "Ten Days with the Armed Forces," that appeared in the July 22, 1950, *Saturday Review*. He wrote of the invitation, "I consider [it] one of the biggest honors and luckiest breaks of my career." Cerf pointed out that the Secretary of Defense wanted leading citizens "to see and hear at first hand . . . how the Department of Defense was carrying out its own obligations . . . and counted on his guests to spread the good word as loudly and vehemently as they knew how. It worked like a charm."

After listening to speeches by generals and admirals, the group was flown to Fort Benning, Georgia. There "a display of our remarkable new recoilless weapons (and other arms still considered secret) had the audience gasping." They also saw the airborne troops begin their parachute training. "It was at our next stop, Eglin Air Force Base, Florida, that I had my unforgettable ride in a jet fighter plane. It all began over cocktails with Hal Stuart, dashing young Assistant Secretary of the Air Force. . . ." After a joke of Stuart's, "I told Stuart, 'If I've got to listen to jokes like that I demand a ride in a jet plane as retribution.' . . . The next afternoon Capt. Jack Fallon, of the Three Thousand Two Hundredth Fighter Test Squadron, equipped me with a Mae West and a parachute, clapped a crash helmet over my head, and strapped me into a two-seated F-80 Shooting Star jet plane." After a harrowing thirty-one-minute flight "over the Gulf of Mexico at the modest speed of 510 miles an hour," Cerf "made a speech that sent all the others clamoring for jet rides. The air was full of petrified VIPs the next day. I must have cost the Air Force a pretty penny."

Cerf concludes: "I came home revitalized and simply busting to shout from the housetops this deep-felt conviction; when and if a war comes with Russia or anybody else, this country is blessed with the basic equipment and leadership to knock hell out of them. We need more fighter planes and more carriers. We need more men in the Armed Forces. Our intelligence and propaganda departments need bolstering most of all. The money already allotted to defense has been on the whole wisely spent. In light of day-to-day news developments, increased appropriations are not only a wise investment but an absolute must."

In recent years, a number of participants in the orientation conferences have been from defense firms, and as Senator Fulbright suggested, "would appear to be already familiar with Defense activities and no doubt assist in influencing the views of their fellow participants."

In the past two years, 188 VIPs have enjoyed Navy hospitality on thirteen "orientation" cruises, most of them destined for Hawaii. One guest, Bertrand Harding, at the time director of the Office of Economic Opportunity, apparently liked his September 1968 trip to Hawaii on the USS Coral Sea so much that he went back in March 1969 aboard another aircraft carrier.

Popular spots in the Air Force's "distinguished visitor program" include Las Vegas, Hawaii, and Florida. Ogden and Salt Lake City civic officials made a trip to the Lockheed Plant in Marietta, Georgia, and "received a briefing on the C-5A and its meaning to future Air Force logistics." Newsmen from Kansas City traveled to Cape Kennedy "to build rapport and improve media relationships between this headquarters and greater Kansas City news media." Texas attorneys journeyed to the Air Force Museum, in Wright Patterson Air Force Base, Ohio, for an opportunity "to become more familiar with the Air Force's history and mission." The Strategic Air Command's most recent community-relations report listed five groups of "distinguished visitors" from Boston, Minneapolis-St. Paul, New York City, Los Angeles, and San Antonio—and twelve "specialized groups," ranging from the Smaller Business Association of New England to New York artists, as visitors over a six-month period.

The Air Force Systems Command noted that more than five hundred influential Americans had participated in its orientation program, which was awarded the Freedom Foundation of Valley Forge's James Madison Honor

Certificate "for outstanding achievement in bringing about a better understanding of the American way of life." The program centers on a three-day tour that includes the Arnold Engineering labs in Tennessee, Eglin Air Force Base in Florida, and the Air Force Earth Test Range facilities at Cape Kennedy. Mr. F. H. Orbison, president of Appleton Mills and chairman of Wisconsin's Young Presidents Organization, wrote the Air Force after his tour, "We certainly learned firsthand the reasons why our military technical programs require the vast sums of tax dollars and the people they utilize."

In some instances, military visitors' programs are designed with a specific purpose in mind. A fact sheet on the Army Air Defense Command's (ARADCOM) public relations program, Operation Understanding, states: "Poised on the doorsteps of America's mightiest cities, guarding against air attack, stands a phalanx of lethal Nike-Hercules and Hawk missiles, the muscle of the Army Air Defense Command (ARADCOM). These surface-to-air missiles, and their forebears, have defended city gates for more than ten years. Despite their protective role, their advent was not always welcome. City officials often opposed government acquisition of choice municipal land. The public did not always relish the idea of troops and lethal missiles in their back yards."

Operation Understanding was established in 1956 "to stem the aroused fears of communities near Nike-Ajax missile sites." The highly successful program won a "Silver Anvil" award from the Public Relations Society of America in 1958 and was listed as one of the nation's ten outstanding PR programs by *Public Relations News* in 1967.

The pilot run of Operation Understanding came in May 1956, when ARADCOM took newsmen on a tour that included a trip to Red Canyon Missile Range, New Mexico, to view the firing of a missile, and a visit to

ARADCOM headquarters in Colorado Springs. A year later, Operation Understanding faced its first public test. The Los Angeles International Airport had been picked as the site for a nuclear Nike installation, and local citizens were upset—demonstrations, critical news stories, and grumblings by legislators followed the announcement. The Army invited the mayor, other civic officials, prominent citizens, and newsmen on a tour. "When Mayor Norris Poulson went on the air," explains the fact sheet, "the opposition dissolved. He declared, 'I wish all the people of Los Angeles could have seen for themselves what the Nike can do for our city. Seeing is believing.' "

The Army notes that close to eight thousand guests have participated in over four hundred tours in the years following the first junket for newsmen in 1956. The Pentagon estimates that twenty-eight to thirty tours occur each year. The Army considers the program a dramatic success and boasts that "results are dramatically apparent. Following a New Jersey missile site explosion in 1958, enlightened communities in the area responded with sympathy and understanding; criticism was restrained and minimal. Missile men and their families had become accepted as valued members of the community, not as a 'necessary evil.' "

The 1967 fact sheet points out how the program fits in with Nike-X, the development from which two ABMs—Sentinel and then Safeguard—have emerged. It states that an "enlightened public" can be counted on to aid in the acceptance of future Nike-X sites, and concludes: "In short, air defense for the future has found the key to public support and acceptance—by laying the groundwork today, through a highly effective community-relations effort, namely Operation Understanding."

Lessons in Patriotism–Military Style

The military is not content to charm influential citizens with fancy tours, impressing them with the physical awesomeness of America's armed might; it also aims to provide them with a proper politico-economic outlook on the world.

Established in 1948 by the Industrial College of the Armed Forces, the National Security Seminar program has been conducted in 163 cities, with a total audience of 180,000. The "purpose of the seminar program," explains *Air Force and Space Digest,* "is to present briefly and plainly the relationships among the military, political, economic, and social factors that contribute to national power, together with a panoramic view of U.S. interests in a troubled and changing world." Those who attend the two-week sessions in selected cities each year include reservists from all the services, and civilians from business, professional, and community organizations. The seminars consist of a series of lectures by officers from the faculty of the Industrial College. In each city, the program is jointly sponsored by a military and a civic organization; a reserve headquarters is designated as military sponsor, and reservists who attend are awarded retention, promotion, and retirement credits. The civilian sponsor, usually the local chamber of commerce, provides the auditorium, meeting facilities, and publicity.

Information is even given that is sometimes news to Congress. Participants are told that "the U.S. has treaties with both Turkey and Iran–to defend them against Russia if need be." (none that the Senate has ratified)

Judging by the responses cited by the Industrial College, support for the educational program appears enthusiastic. A congresswoman said, "And thank goodness we have, in our democratic society, an informed military which is not only allowed, but encouraged, to share its knowledge with the public in seminars such as this." A clergyman from North Carolina wrote: "I attended the last seminar six years ago, and was so impressed and so well informed, that as a concerned citizen, I could not afford to miss this one. You can be assured that I will not contain this information within myself but shall spread it abroad."

Each service holds its own annual strategy seminars for prominent citizens. Naval Reserve Public Affairs units in communities around the nation nominate "outstanding leaders of the area," ranging from department-store owners to social scientists, to visit the Naval War College for political discussion. The Air Force conducts a National Security Forum for fifty-five distinguished civilians each year at the Air War College. The Army hosts more than one hundred twenty prominent civilians and military at the Army War College, Carlisle Barracks, Pennsylvania, who meet with two hundred students "to develop a national strategy through sharing knowledge gained in their particular occupation."

The Military Rap

These spokesmen do not, however, limit their eloquent remarks to the audiences of these special seminars. Public speaking is a weapon in the military's arsenal that it actively uses to enlist public support. "The military establishment must learn, as successful industry already has, to use its own qualified speakers or 'salesmen,'" writes an instructor at the Defense Information School. "Proper use of such speakers is the best method of creating the 'true image' of the military services in the mind of the public and inspiring public confidence in the military, which is essential to the continued success of the military 'corporation.'"

The Public Affairs office of the Defense Department, in the Pentagon, operates a speakers' bureau for high-ranking Pentagon officials. In late 1969, a flurry of activity surrounded President Nixon's policy statements on Vietnam. Military leaders addressed Rotary Clubs, ship launchings, Red Cross meetings, taking a hard line, often more forceful than Vice-President Agnew's. The most prolific speaker was General Lewis Walt, assistant commander of the Marine Corps, who delivered in October and November 1969 (the key Moratorium months) the same basic speech, twice a week on the average, to such groups as the Rotary Club of Pensacola, Fla. (October 21) and the Florida State convention of the American Red Cross (October 10).

"In the past year, over ten thousand Americans have been killed in Vietnam," Walt told the Red Cross. "Those who dissent may not have fired the rifle or thrown the grenade. But they must bear a part of the responsibility for the losses of those gallant Americans." In a November 6 speech to the Annapolis Rotary Club, Walt said, "Those who are in positions of authority know the potential cost of a premature pullout. They know that the blood of millions of Vietnamese would be on their hands. . . . Our premature withdrawal from Vietnam would become a major victory for the forces of international communism."

Early in 1965, a Navy Department Speech Bureau was established within the Navy Office of Information in the Pentagon. This is not simply another speakers' bureau; as a Navy publication points out, "The Navy Department Speech Bureau is the only known activity within the Executive Branch of the Federal Government which provides both speakers for public events and speech materials to be used by those speakers from a single office." One of the first acts of Rear Admiral H. L. Miller, Navy Chief of Information, was to publish a *Navy Speakers Guide,* designed to assist Navy speechmakers in their preparation and delivery of public addresses. The Navy also publishes *Speech Points*—a quarterly list of suggestions and references for speech topics. Speeches are collected in a yearly volume, *Outstanding Navy Speeches,* and selections of useful quotations are published each year in *Quotable Navy Quotes.*

The 1968 *Navy Speakers Guide* includes over twenty-five articles by Navy and Army officers, speech professors, and professionals from the fields of TV, radio, and journalism. Members of the National Society for the Study of Communication and of the Speech Association of America prepared special articles on request for the guide, which includes such useful discourses as "The Framework of a Dynamic Speech," "Mental Attitude and the Speaker," "How to Speak on TV," and "Speaking from Manuscript." The importance the Navy places on speechmaking is underscored by advice given by Henry G. Roberts, a former professor at George Washington University who spent twenty-three years teaching public speaking to naval personnel. Roberts tells would-be orators, ". . . the very fact that you plan to make a speech is news. Every time you accept an invitation to address a woman's club or a chamber of commerce luncheon, you give the newspapers two good stories. . . . Every time you make a speech, you kill two birds with one stone—not only do you carry the Navy's message to the men and women in your audience, but you also reach the wider reading audience by putting the Navy's name and its story in the columns of your community newspapers."

In addition to the speakers' bureau, the Navy provides training in the electronic media for its speechmakers. The Naval Photographic Center in Washington, D.C., has all the equipment used in commercial TV and film production and provides "coaching rehearsals for Naval and Marine officers and civilians. These practice sessions include work with live cameras and teleprompters with videotape equipment to allow the speechmaker to watch himself on playback." Located within the Speech Bureau in the Pentagon is the Navy Speech Evaluation Laboratory, which is available on request to assist Navy speakers in improving their speech delivery through practice and self-evaluation. Equipment in the soundproof lab includes a modified Ampex model 7100 Videotrainer system, consisting of two Ampex 324 closed-circuit television cameras, a videotape recorder, lighted podium, microphone, small monitor, required lighting and switching gear, and a twenty-one-inch television for playback purposes. Naval officers who are in the Washington area are encouraged to use these facilities. "If you cannot come to Washington," notes an article in the Navy *Speakers Guide,* "check with your Public Affairs Officer or Training Officer in regard to local opportunities for studio practice."

Through the Army's speakers' bureaus, which each post is encouraged to maintain, an estimated one thousand audiences a month are provided with Army speakers. Young, returned Vietnam veterans are encouraged to address public gatherings; *Army Digest* noted proudly that, since returning from Vietnam, a Colonel John G. Hughes delivered 240 speeches. The Washington *Post* reported in December 1969 that an Army major was used by the Pentagon to provide public counterattacks to critics of the Vietnam War. Major James Rowe, who spent five years as a captive of the Vietcong, filmed twenty television interviews and cut six radio tapes with congressmen; the tapes were sent to the home stations of the congressmen and used in Army information programs.

In several of these appearances, Rowe questioned the patriotism of Senator George McGovern and charged that the American liberal press was printing material that breaks the morale of American prisoners. "If you take a broad look at the news coverage in the United States, . . ." Rowe said in a color TV program with Representatives Thomas D. Downing (D-Va) and G. William Whitehurst (R-Va), "it is the most biased I have ever seen." According to Colonel Lloyd L. Burke, an Army legislative liaison officer and Rowe's sponsor in Washington, the Army's Chief of Staff, General William Westmoreland, "knows of all his [Rowe's] activity on the Hill and approves of it."

Information officers are taught to seek out speaking engagements in the community, as is shown by a sample letter sent to heads of service, fraternal, religious, and professional groups that is used for instructional purposes at the Defense Information School, Fort Benjamin Harrison, Indiana. The letter is addressed to a local clergyman and reads:

Dear __________:

Did you know that Fort Jackson maintains a Speakers Bureau, listing capable public speakers who are knowledgeable on many academic, business, and military subjects?

If you have had difficulty in finding a qualified speaker to address a meeting of your organization, we may be able to help.

As soldiers, we can speak best about our mission of training young men for the United States Army. But, we are also engineers, conservationists, law enforcement experts, dentists, lawyers, and similarly qualified professionals. . . .

If this active Speakers Bureau is of interest to you, please contact ________.

Officers are encouraged to participate in the speaking program. Information officers are instructed to mail personal letters to prospective officers in an effort to solicit speakers for the bureau; it is suggested that base commanding officers send letters of appreciation to participants in the speakers' bureau. In a sample letter, the commanding officer informs a captain, "Your voluntary participation in the Fort Jackson Speakers Bureau program has been brought to my attention. The four speeches on the U. S. Army and Vietnam which you have presented to civilian groups in the past three months have been informational and well received. . . . Your actions have reflected credit upon the military service and Fort Jackson, and have been in the spirit of the President's program for provision of services and communications to the public."

Going to the People

The list of military public-relations activities does not end with films and speeches. Under the rubric of Community Relations, the services operate traveling exhibits that crisscross the country telling the military "story," and maintain working contact with hundreds of organizations in every local community. The Army's Community Relations Branch estimates that some 13.5 million people viewed the twenty-two Army exhibits that traveled the country in the last six months of 1968. The exhibits included such displays as "Communist Equipment in Use in Vietnam," "How the U. S. Army Meets the Third Challenge," "Adapting to Living in the Nuclear Age," "Chaplains Showcase," and "The Airmobile Soldier." The Air Force's traveling exhibits, operating from Wright-Patterson Air Force Base, Ohio, include a gigantic Titan missile and a Minuteman missile—but the most elegant exhibit is the Air Force traveling art show.

The traveling art shows are displayed primarily in shopping centers around the country. "After all, it's where the people are these days," a briefing officer with one exhibit explained.

Two Air Force personnel are assigned to each traveling exhibit. They work with the sponsor of the exhibit, usually the chamber of commerce or the shopping-center association, to see that the exhibit is properly arranged and given adequate publicity. The sponsor is responsible for electricity, security after hours, parking area for the van, and men to assist in assembling and disassembling the display. The Air Force provided the sponsor with news-release forms for newspapers, TV, and radio, which state, "A unique art exhibit featuring more than 40 original paintings from the U. S. Air Force Art Collection is now on display. The paintings portray dedicated American airmen serving in many lands and many ways . . . all preserving and extending freedom."

The thousands of Americans who wander through the exhibit at their local shopping centers gaze at dramatic renderings such as *The Cross and the Sword,* a painting depicting an F-102 fighter interceptor in the skies above a church in a remote Eskimo village north of Thule Air Base, Greenland, and *Fighter Pilot's Equipment*–"Eglin Air Force Base, Florida, a pilot's equipment was placed in readiness prior to a ground support demonstration in an F-104." Other titles listed in an exhibition pamphlet include *"Air Force Airlift for the UN–Kimina, Congo, Sept., 1960, Buying Souvenirs in Seoul, Pilots on Alert Duty Playing Chess, An Air Base at Zaragoza, Spain, Deterrent, C-130 in India,* and *Good Old Pemmican, Air Force Survival Training.*

This art is not produced by resident Air Force artists–it is the work of professional artists specifically recruited for the task. In 1954, the Air Force invited members of the Society of Illustrators in New York to visit Air Force installations around the world. The first group visited bases in Europe; subsequent groups were flown to the Far East, to South America, to the frozen tundra of Alaska, and into the North African deserts. According to an Air Force fact sheet:

"There they [the artists] were able to see and paint the

Air Force Story as they experienced it. Much of their work was done under rigorous conditions. Sketching was handicapped by cold, stiffened fingers, sweaty palms, sand fleas, and mosquitoes. Some paintings were completed on location, but most were finished in home studies from sketches, photographs, notes, and remembered impressions."

In 1960, the Society of Illustrators in Los Angeles joined the program, followed soon by the San Francisco branch. A special art unit in the Air Force Office of Information in the Pentagon arranges for the artists' trips to far-flung posts of the world. The artists are given uniforms and the simulated rank of colonel while on the job. "It makes things easier for them," said an Air Force official, "and there is the prestige involved." The Air Force foots the bill for travel and expenses; their work becomes the property of the Air Force. If the Air Force does not like a drawing, it will not display it. "We're not going to hang anything that we think is unflattering to the Air Force," explained an Air Force information officer.

Each year, in October, all the artists who have completed work for the Air Force are invited to dinner in Washington, and a reception at Bolling Air Force Base, where new acquisitions are displayed. Besides this first-class treatment, the Air Force has arranged with the Internal Revenue Service that the artists can deduct the value of the paintings they "donate" to the Air Force.

It is the official duty of the Air Force to maintain close relations with the Boy Scouts of America. "Continuing contact between Air Force personnel and members of the Scouting movement will help assure our nation of capable leaders in the future," says Air Force Chief of Staff John P. McConnell. The Air Force program with the Boy Scouts is administered by the Continental Air Command, which is responsible for providing Air Force resources to the scouting movement. This includes arranging tours, air flights, films, and briefings for scout troops. The Tactical Air Command sponsors a specific Air Explorer Wing, officially Explorer Post #54.

Twelve Air Force officers are stationed at Air Force bases located as close as possible to the Boy Scout Association (BSA) regional officers of the twelve BSA regions. According to *The Airman,* official magazine of the Air Force, "Each Air Force facility is required by regulation to appoint a Boy Scout Project officer, who is the contact for the liaison officer of the region." The duties of the base liaison officer—in addition to arranging for Boy Scout use of Air Force facilities—include "briefing and indoctrination of the professional Boy Scout staffs of councils throughout his region."

Since 1948, the Army has appointed for two-year terms a number of Civilian Aides to the Secretary of the Army. "In private life, the Aides are leaders and authorities in their communities and in their respective fields," says the *Army Information Digest.* "Some are nationally renowned engineers, bankers, attorneys, scientists, editors, industrialists, surgeons, and educators. Most of them have a military background of their own and are, therefore, acutely conscious of the problems of the local commander. . . ." The Civilian Aides, who meet periodically with the local base commander, "recommend and assist in ways of enhancing understanding between the Army and the civilian Community." Each year, a national conference of Civilian Aides is held in Washington.

The Navy, however, has a better idea than Civilian Aides. Scattered strategically around the country are thirty-one Naval Reserve Public Affairs Companies consisting of 409 officers and six enlisted men. Each company must submit an annual public-relations plan to the Navy Office of Information on its selling activities in the local area. The basic duty of the companies is to "canvass local civic groups and organizations concerned with welfare and recreation of young men, e.g. PTA, school boards, and church groups, with the purpose in mind of selling Navy as a future career for young men." These companies sponsor a "Day in the Navy" for high school journalists, and a high school Navy Science Day. They try, according to a Navy Office of Information report, to "promote the playing and singing of the Navy Hymn in local churches," particularly on the Navy Sabbath. In the Navy Science Cruiser Program, 220 boys and girls are selected from regional science fairs to ride on a Navy ship. In 1969, the Chicago Naval Reserve Public Affairs Company set up a project "to aid the Navy's 'Hands Across the Sea' program by providing six tons of chewing gum from the Wrigley Company for distribution in Spanish-speaking countries."

By 1972, there will be three times as many high school JROTC cadets in the country as enrollees in the college officers' training program. This, too, is a community relations program. The program cost the Defense Department five million dollars in 1969. The 1964 ROTC Revitalization Act established the JROTC program for the Navy, Air Force, and Marine Corps (an Army program already existed, with units in 295 high schools). Congress set a limit of twelve hundred units–650 for the Army, 270 for the Air Force, 245 for the Navy, and thirty for the Marines.

The official Defense Department justification for JROTC is ". . . since a major portion of the Federal budget is for the purpose of national defense and since all young men are subject to possible military service, it is considered beneficial that our high school students, as future taxpayers, voters, and soldiers of America have an opportunity to learn about the basic elements and requirements for National Security and their personal obligations as American citizens to participate in and contribute toward National Security."

Patriotism is the key word in the JROTC program. There is little career advantage for a student who enrolls in the high school program; he can enter enlisted service at the E-2 rather than the E-1 grade, in which other enlistees must serve three months, and he can transfer a limited number of JROTC credits to the college ROTC, but that is about all. An exchange between Representative Glen R. Davis (R-Wis) and Vice Admiral Charles K. Duncan, Chief of Naval Personnel, at 1969 hearings of the House Appropriations subcommittee on defense, make this clear:

Mr. Davis: What do you have of benefit to the Navy, once a young man has participated in the junior ROTC and has graduated from high school? Then what do you expect of him?

Admiral Duncan: I believe the main benefits, Mr. Davis, are really to improve his citizenship and, hopefully, to give him an initial motivation toward the Navy. The Junior ROTC graduate enters one grade higher?

Mr. Kenyon: Yes, sir; E-2.

Admiral Duncan: He may enter the Navy as an E-2, but the main benefits are, as I said, citizenship and some initial motivation.

Major General Tom E. Marchbanks, Jr., Air Force Reserve Chief, told the same House Committee that the mission of Air Force JROTC is "to acquaint secondary school students with the aerospace age, to develop informed citizens, strengthen character, and to motivate students for careers in the Air Force."

Commander Ralph T. Williams, head of JROTC activities for the Navy, told the Washington *Post* that the Navy JROTC program "is young, and therefore the Navy has no statistics to validate its worth as a recruiting program or even as a positive motivation plan for involvement of students in NROTC. However, there are clear indications that these are reasonable expectations. The program must be considered primarily an 'image' in its current state of development, that is, a project which exhibits the Navy to the public eye and introduces the Navy to the community through the youth of the nation. Add to this the demonstrated effects of better citizenship that are evident where Navy JROTC units exist and the effort and expenditure of funds must be adjudged worth while."

Nearly all JROTC units are in public schools—distributed throughout the country on the basis of population. Instructors are usually retired officers or non-commissioned officers who receive retirement pay, plus a supplement to equal active-duty salary. The service and the school pay half the supplement. Uniforms except for shoes, and weapons and texts, are furnished by the military; the schools provide classroom facilities and drill space. The approximate cost of setting up and operating for a year a 170-cadet unit is $38,350, which drops to $17,500 after the initial outlay.

The role of the ROTC instructor is not limited to his classroom duties; he is also something of a community organizer. The *Infantry Journal,* discussing the role of the Army JROTC teacher, wrote that the "job is one of public relations—Kiwanis club on Wednesday, speaking to the Sons and Daughters of 'I Will Arise' on Friday, cooperating with the Campfire Girls in their new project on Rifle Marksmanship . . . training the girls' marching unit with the thought in mind of making them a 'Corps of Sponsors' for the ROTC sometime in the future." The increase in the number of JROTC units will, of course, increase the number of such teachers in high schools throughout the country.

How Effective Is the Military Propaganda Machine?

This question is important, and naturally enough, is of concern to the defense establishment. For example, in 1965 the Navy hired Louis Harris and Associates to conduct a public opinion poll on how Americans view the Navy and Marine Corps. The Harris poll summary concluded, ". . . the Navy's reputation as a fighting force has diminished since World War II. That of the Marine Corps has remained high, perhaps increased." This finding was, the report suggests, due to the changing nature of warfare in the previous two decades; Harris also noted that movies like *Mr. Roberts* and TV serials such as "McHale's Navy" and "Ensign O'Toole" provided an inaccurate picture of Navy life. ("McHale's Navy" especially angers information officers because, as one told me, "It shows blatant disrespect for authority.") "In the absence of popular fare to the contrary," say the pollsters, "the image of the Navy as a fun-loving, easygoing institution remains. . . . An element of toughness and discipline is missing . . . the feeling of 'easy' must be turned into a challenge of no-nonsense." The Marine Corps, on the other hand, has no need for programs to improve its image, but "the only potential danger is that the picture may be carried too far, that a reputation for too much toughness, for being overly rugged, for excessive discipline may begin to grow. . . ."

Such results are, it seems, trivial. Americans like a good laugh, even at the expense of the Navy (or any other service), and there is a tradition of making fun of the sergeant (Beetle Bailey comics, for instance)—but this does not mean that Americans question the underlying need for a large military establishment and the foreign policy it serves. The effect of more than twenty years of military propaganda coupled with the continual anti-Communist statements by civilian policy makers has been to give the public a Cold War vocabulary and teach them to see the world in those terms. The evidence (regardless of any poll) that this has worked is the willingness of the public to support larger and larger defense budgets. It is possible to say that Americans have been patriotic, in the sense that the military desires, by paying for what the military wants. Representative Mendel Rivers, chairman of the House Armed Services Committee is correct when he claims, ". . . the funny thing about it, the American people are not interested in a balanced budget when it comes to security. . . . I have traveled the length and breadth of this country. They say, 'We will forgo anything but our security.' "

The belief that national security can be purchased by spending more money for weapons systems, and deploying more Green Berets around the world, has been inculcated in the public. Patriotism is synonymous in this view with militarism; love of country is equated with an open pocketbook and sending one's sons proudly off to die in a senseless Asian war. A letter from a housewife in the midwest gives a concrete impression of this manifestation of loyalty in the daily lives of millions of Americans:

> To make a beginning, since May 1 the County has celebrated several occasions you should know about. May 1 is Loyalty Day, a fairly new holiday somebody thought up to counter Communist May Day observances in other countries. High school students marched with homemade posters. Sample: a sign showing a flag-draped coffin and the legend "Better Red than dead? Ask him." This was not an anti-war poster—the inference is that if you asked, a cheerful voice from inside the coffin would sing out, "You Betcha."
>
> Armed Forces Day is May 18; in addition to the local observance, we are not far from Glenview Naval Air Base and the spectacular air shows there. On May 30, of course, we

honor the war dead. Skinny ten-year-old baton twirlers wearing side arms march out to the cemetery, along with the veterans, auxiliary ladies, Scouts, etc.

In June we have Flag Day; later the Glorious Fourth, but we're just warming up. Locally we also celebrate Marine Day, and a little later V-J Day (yes, that's too early but if we waited until the V-J Day anniversary in September it might rain on the parade–which includes girls in bikinis with the customary banner across the bosom, "Miss Corregidor," "Miss Bataan"). . . .

But don't over interpret. Despite seven major patriotic-military observances in about seventy days, there is no pro-war sentiment here; indeed, anti-Viet Nam feeling is freely expressed. Most of what I've just described is simply traditional–mindless, vulgar, silly, and traditional. That's what makes it so hard to come to grips with it. One can't run into the streets and protest side arms on ten-year-olds, because all it means, really, is that Miss Darlene, their teacher, thought it looked cute.

Nevertheless, these people have only one way to think or speak about their country and its policy, one vocabulary. They are loyal Americans, and you express loyalty with military or para-military display and rhetoric. That rhetoric infects 75% of all the sermons, all the graduation exercises, all the prayers before Kiwanis and Rotary meetings, all the Campfire Girl proceedings, every page of the local papers, including full-page ads for automobile dealers and dry-goods stores, all the week-long pageantry of the County Fair. . . .

This description adequately fits the land of the Silent Majority. They are not bloodthirsty killers, they do not inherently desire to plunder the Third World, and they certainly don't want a nuclear confrontation with the Soviet Union–it is that they have no alternative way of being Americans. There is no other citizenship open to them. Their choice of actions has been defined by the defense establishment (in concert, of course, with the elite policy makers, and with the help of the media) and it is difficult for them to imagine any other way of thinking, let alone acting. Thus, the protest movement of the young is seen as un-American (rather than in the American tradition). The individual has become subordinated to the state; the news stories about how people refuse to sign a petition endorsing the Bill of Rights are not trivial.

Where Is Congress?

If the people have, to a large extent, been brainwashed, what of their elected representatives?

As one information officer explained, "Congress is our real public. We try to get at Congress through the general public, but we also go directly after them." In the lobbying and persuading of Congress, the military is joined by the large defense contractors. Hand in hand, the military-industrial complex does everything possible to sell its programs to Congress. The Pentagon maintains a four million dollar a year legislative liaison staff in the House and Senate. Each service has its own office on Capitol Hill, under the general supervision of a Pentagon lawyer, an assistant to the Assistant Secretary of Defense for Legislative Affairs. In fiscal year 1970, 140 military and 199 civilians operated these legislative offices (the Veterans Administration is the only other executive agency to have quarters on Capitol Hill).

The Pentagon maintains that these offices simply answer queries, make arrangements for committees traveling abroad, and prepare background material for defense officials who testify before Congressional committees. While the legislative liaison offices may do these things, their activities are not limited to them.

A document entitled "FDL Public Affairs" produced by the Navy legislative liaison office (and then released to the press by student investigators) provides a case example. The paper, dated January 1967, gives a detailed rundown on the lobbying efforts that surrounded the Navy's Fast Deployment Logistic Ships program. A number of key congressmen are listed under the heading "Completed Actions and Results," followed by the individuals who visited them to discuss the FDL program. The paper notes that "Mr. Dan Houghton (Lockheed) talked to Senator Russell. The Senator was not responsive. Direct contact by Navy personnel required." Senator Kennedy and Congressmen Burke were "contacted by Mr. Roger Lewis (General Dynamics), who explained the over-all merits of the program. Follow-up briefing required."

The paper notes that on December 30, 1966, Admiral Sonenshein, the program manager, briefed staff members of the Armed Services, Merchant Marine and Fisheries, and Government Operations committees: "The discussion following indicated that MM&F staffers are still opposed to the program and that other staffers may still challenge the program. . . . It is necessary to get to the Congressmen and Senators directly."

Admiral Sonenshein addressed the National Defense Transportation Association in San Francisco, in January 1967. "Mr. Dewey, President American Steamship Association, followed Admiral Sonenshein and prefaced his remarks by commenting that the Admiral's FDL presentation was the finest and most informative he had heard concerning the FDL program. Mr. Dewey's remarks were somewhat critical of the program though his speech might have been different had he been aware of the whole program rationale beforehand."

A second section of the paper is entitled "Specific Adverse Indications." Congressman Leggett (D-Calif) and Senator Russell (D-Ga), both of whom criticized the FDL program, are slated for follow-up briefings. Congressman Garmatz expressed opposition to the FDL because he felt the program would be detrimental to the

Merchant Marine. "He is attacking the concept of the FDL vs. Merchant Marine rather than the military necessity," notes the public-affairs paper. "Since he does not understand the 'instantaneous response' requirement, a briefing is in order and will be scheduled."

The public-affairs paper expressed concern about the reaction of shipbuilders and maritime unions. It states that "the Maritime Unions are opposed to the program, as it appears to them to be a threat to the Merchant Marine. Arrangements are being made to brief the Union executives and the people who write speeches and press releases."

Congressmen who disagree with the program are put down rather sharply. The paper states that Representative Lennon of North Carolina, who opposed the FDL program, "has heard only one side of the story. Briefing required."

The last section of the paper, "Schedule," lists congressmen who must be "briefed," meetings with Maritime Union groups, and lunches for Admirals Galantin and Sonenshein with the head of the Industrial Union of Marine and Shipbuilding Workers of America.

While the FDL program did not receive a full go-ahead from Congress (mostly due to Senator Russell's strong opposition), the public-affairs program, which was designed to gather Congressional, union, and industry support, is not extraordinary. Similar public-affairs lobbying plans are made and carried out for every major weapons program proposed by the Army, Air Force, and Navy.

During the 1969 fight over the military budget in Congress, the Pentagon created a special task force headed by William Baroody, special assistant to Secretary of Defense Laird, to assist Senator John Stennis, chairman of the Senate Armed Services Committee, in the floor battle on the military spending bill. A description of the activities of this task force is revealed in a memo signed by Joseph

J. F. Clark, Air Force Deputy Director for Legislation and Investigation, Legislative Liaison Office, which was printed in the Washington *Post.* The memo, directed to Air Force Secretary Robert Seamans, says Baroody ". . . heads up one task force to provide material to Chairman Stennis to refute statements and arguments being made by various Senators in their efforts to reduce or eliminate programs. The C-5, AMSA, and F-15 Air Force programs are all involved in this effort.

"In addition, we have been asked to submit a point-by-point analysis of the statements made by Sen. Proxmire in support of his amendment to eliminate money in 1970 for the fourth squadron of C-5 aircraft. This analysis will serve as a basis for response by Chairman Stennis or other Armed Services Committee members during the floor debate which will resume next week."

The memo also mentions that a staff member of the House Armed Services Committee "has asked for a detailed analysis and rebuttal" to several documents, including the report on military spending prepared by Members of Congress for Peace Through Law, a bipartisan group led by Senator Mark Hatfield (R-Ore), and the "Fact Book" of the Democratic Study Group, a caucus of House liberals. It concludes that this rebuttal material "is to be provided to the House Armed Services Committee for use during floor discussion of the procurement bill in that body."

Baroody says, "It is perfectly legitimate" for a senator to ask the views of the Defense Secretary on military questions. He does not mention the fact that Secretary Laird and a host of other Defense Department officials had already testified at length before the House and Senate Armed Services committees.

The Washington *Post* also reported that "outside the Pentagon itself, military contractors are helping their allies in Congress with speeches. At least one contractor has helped answer the questions one senator posed to the Air Force on the AMSA bomber."

A memo from the office of the Assistant Secretary of Defense for Procurement entitled "Fundamental Problem Areas, Key Areas Worthy of Joint Exploration by DOD and Industry in Calendar Year 1969" listed as a primary activity for the coming year: "Devise programs for use both by DOD and Industry which will regularly communicate significant information to Congress, the press, and the public (in contrast to today's tendency to react to criticism)." Senator Proxmire, who has become increasingly critical of the defense establishment, notes in November 1968 hearings, "These [memos] are designed for what you can do about the inquiries by Congress into these matters [the procurement process], how you can best meet them, and the implication is very strong of how you can best mute them or cut them off."

The correctness of Proxmire's assessment was evident a few months later, when the Washington *Post* uncovered a memo from Secretary of the Army Stanley Resor on the public relations plan for selling the ABM. Resor's proposals directed to Secretary of Defense Clark Clifford were a follow-up to a public relations campaign launched in March 1968 to convince Congress and the country that the ABM system was needed and should be approved. Resor noted, ". . . there is public confusion regarding the necessity for the Sentinel System deployment decision and of our need to acquire particular geographic areas for use as Sentinel operation sites. I feel it essential that the Army undertake a time-phased public affairs program to provide information to dispel this public confusion." Resor suggested that the campaign to win over hostile senators and representatives with personal visits from high officials be stepped up; a program of "orientation visits" for a wide assortment of state and local officials be expanded; special calls on local editors and publishers be increased; a "transportable display exhibit" for use in communities and featuring "pre-taped voice commentary," visual aids, etc., be put into action; support of the ABM be written into the State of the Union message; and that newsmen be invited to witness firings of the Sprint missile at White Sands Missile Range in New Mexico and the Spartan at Kwajalein to "bring home to the public" the message.

The five-page Resor memorandum was accompanied by a longer, more-detailed, seventeen-page public relations plan signed by Lieutenant General Alfred D. Starbird, project manager of the Sentinel program. The Starbird memorandum—in addition to a discussion of the public relations activities mentioned briefly by Resor—envisions an interplay between Army and defense contractors engaged in ABM work. The memo includes the instruction that "personnel affiliated with the Sentinel Public Affairs program will cooperate and co-ordinate with industry on public relations efforts by industries involved in the Sentinel Program. Like the FDL public affairs program mentioned earlier, such activities are standard practice. The *Post* stated that the memo exemplified "the resourcefulness of the Army's public relations operations, and the apparent indifference of the Army to the question of whether what they are propagandizing across the country has become, with Congressional funding and approval, an actuality or merely as Administration proposal." If Congress has been ineffectual in countering the propaganda of the Pentagon and the defense contactors, what might be asked of the press? The story is, in general, a sad one, for the press, particularly the Pentagon press corps, has been—in most cases—an arm of the defense establishment. The Pentagon, as might be expected, has done everything it could to curry favor with the press, and it has been quite successful.

The Office of Public Affairs in the Pentagon maintains

a magazine and book division, which assists writers in preparing articles and books on the military. Friendly authors, of course, receive warm treatment. When Robin Moore, a former public relations man for Sheraton Hotels, decided to write a book about the Green Berets, the magazine and book division arranged for Moore to participate in action training at the Green Beret School at Fort Bragg, North Carolina, then to accompany Special Forces in action in Vietnam. The Directorate for Defense Information handles interviews, processes and releases speeches, and deals with newsmen. In fiscal year 1969, the Directorate issued 1604 press releases.

Reporters who faithfully report the "party line" receive good treatment from the Pentagon press section. For years, there existed a system of off-the-record dinners with the Secretary of Defense or other high-ranking Defense Department officials and generals for such newsmen. The meetings were finally abandoned when George Wilson of the Washington *Post* described the séances in an article. Most members of the Pentagon press corps accept the assumptions of the military and are not inclined to probe into the Pentagon's activities in a critical manner. A former Pentagon correspondent for a major wire service tells a story that describes, in part, the situation of the Pentagon journalist.

"A group of us used to eat together in one of the general staff dining halls," he related, "and we would sit around and talk about what liars the public affairs men were. How you couldn't trust the Pentagon's word on the weather. Then, after this bitching, one of the guys would go out and write an exclusive which caused a little flak in the building, and his buddies would rush to the Public Affairs press conference and write their story with 'Today the Pentagon denied. . . .'

"Most of the correspondents didn't even know where the library was," explained the reporter. "Besides, there was no premium on writing critical stories. It just got you in trouble."

The reporters who, in effect, "explain" the Pentagon to the public have the opportunity to write for the various military journals such as *Navy* and *Army*.

During the Kennedy and Johnson administrations, a reporter who wrote an unfriendly story or broke information that the Pentagon did not want released was often investigated. The FBI, or one of the special detective branches in the Pentagon such as the Civilian Security Agency, would harass the reporter, question him about his sources, and, although it cannot be proved, tap his phone. Such treatment was dealt reporters of such reputable organizations as *The Wall Street Journal,* the Associated Press, and *Newsweek.*

Not only do such techniques make it hard for the newsmen to do a decent job; they have the effect of scaring potential news sources. While McNamara was Secretary of Defense, he enforced a rule that at the end of each working day every Defense official must report all contact with newsmen in writing.

All the services deal with newsmen in a similar fashion: reward the "good" reporters, and harass the "bad." Twice a year, the Navy invites a group of newsmen to spend a few days aboard ship. One of the duties of the thirty-one Naval Reserve Public Affairs units is, according to instructions issued in 1968 by the Secretary of the Navy, to "nominate top media executives for two yearly trips to Hawaii (fifteen per trip) on an aircraft carrier and return via Navy air to the West coast." Newsmen are, of course, included in the orientation programs described earlier. An Air Force public affairs report notes, ". . . the use of this airlift [of newsmen], although not authorized in advance through OASDPA, further cemented the fine public and community relations support of an influential segment of the local press, radio, TV, and civilian leaders in the community. Exceptionally good coverage of the five Outstanding Airmen of the Year from Colorado resulted from this trip." Local military units are encouraged to seek out the community press to assure that the military's "story" is being told. Instructions for the Naval Public Affairs reservists includes: "If the news is devoid of Navy activity, call the media and ask the simple question, 'Where is the Navy news today?' "

Each service also maintains a home-town news service, which supplies local papers and TV stations with stories, photos, and film on the service activity of local soldiers. The Air Force Home Town News Center is located at Tinker Air Force Base, Oklahoma; it became operational in October 1961. A fact sheet from the center states that "every Air Force information officer has the mission to develop and maintain–inside and outside the Air Force –a climate of opinion that will assist the Air Force in meeting its worldwide responsibilities. A part of this duty includes telling the Air Force story, through individual airmen, to the people of America. The HTNC was established for this purpose."

The half million dollar Army Home Town News Center in Kansas City, Missouri, estimates that in fifteen years it has issued thirty-two million written releases, a million and a half stills, 175,000 taped interviews, and forty thousand motion pictures, to fifteen thousand newspapers and radio and TV stations. The Navy News Center is located at Great Lakes, Illinois. The Home Town news-release operation is important in maintaining good relations with the families of the boys who have to serve in the military; glossy stories on military life, no doubt, make it easier for Americans to accept the draft (not to mention the transmitting of an aura of adventure–join the Navy, see the world, and so forth).

Fighting Anti-Communism

Too much can be made of the military's public relations activities. The American people are not automatons, and blacks and students through their own reading and experience have rejected the Pentagon's propaganda. Nevertheless the problem is that the great majority of the American public has been affected by twenty-five years of Cold War propaganda, and that there is no countervailing source of information.

Those who wish to dismantle the military-industrial complex, and radically alter America's foreign policy, are finding it necessary to counter the Pentagon's public relations machine with their own education program.

To counter military radio shorts, San Francisco peace groups have prepared a series of anti-recruitment ads ("See your draft counselor, not your recruiter"), and have requested northern California stations to broadcast them. The basis for their request relies on the fairness doctrine of the FCC and the manner in which that doctrine has been applied to cigarette advertisements. In a letter to a local station, the peace groups' lawyer contends that military service today "is a controversial issue of public importance–far more controversial and far more important than the issue of whether an individual ought to smoke cigarettes."* Anti-war groups in other cities are following this lead. A group of business executives opposing the war in Vietnam have compiled ten-second anti-war radio messages from leading military men such as former Marine Commandant David Shoup.

* In June 1970, the FCC (with Commissioner Johnson dissenting) denied the peace groups' request, ruling that military recruitment ads do not raise "a controversial issue of public importance requiring presentation of conflicting viewpoints."

In December 1969, returned Vietnam veterans opposed to the war held a "Trial of the Army" at the University of Washington in response to official harassment of the GI coffeehouse, The Shelter Half. A jury of GIs and a crowd of 1200 heard testimony against living conditions in the Army and the conduct of the war. Fred Gardner, one of those responsible for the coffeehouse movement, wrote that "the passion of the speeches and the impact on the crowd convinced some observers that the time is ripe for setting up a speakers' program for GIs and Vets. . . . There are so many men back from Vietnam now, yearning for a chance to dissociate themselves from the war machine, that we could confront the Army flacks whenever and wherever they ply their trade. And if a speakers' network were established, it would be the basis for a vets' anti-war organization that had roots in real work."

In January 1970, the Businessmen's Educational Fund, an outgrowth of the Business Executives Against the War group, which supported the candidacy of Gene McCarthy, hired Ernest Fitzgerald, the efficiency expert who was fired by the Pentagon for exposing cost overruns in major weapons systems, and is sending him on a nation-wide speaking tour to discuss how the Pentagon wastes taxpayers' money. Fitzgerald is the first in a line of speakers critical of the military, that the group plans to organize into a speakers' bureau. In Peoria, Illinois, the local peace-action council is organizing counterseminars to be held when the National Security Seminar program comes to town in May.

Such education activities are just beginning. They must be greatly expanded and multiplied if the anti-Communist reflex and the belief that the way to national security lies in more military spending are to be seriously challenged.

NOTES

Parts of this paper are based on interviews conducted with military information officials in the summer of 1969 in the Pentagon, at the Los Angeles branch office, and at the Defense Information School, Fort Benjamin Harrison, Ind.

The best, and one of the few, sources of information on military publicity programs in the immediate postwar period is a pamphlet, *Press Agents of the Pentagon,* by John Swomley, Jr., published by the League Against Conscription, in 1953. Copies of the booklet are available by writing John Swomley, Political Science Department, St. Paul School of Theology, Kansas City, Mo.

The single most valuable printed source on military publicity activities is the material placed in the Congressional Record by Sen. William Fulbright. Many of the quotes from military documents and from newspaper articles in this paper can be found there. See: *The Congressional Record,* Dec. 1, 2, 4, and 5, 1969.

Copies of the report of the Comptroller General on the making of the movie *The Green Berets* are available on request from the office of Congressman Benjamin Rosenthal, House of Representatives, Washington, D.C.

Military films are listed in two publications: "Selected List of Armed Forces Films for Public Exhibition" and "Catalog of Current Information Materials Produced by the Armed Forces Information Services." For copies, write: Office of Assistant Secretary of Defense (Public Affairs), Department of Defense, Washington, D.C. 20301.

A fact sheet of Operation Understanding can be gotten from ARADCOM Headquarters, Colorado Springs, Colo.

Excerpts from lectures used in the National Security Seminar Program, 1968–69, can be found in hearings on the Nuclear Non-Proliferation Treaty, held before the Senate Foreign Relations Committee, Feb. 18, 20, 1969, Part I, pp. 506–14.

See also: "National Security Seminars," *Air Force and Space Digest,* Sept. 1969.

The *Navy Speakers Guide* and other publications can be obtained by writing: Navy Department Speech Bureau, Office of Information, Department of the Navy, Washington, D.C. 20350.

A fact sheet on the Air Force Art Program is available from the Information Officer, Wright-Patterson Air Force Base, Ohio.

The Air Force program with the Boy Scouts is discussed in "Building Better Men Together," by Ted Strum, *The Airman,* Nov. 1967.

References to High School ROTC can be found in *Hearings Before the Subcommittee on Defense of the House Appropriations Committee,* Part 1, 1969, p. 270. See also: "High School ROTC Growing," By Richard Homan, Washington *Post,* Aug. 3, 1969.

Copies of the Harris poll are available in the Navy Office of Information, the Pentagon.

The FDL Public Affairs paper is printed as an appendix to the report of the Summer National Security Research Project, which appeared in the *Congressional Record,* Nov. 6, 1969, pp. E-9417–23.

Further information on Pentagon public relations programs can best be obtained by applying in person at the Army, Navy, and Air Force offices of information. Public affairs officers on local bases are also quite useful.

II. INTERVENTION

President Nixon's self-proclaimed doctrine of American military disengagement from the Third World, particularly Asia, has a familiar ring. President Kennedy stressed the importance of self-reliance for the less developed nations, and President Johnson stated that American boys would not be sent to do the job of Asian boys. Such rhetoric should not be mistaken for policy.

America has, throughout its history, practiced interventionism. The State Department has identified fifty acts of American intervention in foreign nations between 1900 and World War II. But the emergence of this country after 1946 as the most powerful nation on the face of the earth led us to intervene unilaterally in country after country around the world. Indeed, the Navy informed Congress that there had been fifty "wars or near wars" in which it had played a role *since World War II.* While this listing included such shows of strength as raising the flag off Jordan and demonstrating the U.S. presence during the Zanzibar riots, the statement is indicative of America's stance as the world's policeman.

Examination of official policy documents, and interviews with government officials, lead to the conclusion that American foreign policy for the Third World has not changed in its essence from the days of Truman, and will not be changed by the Nixon administration.

The activities of the CIA and the Green Berets in Southeast Asia have raised serious public concern as to whether Congress has any control at all over foreign-policy operations. The CIA has built up a worldwide network of agents, skilled and ready for intrigue, and the Army's Special Forces have been trained and deployed to combat insurgencies in Asia,

Africa, and Latin America. The Special Forces, according to a reporter who visited their headquarters at Fort Bragg, North Carolina, "anticipate almost endless insurgencies in the underdeveloped countries of the world. And they are counting on American intervention in many of these situations."

The papers in this section suggest that, if present trends continue, the American military presence in the Third World will not diminish. William Stivers' paper deals with the perceptions that drive American policy makers to attempt to control change in the Third World. Given the outlook of the President's advisers and his own statements that the United States will live up to all its prior commitments, future interventions are unavoidable. Tom Klein's paper describes the steps taken by Secretary McNamara to increase dramatically America's air and sealift capacity. As his paper shows, America now has the capability to intervene anywhere she wants to in a matter of days. When a nation possesses such a capability, the temptation to use it is overwhelming.

The Third World, because it is in the throes of development—a process that is often violent and chaotic—will not march orderly to an American beat. Failure to allow these nations their own destinies will doom America to a counterrevolutionary role in the coming years. It will precipitate further upheaval and social conflict at home, as segments of the population rebel against the aspirations for empire and the neglect of social justice and a decent life for Americans in their own country. The response of the National Security State may well be to import the military techniques it utilizes on the people of the Third World in order to "pacify" its own citizens.

THE WILL TO INTERVENE

by William Stivers

EACH major conflict in which the United States has engaged during the twentieth century—World War I, World War II, and Korea—was intended to be the last. In each case, the circumstances leading to conflict were analyzed by policy makers and turned into a body of holy writ, or "lessons," and then applied in various schemes designed to decrease the likelihood of another such war. In each case, our public leaders, and the American people, vowed "never again." Now, even as the war in Vietnam continues, we are seeing a repetition of this familiar pattern: President Nixon campaigns on the promise of "No More Vietnams," and declares, after election, that there will be no new American commitments in Southeast Asia. In the Senate, hawks and doves alike join in the overwhelming passage of Senate Resolution 85, declaring that a national commitment to a foreign power cannot be made at the sole initiative of the executive. High officers of the Joint Chiefs of Staff proclaim their aversion to any more counterinsurgent actions involving U.S. personnel in a combat capacity. And no less an architect of the Vietnam War than General Maxwell Taylor states that the Vietnam War has been far too costly in relation to our objectives, that it has caused an unacceptable dissipation of our strength, and that we must be far more selective and self-interested in making future commitments—even willing to write off a country if the cost of saving it appears too high.

Yet all the hopes for no more Vietnams will mean very little if they are not backed up by a thoroughgoing change in the assumptions that spawned our adventure in Vietnam. For, contrary to the view expressed by many critics of the war, Vietnam is not just the result of a miscalculation: the executive branch, including especially the defense establishment, miscalculated only to the extent that it underestimated the ability of the enemy to resist. Surely, if the war had been won at minimal cost, and with the political repercussions at home confined to a few fuzzy-minded moralists, the glamorous image that emerged at the inception of the counterinsurgency doctrine, with Sergeant Barry Sadler crooning "The Ballad of the Green Berets," would remain untarnished, and no political constraints would exist to forestall similar engagements in the future.

If, in the light of our experience, we now wish to prevent a recurrence of another Vietnam War, we cannot depend on a continuation of the present political climate: while political climates are transitory, policy premises and the bureaucracies that promulgate and implement them have a capacity to weather adversities and emerge largely intact. If the principles that led us into Vietnam continue to guide our policy, then the assurances of Presidents and generals are valueless.

It is well to note that there was only a ten-year interval between the end of Korea, when America resolved never to fight another land war in Asia, and the start of our combat commitment in Vietnam. As a colonel in the counterinsurgency section of the Joint Chiefs of Staff told me with unusual frankness, "We are going to be very reluctant to use American troops in combat for the time being. We'll do anything not to get involved. But circumstances change; maybe conditions will be such that we will get involved again—when the heat from Vietnam is off."

The Basis for Intervention

Far from being merely an error or an unpleasant turn of events, the Vietnam War was a logical, perhaps inevitable, outcome of the official doctrine concerning America's role in the world. The Vietnam conflict, said President Johnson in his 1966 State of the Union message, "is not an isolated episode, but another great event in the policy that we have followed with strong consistency since World War II."

The center of the postwar conception of our security interests is a belief in the indissoluble connection between the disruptive forces loose in the world and our own well-being. The world has shrunk; events in one region will have global repercussions from which we cannot escape. It is impossible to retreat to nostalgic but fallacious notions of isolationism, for the preservation of American security and the growth of our economy are tightly bound to the maintenance of a congenial world environment. Adopting a Fortress America policy, warned Robert McNamara, would force us to reorient our industry and commerce toward self-sufficiency, with lower standards of living for our people and less economic freedom; we would live in an uncertain world, "surrounded by a sea of struggling, envious, and unfriendly nations." Thus, world stability is a prerequisite for the protection of our economic position and our democratic institutions. Visions of hostile and desperate forces emerging from the flames of revolutionary turmoil, antithetic to our political ideals and to our very civilization, are seen as horrors possibly as fearsome as nuclear war.

The lesson learned in World War II was that we cannot develop a stable world order unless the "peace-loving states" make arrangements to punish those states that do violence to the principles of international law. In the past, according to such men as Admiral Arleigh Burke, former Secretary of State Dean Acheson, and former Undersecretary of State George Ball, the longest periods of tranquillity were realized when great centers of power assumed the duty of thwarting disturbers of the peace: "International peace," wrote Admiral Burke, "is a consequence of the rational use of national power by a dominant and dominating power center." Acheson heaps praise upon the Concert of Europe, which, bolstered by the British Fleet, provided a degree of political coherence unequaled since the Roman legions enforced the Pax Romana. The trauma of the two world wars, however, dissolved the old centers of power that had been responsible for containing conflict, and old arrangements were altered beyond recognition. The revised power arrangements left only two major power centers—the United States and the Soviet Union—while the dismantling of the colonial power structure created, in the words of Mr. Ball, "power vacuums and power dislocations of major dimensions," which we rushed to fill because we "abhorred tyranny." The benevolent role of the British imperium had been cast upon us, and, driven by unalterable necessity and humanitarian purpose, we accepted the imperial burden as ours.

The growth of aggressive Soviet power made necessary a counterpower, consisting, in Dean Acheson's vision, of a secure "non-Communist world system." A farsighted analysis of our interests would reveal that the export of capital, through favorable aid and economic-assistance pacts, could stimulate the expansion of industries needed for military strength and foster the growth of the integrated economic system so fundamental to the achievement of political unity.

Military power, nevertheless, is the basic relationship between states. "Peace," according to Eugene V. Rostow, "is a function of power." Events preceding World War II amply demonstrated that, if an aggressor power is not confronted with a united force prepared to repel its aggressions, its appetite will be whetted as its power becomes greater and more difficult to contain. Aggression cannot be tolerated anywhere, for to do so only makes the peace ever more uncertain and increases the likelihood that the peace-loving states will have to fight a larger war under far less favorable circumstances.

This belief that peace is indivisible—that our own security could be ultimately imperiled if an aggressor gets away with the use of military force anywhere—led to our post-war alliance structure and our reliance on collective security systems, embodied in bilateral or multilateral agreements with forty-two countries. And since formal treaties were insufficient to maintain our interests, Dean Rusk, testifying before the Senate, added ". . . no would-be aggressor should suppose that the absence of a defense treaty, Congressional declaration, or U.S. military presence grants immunity to aggression."

The mere existence of an alliance structure will not, of course, act to deter aggression. "There can be no doubt," writes a military officer, "that the strategy is but a hollow bluff if we are not determined to expend our national blood and wealth to validate it." Our alliance structure must not only exist, but it must be credible. If our enemies, real or potential, come to doubt our readiness to back up our commitments, the whole structure upon which rests the peace of the world will be shaken, and our allies may feel the need to be more accommodating to our adversaries.

It was upon this reasoning that Dulles justified our support of the Bao Dai government in Indo-China and our aid to the French during that war: "There is a civil war in which we have, for better or worse, involved our prestige. Since that is so, we must help the government we back. Its defeat . . . would have further serious repercussions on the whole situation in Asia and the Pacific. It would make even more people in the East feel that friendship with the United States is a liability rather than an asset." Any crack in the collective security system, irrespective of whether our interest in a conflict is vital or direct, will threaten the entire edifice.

As long as the Soviet threat against Western Europe was the prime concern, the work of preserving the international power balance was a relatively simple task with built-in limitations: it easily translated into the relatively restricted objective of containment in Europe. Under the tenets of the Truman Doctrine, however, the United States became concerned with supporting all "people who are resisting attempted subjugation by armed minorities and outside pressures." As we carried to its logical conclusion the idea that freedom and security were indivisible, the scope of our interests expanded beyond Western Europe, and the crusade for stability and an orderly power balance became a global engagement. Thus, writes Robert Tucker, ". . . a policy initially designed to restore and maintain a balance of power in Europe has been replaced by a policy that scorns so modest an objective. A policy once reasonably tolerant of revolutionary change has been succeeded by a policy intolerant of such change, because of an obsessive fear of communism and an equally obsessive fear of revolutionary change with communism. Finally, a former reluctance to employ force, save on behalf of narrowly construed vital interests, has given way to the assertion of a right, and indeed, an obligation, to take whatever measures are deemed necessary to prevent violent changes in the status quo."

Further confusion set in as the bipolar world dissolved into a welter of competing interests, each a potential source of hostility. The breakup of the Communist world into nationalistic units, each pursuing its own objectives, did not signify less danger for the United States, only more troublemakers to contend with. "The United States can no longer be a one-eyed Cyclops," writes General Taylor. "Its power of attention must partake of the many-eyed vigilance of Argus—constantly watching in all directions in anticipation of the emergence of forces inimical to our national purposes." In addition to the Soviet Union, we have to contend with the danger other expansionist countries pose to the geopolitical balance and, hence, to our vital security interests. Their capacity to create disorder is augmented, moreover, by the innate vulnerability of the emerging states of Latin America, Asia, and Africa.

The stresses of a multipolar world have brought some uncertainty as to how we determine whether a given situation, especially a local insurgency, constitutes a threat to our vital security interests, which should be met by some form of intervention. In the 1966 hearings on Worldwide Military Commitments, Secretary of State Rusk pointed to ten political crises and critical situations in which the United States became directly involved, and twenty-seven crises in which we had only indirect or limited involvement. Clearly, then, we need not intervene in all situations disruptive to the peace.

Here we arrive at the crucial question: what criteria are used to determine the circumstances and extent of our involvement? On this matter, there are two general views. One identifies worldwide turbulence with Communist expansion. The prime objective of the Sino-Soviet bloc, wrote Roger Hilsman in 1962, ". . . is to enhance total Communist power relative to that of the United States and its allies." Our response to the invasion of South Korea taught the Communists that overt aggression does not pay, and they were forced to adopt what Hilsman called a "new tactic": wars of national liberation. By attempting to further their aims through fomenting internal conflict, the Communists employ a form of aggression that costs them little and affords immunity from retaliation. This does not necessarily mean that an insurgent organization will be a stooge of either Russia or China, or that genuine popular grievances and indigenous support are not essential to the success of the revolutionaries. What it does imply—and this is the focus, in this view, of U.S. worries—is that the installation of regimes friendly to the Communist powers would alter the power balance and lessen our influence over events in the affected areas.

A second view is concerned less with the factor of communism than with the balance of power itself. An example of this orientation is contained in Eugene V. Rostow's State Department pamphlet *The United States and the Communist World.* He embraces the balance of power as a goal of national policy. The objective of our security policy is not, says Rostow, based on ideological opposition to communism, but on preserving our national interests in a balance of power. It is true that the troublemakers who threaten the vital power balances are mostly Communists, but this is not always an integral characteristic. For the maintenance of the balance of power is tied to the maintenance of our influence; even should a non-Communist revolution threaten our influence in an area we deem vital, we must be prepared to respond, lest matters escape our control.

Rostow's position, albeit superficially more flexible than simple anti-communism, is in operation a position that produces a far more expansive conception of our national security. Instead of perceiving a revolutionary movement as a threat to our interests because our intelligence discovers it to be controlled by Communist elements, we perceive a revolutionary movement as threatening simply because it is revolutionary, and therefore disruptive of existing patterns of order and influence. The policy then becomes one of containing disorder rather than containing communism. Not that we oppose change;

change is required if we are to lay ax to the root problems that cause revolutionary instability. The essential demand we make is that change be evolutionary, that no radical convulsions occur, which may alter existing power relationships. As Robert Osgood said in 1957:

> The external interests of democratic powers are not necessarily identified with the status quo in all respects, nor do they require the rest of the world be democratic. However, they do require that the inevitable adjustments and accommodations among governments and peoples be sufficiently moderate and gradual to permit orderly change. Long-term interests as well as immediate interests of democratic nations lie in preserving an external environment conducive to relative security and stability in the world.

The foregoing suggests that in either view, our local interventions are governed by considerations of global strategy. The question asked is: "How do events in region X affect the Free (i.e., non-Communist) World?" or "How do they relate to our grand design—the promotion of a stable world environment?" In either case, policy is implemented through collective security treaties or informal but nevertheless clearly comprehended commitments serving notice on potentially hostile forces that these interests are not to be violated. If we allow violations of our interests at any point, the credibility of the commitments is lost. The importance of any particular country is thus determined by whether or not in prior times we have included it in our security arrangements.

In accordance with the necessity of assuring credibility, prior commitment becomes a rationale for further commitment. Although the United States has been fairly tolerant toward revolution and instability in nations that have not become client states in the grand design, it conceives the loss of client states as not permissible. Hence, a collective security system assembled in one era, to meet a particular threat, has entangled us in an illogical, inconsistent posture that can produce only never-ending conflict.

The Collective Security Psychosis and Vietnam

There is no way to maintain the credibility and integrity of a deterrent threat save by manifesting a willingness to oppose forcible Communist expansion, particularly directed against an ally, and this even though such expansion is directly undertaken–indeed, independently undertaken–by a small Communist state. For the deterrence of other, and larger, potential aggressors, however disunited, is dependent on the deterrence of all aggressors.

–Robert Tucker, *Nation or Empire?*

Considering the premises on which our national security policy has been built, our involvement in Vietnam should not be a cause for wonder; on the contrary, we can only profess perplexity over why such an involvement did not occur sooner. For, after dispensing the familiar litany of democracy and freedom, official statements justifying our role in Vietnam have almost invariably invoked the considerations of power politics described in the previous section. The argument was usually developed as follows:

The allegiance of the Third World was going to determine the outcome of the power struggle of the sixties. In Southeast Asia we had to guard against domination of the region by Red China. Even if North Vietnam were not entirely controlled by the Red Chinese, any diminution of American power would alter power ratios and bring, perforce, a strengthening of the Chinese position. Although we had shown the Chinese, via our actions in Korea, that overt aggression would fail, they had changed tactics and looked to the promotion of revolution as the only means they have of setting up a regime friendly to them. If we allowed China to enhance her power through this devious route, we might have to engage her later, when she was a far more powerful adversary.

Our Asian allies would thus lose faith in our determination to protect their interests and would have no recourse but to seek a *modus vivendi* with Chinese power. Loss of the conflict, moreover, would have adverse ramifications world-wide: "I am deeply convinced," writes General Taylor, "that such a disaster would propel a shock wave of dismay which would spread rapidly from the epicenter in South Vietnam extending around the globe, which would affect every international relation we have and every alliance, including NATO. If our other allies witnessed an American failure in South Vietnam—particularly if it were accepted voluntarily and not imposed by a superior enemy—they would raise the inevitable question, 'Can we count on the Americans any more anywhere?' "

Our interest in Vietnam, therefore, was not defined merely by our concern for the country itself. If the insurgents were allowed to succeed, then the enemy would have proven that the United States could not defeat a war of national liberation, and this would lead to assaults on U.S. power elsewhere, as revolutionary movements would sweep the globe. The house of collective security would become a house of collapsing cards.

On the other hand, we need not have drawn the line in Vietnam; we could well have picked another place to prove our point. But the circumstances seemed propitious. Having anticipated the importance of counteracting revolutionary warfare, the Kennedy administration had begun preparing new techniques for fighting guerrillas on their own terms. At the Special Warfare School in Fort Bragg, men received training in fighting guerrilla-style: they swung through trees, practiced living off the land, and practiced with walkie-talkies, helicopters, and various other devices that had been newly developed for counterinsurgency purposes. After a long and unsuccessful fight during the Eisenhower administration, the Army finally realized its wish for expansion of its air-mobile capacities, with McNamara overruling the protestations of a jealous Air Force. Programs were launched to redesign and modernize conventional weapons—a part of our arsenal that had been neglected during the "more bang for the buck" era of the fifties.

If the time seemed right to conduct a counterinsurgency campaign with the doctrines available and the capabilities in hand, it also seemed right politically. The Kennedy administration's initial decision to aid South Vietnam occurred at a time when some assertion of its power seemed imperative. The Bay of Pigs fiasco, the Kennedy-Khrushchev confrontation in Vienna, and our nonintervention in Laos—". . . each," explained Adam Yarmolinsky, "argued in its way for some countermove to demonstrate America's firmness in the face of Soviet or Soviet-backed probes, whether verbal or physical. In some situations, timing becomes all important; and if Vietnam was the wrong place to increase our military commitment, it looked like the right time. A new administration is likely to be optimistic about new ways of doing things—even of fighting wars—and Vietnam turned out to be a testing ground for these new kinds of forces and techniques. And once the initial commitment was made, there was little chance for escape. For as our presence became more visible, the engagement became a test of our dependability and determination. Once that juncture was reached, the tenets of collective security closed in upon us like a Venus fly-trap."

The Failure of Vietnam

In his *Report on Operations in South Vietnam, January 1964–June 1968,* General Westmoreland stubbornly refuses to admit the failure of our effort in Vietnam. Citing casualty ratios, weapons losses, figures on the progress in pacification, advances in the combat capacity of the South Vietnamese forces, logistical successes, and, most of all, the fact that the Viet Cong is not in complete control of the country, he concludes that the "significant trends in the war" clearly favor the "Free World Forces."

General Westmoreland's roseate analysis is not shared, however, by others in the national security establishment. Our intervention, we must remember, was not undertaken solely to save South Vietnam from collapse, but to show that we could defeat revolutionary warfare and would be willing to stamp out troublemakers throughout the world. Our success in prosecuting the war was thereby to have a deterrent effect on insurgency movements in other areas. But the form and extent of intervention must be tailored to its justification. Escalation, as Paul Kecskemeti has pointed out, has instead destroyed whatever deterrence the war was supposed to exercise. The very cost of Vietnam lessened our credibility. To be successful, we would have had to win with limited and low-cost means, but as our involvement intensified, the costs soon outstripped any possible gains. Knowing that the United States would have to pay an unacceptable price to resist an insurgency, potential insurgent organizers will in the future have serious cause to doubt our willingness to risk being bogged down in other such ventures.

Even though many officials in the defense establishment recognize the damage the war has done, this does not signify any questioning of the basic premises that propelled us into this costly entanglement. On the contrary, the security managers and private defense analysts still retain the same concerns and most of the same preconceptions that sent American forces thrashing about in the jungles of Vietnam. Indeed, their greatest worry is that public dissatisfaction over the cost of the war, combined with the uncertainty, if not the dismal quality, of the outcome, may lead to a pulling back or to a withdrawal. Such an action would have grave implications; Chinese power is still a threat, writes an Air Force colonel in the *Air University Review,* and until China begins to behave herself, our continued policing of Asia cannot be avoided. Guy Pauker of RAND agrees that "China is not likely to abandon her policy of achieving Asian hegemony." And China, says Secretary Laird before the House Armed Services Committee, has "the possibility of being one of our gravest national security problems in the 1970s."

High officers interviewed in the Office of the Joint Chiefs of Staff demonstrated in no uncertain fashion that their conceptions of the nature of insurgencies and of American security interests have changed little. "We were not just confronting the Communist bloc. The war is a major confrontation between world powers; it was the next move on their part after Korea." A colonel in the office of the Special Assistant for Counterinsurgency and Special Activities concurred. "This is what we're after," he stated as he leaned backward in his chair and tapped his pencil on a map of China. "A national liberation movement," said another colonel in the counterinsurgency section, "is just the way the Communists paint the threat a different color. They want to build up an insurgency slowly, then strike, and present us with a *fait accompli.*" An analyst with the Army's think-tank, the Research Analysis Corporation (RAC), cast the problem in terms of immutable patterns of human history. "The real world," he said, "is a conglomerate of nation-states, some of which are aggressive and expansionist. As long as the nation-state system exists, conflict will recur. We worry about insurgencies, which are tactics of an expansionist power and which threaten to upset the international system. . . . The Vietnam War," he continued, "was part of North Vietnamese expansion. They dressed up troops in peasant costumes and sent them south because this was a cheap way of thwarting the United States. And you know? They succeeded. If you were Ho Chi Minh, would you stop?"

Southeast Asia, furthermore, is not the only area demanding an active American posture *vis-à-vis* the threat of insurrection. Although the situation in Latin America is seen as fairly encouraging, the region's social problems —the maldistribution of wealth, the structural imbalances of Latin American societies, the rapid rate of population growth—offer manifold opportunities for Communist initiatives.

The danger is viewed as especially imminent in Latin American cities, where the concentration of population, added to the restiveness of the intelligentsia and working classes, makes urban centers relatively easy targets for total disruption. (There is, indeed, more danger from urban insurrection than from peasant insurrection, since the political consciousness of the urban populace is more extensively developed. In the Dominican Republic, the support for the constitutionalists in 1965 came entirely from Santo Domingo, whereas the rural areas were conservative strongholds. Here, again, our fears do not derive so much from apprehensions that revolutionary movements in Latin America will come under Soviet domination or will pose an insufferable military and economic threat to our interests but, rather, that our prestige and world influence would be impaired if we had to suffer such another loss of influence over our traditional domain. "To lose another Latin American country is simply not allowable,"

I was told by a high State Department official. "This would seriously affect the world's perception of our ability to keep our own house in order."

Africa is another potential crisis area. Kecskemeti of RAND fears that an outbreak of civil war in South Africa would endanger Western interests. The analyst from RAC saw evil happenings even in Ethiopia: "We have a vital interest in seeing that Haile Selassie doesn't fall," he said. "The Soviet Union has long had designs on the Red Sea —in order to give them access to the Indian Ocean. They already have Egypt under their thumb. Now they are trying to filter down through Ethiopia by supporting an insurgent movement against Haile. If they can overthrow him, they could then fill the power vacuum in the Indian Ocean. Even here, you have this interplay of great-power conflicts."

In brief, the national security establishment clings steadfastly to its belief in the ability of foreign powers to instigate insurrection and in the necessity for our intervention. Talk of confrontation and the balance of power is still central; the feeling that American security is dependent on upholding world order is largely undiminished, and there is little indication of a willingness to run any risks of losing control.

This is not to contend that there has been no change; the sheer cost of Vietnam would force even the most rigid organization to reappraise its actions. For the military, an examination is inevitable, since no other group in American society has suffered so much loss of prestige, trust, and political power as has the military from Vietnam. If the military is to regain its former esteem, it has to lie low for the time being and try to avoid the kind of wars that may cause domestic political disruptions. Hence, for acutely practical reasons, the military desperately wants to avoid active involvement in combat. "We'll do anything not to get involved," said a colonel, echoing the predominant theme of his colleagues.

Yet it is doubtful whether the hopes for non-involvement can be realized under the present set of policy assumptions. While the will for non-involvement clearly exists, if for no other reason than political expediency, old patterns of threat perception and response remain unaltered. If it is still to be our role to be "the guardian at the gates" (in Lyndon Johnson's Romanesque phrase), then the most profound outpouring of wishful proclamations will not prevent intervention and the incalculable risks it entails.

Nevertheless, from the perspective of the security managers, the war has taught us valuable lessons. From World War II and Korea, we thought, we learned the indivisibility of freedom and the need for collective security systems. The lessons of Vietnam have been equally valuable, for we have learned how to defend our interests at more acceptable levels of cost. We have learned to be more selective about choosing the next locale to prove our point, and we have seen the need to formulate more-suitable tactics.

The Locale of the Next Vietnam

Future Vietnams must be avoided, because the high cost of such engagements saps our strength and weakens our power position. One of our problems in Vietnam was that we failed to make an adequate assessment of our chances for relatively painless success. In the future, we will be reluctant to commit ourselves on behalf of a country whose government is marginally viable and cannot control its own populace. "We cannot," says General Taylor, "afford to stake our world standing on a lost cause or on one with unduly high risks of failure."

The need for selectivity is particularly important, since military planners now perceive that an initial commitment impels an often relentless momentum for subsequent commitment: "Intervention on any scale," said a colonel in JCS Policy and Plans, "leads to further intervention. . . . This," he continued, his brow furrowed with pensive strains, "is a sticky wicket. In the future, any cause will be much more carefully examined, and our response much more carefully assessed." An officer in the JCS Counterinsurgency Division explained that, in future insurgency situations, "we are going to make a more careful assessment of geography and historical circumstances. If these factors make the situation favorable, we should be able to win without risking involvement of combat troops, which is something we deeply desire to avoid." By way of illustration, he further explained that "the historical circumstances of Thailand make it a good bet. Unlike South Vietnam, it is a nation, to begin with. It has experienced centuries of stable governments, has religious and social cohesion, has a secure economic base, and is included under treaty arrangements with the United States." Walking over to a map of Asia, he planted his finger on Burma: "Here would be a country we would have second thoughts about protecting from the simple standpoint of geography. It has a long border with China, which would give the insurgents a secure sanctuary and would allow an almost painless infiltration of men and supplies." Moving his finger over to the Philippines, his eyes brightened and his voice perked up: "In the Philippines, however, there is a chance to assert our naval power. The country is surrounded by water, so it would be impossible for an insurgent movement to receive outside aid. There, sources of weapons could easily be dried up."

It is abundantly evident that the defense establishment does not see the prospects for future interventions as being governed by a reassessment of our attitude toward revolution; rather, the question is one of risk calculation. The Vietnam war has failed because we did not adequately analyze the potential costs—the economic, political, and social costs as well as the purely military costs. Since the object of war is to improve our over-all power position, the net gain over the *status quo ante* must be sufficient to justify the expected costs; if it is not, then it would be better to cede some of our local objectives in order to preserve our strength for other contingencies. This, in fact, explains our non-intervention in Indonesia. "We looked at that country," said a high State Department official, "saw nothing more than two thousand islands, and decided there wasn't much we could do. We asked ourselves: What do we lose if we don't get in? What do we lose if we do? We measured our gains and losses, and the losses outweighed the gains." When, on the other hand, the risks are low and potential gains high—or when a loss would be unacceptable, as in Latin America—there are no grounds to refrain from intervention.

The processes for making better risk calculations have become a preoccupation of the national security establishment. Systems analysis, the favorite tool of economic assessment during the McNamara years, is now being seriously considered in professional journals for its application in suggesting and evaluating policy alternatives in terms of risk as compared with outcome. Computer simulation and war gaming have become popular tools in all the upper-level service schools. High- and middle-level officials from the State Department and the Department of Defense regularly participate in elaborately researched manual war games sponsored by the JCS Joint War Games Agency. Scenarios projecting the world situation from two to five years hence are presented to the players, who are divided into groups representing each country. Between turns, a control group, which also represents the world community, analyzes the preceding moves and gives the players a new scenario projection. At the conclusion of the game, a critique is made of the actions and responses. "The primary aim of the game," said an officer of the Joint War Games Agency, "is to gain new insights and to point up the ramifications of actions." "Some games," said General Wheeler, "have caused a revision in contingency plans." While initially the use of war games was restricted to the playing out of large-scale international conflicts, there are now game designs for counterinsurgency that include social and attitudinal factors such as village loyalty, availability of intelligence, political impatience, and pressure from the press.

It is possible that such new-found attention to risk analysis, and the concern for a deeper exploration of the potential impact of policy decisions, may work to prevent Vietnam-type imbroglios. What is more likely is that the adoption of seemingly impressive analytic techniques may infuse the security managers with a belief that they have explored and resolved more aspects of the problem than they actually have. They may dismiss uncertainties, and roll headlong into interventionist adventures, confident that this time the correct calculation has been made.

Techniques for the Next Interventions

The goal of U.S. foreign policy, we have seen, is the preservation of stability and a favorable world order. No high-cost counterinsurgency campaign that drains our power and thereby weakens our credibility can be a functional part of this grand design. If this policy is to be validated, we have to find more-effective, low-cost means of putting down insurgencies that threaten American hegemony.

"Military commanders always live within the mental bounds of the last war," said an analyst from RAC. "What the French did," he continued, "was to train the Vietnamese Army to fight well in France and Belgium. If there were a ground war in Europe, the Vietnamese Army would perform brilliantly. We, too, used tactics that were appropriate to the last war, in Korea, and not to this one. The top positions in our Army are still held by officers from the old Korea generation. But now a new generation of officers who received their baptism in Vietnam is moving up through the command structure, and they can be counted on to bring the lessons they learned in Vietnam into high-level policy making."

The officers educated in Vietnam seek above all to defeat the insurgents with a minimal expenditure of resources and a minimal presence of American personnel. A large infusion of American troops arouses the hostility of the local populace, creates strains on the threatened country's economy, and alters domestic life-styles and social relationships. Indeed, direct U.S. military action could result in a repudiation of our effort by the very people we want to aid–in addition to inciting political opposition at home because of the vastly greater costs in money and lives and the difficulty of bringing counter-guerrilla war to a quick and victorious conclusion. When the only means of saving a country lies in the deployment of American troops, we have already suffered partial defeat.

Fortunately for counterinsurgency planners, revolutions cannot gain full strength in a short period of time. On the contrary, they develop slowly, through stages that, as described in the Special Warfare School's *Counterinsurgency Planning Guide,* unfold as follows:

In the first stages, the guerrillas seek to arouse mass consciousness and destroy confidence in the government. Subversion and infiltration of the political institutions may occur frequently and in organized patterns, but there are no major outbreaks of uncontrollable violence.

In the second stage, the insurgents, having gained popular and external support, initiate armed guerrilla warfare against the established government.

In the third stage, the war becomes a war of movement "between organized forces of the insurgents and those of the established government."

During the second stage, the guerrillas establish political control over some areas of the country, and the insurgent organization becomes a political authority fulfilling the same functions as the "legally constituted government." As an insurgency progresses through this stage, their consolidation of strength makes them harder to defeat, and by the time the last stage is reached, the situation may have become hopeless beyond repair. None of this bursts upon us unforeseen, however, and if the insurgency is detected in its initial stages, we should be able to carry out adequate countermeasures to forestall its further progression. "Vietnam," a colonel in the JCS counterinsurgency section told me, "was not a test of counterinsurgent operations in the proper sense of the phrase. We ended up fighting a limited conventional war on a mobile battlefield. Instead of doing this again, we have to devote more attention to nipping insurgencies in the bud. We have to prevent them from occurring, rather than jumping in after the conflict has escalated."

The prevention of an insurgency is seen to be a political as well as a military concern. "As long as a national social system permits adequate satisfaction of perceived future needs through its institutions and practices," wrote Major John Pustay, "it will remain stable. When perceived needs and desires are repressed, the social system becomes unstable and ready for revolution." If a counterinsurgency campaign focuses only upon killing guerrillas, it totally misapprehends the central problem and will ultimately fail.

The sacred canons of future counterinsurgency operations will be to drastically limit the visibility of the American presence and to foster the social reforms that will undermine the appeal of revolutionary movements. "When a society is in order," said an officer in JCS, "insurgencies don't occur. We are in favor of helping people to make a non-violent, appropriate change."

The mission of the Army is thus expanded to include acting as a catalyst for social change. Although this mission belongs initially to AID, the military often has more men and superior resources. It plays a significant role through the conduct of "civic action" programs, which not only include technical assistance in such activities as road building, construction of schools, etc., but also involve, theoretically at least, using the military as a "change agent." That is to say, the U.S. military would work to encourage the kinds of attitudes and institutions that will insure the continuance of desirable social innovations. As the command doctrine of the U.S. military mission in Iran explains: "The people should learn that they can contribute to their own social and economic development by working side by side with the military in the conduct of civic action. Civic action must be 'self-regenerative.' . . . this means that a project [should be designed so that] users will be motivated to maintain, and hopefully extend, the project when military support is withdrawn, and thus it has the potential of starting a chain reaction that will lead to further economic and social development."

"All mission officers," states a report prepared for the Army by the Human Resources Research Office of American University, ". . . can and should assist by encouraging relevant new behaviors of counterparts, and by reporting such behaviors to their superiors, so that they in turn would comment favorably to the counterparts' superiors."

The American role in the maintenance of internal security is, like our role in civic action, conceptualized as building the capacity of local forces to do the job themselves. We can do this either by augmenting a threatened country's armed forces through the Military Assistance Program, or by emphasizing, instead, the use of civilian police. Having learned in Vietnam that the use of large-scale military force is an ineffective way of counteracting insurgency, the importance of training civilian police for domestic insurgency operations has increased. In an October 1968 speech before the graduating class of the International Police Academy (a Washington-based, AID-supported school), Major William E. DePuy, Special Assistant for Counterinsurgency and Special Activities of the JCS, accentuated this theme: "The military exists primarily to preserve a nation from foreign threats. Where there is a domestic threat, the police possess, and should possess, a legitimacy which the military should not appropriate; . . . the military is not suited for continuing commitment to the special functions of law enforcement."

In his manuscript *The Police Function in Stability Operations,* Joseph Coates, of the Institute for Defense Analyses, elaborated upon the advantages of using civilian police as the primary instrument against insurgent movements. If the counterinsurgent operation succeeds in disrupting the subversive organization, irrespective of other factors, it succeeds in disrupting the subversion. Hence the key to defeating insurgency is to disrupt the subversive organization—a point agreed upon by other authorities, such as Sir Robert Thompson. This cannot be accomplished without good intelligence, and good intelligence is impossible without "a long-term immersion in a particular cultural milieu." This immersion is incompatible with a military approach; it can be realized only by native police: "Whether he is a small-town policeman in Venezuela or a border patrolman in Thailand," Mr. Coates writes, "the officer probably can function more effectively if he is a local citizen living and working in the area he knows, among people he understands. With a permanent tenure of ten or more years, he can establish a rapport with the local citizenry that a transient military man can never hope to achieve."

Wisdom, Old and New

What can we conclude from these trends? Will the increased concern for care in selecting a low-risk situation for intervention and for keeping American personnel out of combat offer an adequate safeguard against future Vietnams?

One cannot help being skeptical. In fact, these fervent proclamations are little more than a body of old doctrine that has been exhumed and garbed in post-Vietnam dress. We did not enter the Vietnam War ignorant of the social causes of revolution; we were not unaware that counterinsurgency operation should have primarily a political focus. Most of all, we were manifestly aware of the necessity to use native forces, and understood that the infusion of American troops was a dangerous and undesirable course. In September 1963, President Kennedy stated that the war could not be won unless the government of South Vietnam made a greater effort to amass popular support. "In the final analysis," he said, "it is their war. They are the ones who have to win or lose it. We can help them, we can give them equipment, we can send our men out there as advisers, but they have to win it–the people of Vietnam. . . ." The Special Warfare School's 1964 *Counterinsurgency Planning Guide* abounds with calls for "co-ordinated programs designed to create a favorable political, social, and economic environment. . . ." It warned that employment of large conventional forces in area sweep operations was to be avoided, leading only to "fruitless and frustrating pursuits." It cautioned, ". . . the primary responsibility for counterinsurgency operations must rest with the local government. Insurgent warfare, by its nature, is an intimate affair normally fought between antagonists of similar ethnic backgrounds. The intrusion of force by an external power, unless carefully applied through the medium of local government, can have a debilitating effect on the government's power to control the affairs of its own nation."

The lessons of Vietnam are then in reality only the old wisdom accrued from studying the histories of previous insurgencies. Rather than acting as a safeguard against further involvements, the new wisdom is a declaration that intervention is still the unquestioned basis of American policy and that further interventions are taken for granted. Under the tenets of the new wisdom, we can anticipate only a more subtle management of intervention: more reliance on clandestine operations, greater emphasis on building the strength of local elements favorable to the United States, and–at least in principle –the withholding of aid from governments that seem too far gone to be saved. The new wisdom implies that if the conditions for intervention seem right–if the threatened country has a stable government, if the insurgents can be easily cut off from sources of outside supply, if we can reasonably expect to accomplish our goals without the commitment of combat troops, and if the threatened country has an established relationship with the United States –then our vital security interests could well lead us to intervene.

The relevance of this outlook to current developments in Thailand is clear and ominous, for Thailand has all the attributes of a situation prime for intervention. Officers in the JCS Policy and Plans Division and in the Office of the JCS Special Assistant for Counterinsurgency Warfare

are confident that the Thai Government, with minimal U.S. aid, could successfully defeat the growing insurgency in northern Thailand; Thailand, in their judgment, is a good bet. Unlike South Vietnam, it is a nation, to begin with; despite the occurrence of several bloodless coups, it has a long history of stable government and an established system of public administration. In the words of the Army's *Area Handbook for Thailand:*

> General conditions of public order and safety are normally good. Habits of obedience and respect for authority have been inculcated in the people by centuries of rule by absolute monarchs whose authority was both secular and religious. The moral sanctions of Buddhism and the pressures for conformity in the village communities were placed on personal restraint and public harmony. A potential source of friction exists in the ethnic minorities, but the vast majority of the population is united by its common heritage of Thai history, language, and tradition.

Thus, Thailand is appropriate to include as a position of forward defense in the collective security structure. And if the insurgency there should grow, we should be able to help the Thais overcome the dissidents at little cost, proving the point that became so elusive of proof in Vietnam.

Yet the logic of commitment makes any visible involvement a risky endeavor. Since the collective security doctrine leads us to define our interests at any point by the extent of prior commitment, any initial obligation turns into a rationale for further commitment. After an American commitment becomes visible, any confrontation is invested with global implications; the issue becomes a test of our resolution to defend our security interests against the forces of instability and disorder. At this juncture, retreat becomes psychologically untenable, for the loss of our influence and credibility will encourage subversive movements elsewhere and make the world environment even more turbulent and inhospitable.

A colonel in JCS, who claimed that the Vietnam war "just crept up on us," touched on this dilemma when he theorized that we "wouldn't have become involved to the extent we did if the Viet Cong hadn't fired on American advisory personnel. If we hadn't been fired on, we may have been more willing to get out instead of escalating." Indeed, what we are here contending with is a common pattern of human behavior: when an opponent does physical harm to oneself or one's comrades, the normal response is not to retire to safer environs, but to seek retribution, to harden one's position, and to counter violence with violence. Wherever there is an American presence, there is the threat of assault upon American personnel, and the concomitant danger that we would react to such an assault by an escalatory response. When a situation worsens, there is little reason to think that policy makers will simply subtract the threatened country from the list of nations considered to be in our sphere of vital interests. On the contrary, the Joint Chiefs of Staff will call for the protection of our men, the State Department will argue for the protection of our client government, and politicians will call for the preservation of our honor.

If the subtraction of commitments is difficult, the addition of new interests seems inevitable. For commitments tend to spread into heretofore undefined areas, a phenomenon one high State Department official termed "creeping commitments." As he explained, "Once we establish commitments in one country, the military will argue that we have to extend them to contiguous areas, to defend the original commitments. A fundamental interest in Indonesia lends importance to Thailand, and a commitment to Thailand leads to the argument that we have to defend Burma. We have given a basic core of commitments, but that is not all, because we have to do other things to make these commitments valid. And there is great difficulty in getting up in public and arguing that we should live up to our commitments, even though retrenchment may be the more rational policy."

In this way, we bring upon ourselves a new range of obligations and feel forced not only to defend client governments, but also to defend areas considered vitally important by our clients. "From the strict standpoint of national security," said another high official at State, "all of Southeast Asia is insignificant to the United States. The whole region could pass into Communist domination and wouldn't make the slightest bit of difference to us. But we have to consider allies to whom the region *is* vital, most notably Japan. We have a defense treaty with Japan, and the well-being of Japan is vital to our interests. And while Southeast Asia isn't tremendously significant to us, it is significant to Japan. We have to defend Southeast Asia in order to live up to our commitment to Japan."

The old policy, then, remains in force. The vocabularies of containment, commitment, and collective security still form the sacred articles of our position. Assurances are given that we will be much more careful the next time, and will not involve ourselves in high-risk situations; we will, it is asserted, make more-judicious calculations based on the valuable experience gained in Vietnam. What is lacking, however, is any consideration of the risk of miscalculation. How do we extricate ourselves if we have again miscalculated and the situation deteriorates? Under the tenets of collective security, extrication is impossible, because retreat would lessen our allies' faith in our determination. "The commitment of 500,000 Americans," writes Presidential Assistant Henry Kissinger, "has settled the issue of the importance of Vietnam. For what is involved now is confidence in American promises. However fashionable it is to ridicule the terms credibility or prestige, they are not empty phrases; other nations can gear their actions to ours only if they can count on our steadiness. . . . In many parts of the world . . . stability depends on confidence in American promises. . . ." If, believing a country constitutes a good bet for our protection, we include it in our security structure and commit ourselves to defending the established government, we will only escalate our support should the threat grow beyond what we initially thought probable. While the defense establishment, clinging to the logic of the past twenty years, proclaims its abhorrence of the commitment of a large-scale American presence, the strength and organization of enemy forces may make such a presence again a compelling necessity.

The impetus of our interventionist policy then leads inexorably to military involvement. If conditions in a threatened country allow the development of a full-fledged insurgency, such ameliorative measures as military assistance, police training, civic action, and other stratagems to "win the hearts and minds of the people" will be of little value, but will only pave the way for greater involvement. American participation in these measures will not be a serious obstacle to the development of an insurgency, if the established government has failed to gain the support of its people in the work of social reconstruction, if the structure of public administration is inadequate, and if there is no sense of national unity and common purpose. These objectives can be attained only through the leadership of an indigenous elite, and, once they are attained, there is no need for an American presence. If the local leadership fails, and falls short in these objectives, a limited American presence will be of no avail.

Change or Continuity?

We have seen how the premises of collective security led to our massive involvement in Vietnam, and how they have persisted with the defense establishment. We have seen, moreover, that any safeguards against future Vietnams amount to little more than assurances that better calculations of risk will be made the next time around.

Few in the defense establishment have dared explore a fundamental change in our conception of security interests. "At the Pentagon," said a former official in the Office of the Secretary of Defense, "there are certain rules of debate that dictate subjects which simply can't be discussed except informally at lunch. There is no challenge in weighing over-all strategic objectives; the basic premise is continued interventionism, and the only topic of debate is the most effective way of configuring our forces to serve this policy. And after initial decisions are made, events just lumber on; the effects ooze down into every part of the defense establishment. At the start of the Kennedy years, great interest and enthusiasm were devoted to counterinsurgency. This became the context in which the services can market their hardware. Each service will invent types of forces and say, 'What programs can we field this year under the rubric of counterinsurgency?' This will probably go on for a decade until the fashion changes."

A member of the defense establishment must therefore express his thoughts within a closed vocabulary and set of assumptions that are immune from outside challenge. If he dares flout the rules, his credibility will slip away, as will his chances for professional advancement if he persists with his deviant behavior. "The whole idea," continued this official, "is not to undermine the structure."

The institutional constraints that restrict thought within

the defense bureaucracy are reflected also in the psychological constraints that govern at the top. Men who have expended a substantial part of their careers, not to mention the lives of American soldiers, in implementing their prescriptions for world order will be loath to question the validity of their position. On the contrary, they attribute failures to simple miscalculation, or else plead that their actions will be vindicated once the furor has died down and events can be viewed in proper historical perspective. Any favorable circumstances, of course, are credited to the working of the present system.

Writing in *The Essence of Security,* McNamara states that the fundamental issues are the same today as they were a decade ago and will be a decade hence. In testimony before the House Foreign Affairs Committee, Eugene V. Rostow reiterated the incantations that constituted the Administration's stock-in-trade in the halcyon days before Vietnam. In testimony before the same committee, Undersecretary of State U. Alexis Johnson vigorously proclaimed, ". . . our security relationships around the world have pretty well proven to have been valuable in moving toward creating the kind of world environment we seek." He promised, furthermore, that while treaty commitments will be re-examined, nothing substantial will change.

There are few institutional restraints on this weight of bureaucratic momentum in the Pentagon and the Department of State. The power of Congress, which has steadily eroded since 1900, is viewed by policy makers as a dangerous hindrance to effective action. The postwar crisis atmosphere led to the belief that the President should be allowed the freedom to determine the American reaction to events in troubled areas. Coupled with the President's capacity as Commander in Chief of the Armed Forces, and his power to deploy forces wherever he pleases, the executive has assumed plenary power over foreign policy.

In hearings before the Senate Foreign Relations Committee, Nicholas DeB. Katzenbach, then an Undersecretary of State, asserted that within the presidency reposes the "responsibility for controlling and directing all the external aspects of the Nation's power." The need for Congress to declare war, he explained, was outmoded; Congressional haggling over foreign-policy decisions and troop deployments could only hamstring the President and frustrate our policy. The proper executive-legislative relationship was for the President to keep Congress informed of what he was doing, and for the Congress to declare its support for his initiatives, lest our enemies doubt America's unity of purpose.

The view under President Nixon's administration is evidently the same. In his comments on Senate Resolution 85, which states, ". . . a national commitment by the United States to a foreign power necessarily and exclusively results from affirmative action taken by the executive and legislative branches. . . ," Assistant Secretary of State William B. Macomber served notice on Congress that the State Department intends to ignore the resolution: "The executive branch," wrote Macomber, "tends to doubt the usefulness of attempting to fix by resolution precise rules codifying the relationship between the executive and legislative branches in the broad area of national commitments."

Even the plenary power of the President, however, is compromised by the nature and the political power of the bureaucratic apparatus. The President cannot command the bureaucracy as much as negotiate with it, and extremes of conflict between them must be avoided. For one thing, the bureaucracy commands channels to Congress and to the information media that could be used to the President's detriment. But perhaps of more importance is the fact that the President is dependent on the bureaucracy for his advice and intelligence assessments and for any eventual action. By the time raw data have been filtered through the policy machinery, the President's scope of decision is restricted to the choices worked out on lower levels. "The options the President exercises over foreign policy are bound to be limited," a high State Department official told me. "There is little possibility that the President can alter basic policy premises. Our conception of fundamental interests is non-controversial; the question is only what you do to promote those interests. What the President can do is develop force configurations; he can decide, for example, whether we should have eight divisions in Southeast Asia or five."

The Requisites for Change

It is clear that, if we are to avoid an endless series of interventionist entanglements, we cannot maintain past policy, but will have to evolve a new way of perceiving America's place in the world. The following are some changes in perceptions and attitudes that should evolve from our experience in Vietnam:

(1) Security is not indivisible. The world is bound to be disorderly, and we will have to learn to live with violent change. To think that violent change anywhere necessarily affects our security interests is to adopt an overblown conception of what our security interests require. Our position is not so weak and perilous that we cannot afford to try a wait-and-see approach.

(2) The Third World is not going to be the decisive battleground in a geopolitical struggle with communism, and is not the kind of area that anyone is going to organize. There are definite limits to the capacity of either side to make headway there, for we have little capacity to control any movement in a country that is not close to our borders.

(3) The Soviet Union is discovering that the maintenance of client states is a troublesome venture, and it may not be so enthusiastic to continue prosecuting the imperialist game.

(4) The threat that wars of national liberation pose to our security is not so great, but the cost of defeating them is. When states have to pay a great cost to support their interests, they come to doubt whether these interests are worth supporting.

Whether or not such modified perceptions can gain ascendancy in the national security establishment will determine whether we will escape from an endless series of interventions.

NOTES

A large part of this paper is based on interviews held in the summer of 1969 with officials in the State Department and the Pentagon, especially in the office of the Joint Chiefs of Staff. These sources are not directly attributable.

President Nixon's position on future American policy in Asia (the "Nixon Doctrine") was disclosed in a background press conference on Guam and repeated in a speech of November 3, 1969 (New York *Times,* November 4, 1969).

Maxwell Taylor's views on the lessons of Vietnam can be found in his book *Responsibility and Response* (Harper & Row, 1967) pp. 42–64.

The Basis for Intervention

Robert S. McNamara's view of our need for world stability is presented in *The Essence of Security* (Harper & Row, 1968) p. 7.

Admiral Burke's quote is from his article "Power and Peace," *Orbis,* Summer 1962.

George Ball's statement can be found in "The Dangers of Nostalgia," State Department Publication #7858, 1965, p. 10.

Dean Acheson's position appears in his book *Power and Diplomacy,* Harvard University Press, 1958, pp. 17–20.

Eugene V. Rostow's statement is from "The United States and the Communist World," State Department publication #8388, 1968.

Dean Rusk's extension of our responsibilities beyond the treaty system appears in *Hearings on Worldwide Military Commitments Before the Preparedness Investigating Subcommittee of the House Armed Services Committee,* Part 1, 1966, p. 8.

Our need to expend "national blood and wealth" to validate our commitments is expressed by Lt. Col. Don H. Payne in "What Happens After Vietnam?" *The Air University Review,* September 1968.

John Foster Dulles' statement of the "domino theory" appears in his book *War or Peace* (Macmillan Company, 1957) p. 231.

The statement of the Truman Doctrine is in his message to Congress of March 12, 1947, reprinted in *Vital Speeches.*

Robert Tucker's statement of our policy appears in his book *Nation or Empire?* (Johns Hopkins University Press, 1968), a work that is essential reading for anyone concerned with the matter of foreign policy.

General Taylor's expression of the need for this country to be "watching in all directions" for danger appears on page 6 of his book *Responsibility and Response.*

Roger Hilsman's description of the Soviet objective appears in "The Sino-Soviet Economic Offensive Through June 30, 1962," Department of State, Bureau of Intelligence and Research Memorandum RSB-145, September 18, 1962.

Robert Osgood's description of the need for gradual change appears in "The Theory of Limited War," in *American Defense Policy,* Mark E. Smith and Claude J. Johns, eds. (Johns Hopkins University Press, 1968). Dr. Osgood told us in private conversation that he no longer holds to this theory.

The Collective Security Psychosis and Vietnam

General Taylor's description of the domino theory appears on page 21 of *Responsibility and Response.*

The new weapons and techniques for conventional and counter-insurgency warfare are described by John S. Tompkins in *The Weapons of World War III* (Doubleday & Company, 1966).

Adam Yarmolinsky's description of the motives for intervening in Vietnam appears in *No More Vietnams,* edited by Richard M. Pfeffer (Harper & Row, 1968) p. 23.

The Counterinsurgency Planning Guide (1963), a publication of the Army's Special Warfare School (now the John F. Kennedy School for Military Assistance, Fort Bragg, N.C.), is available in the Army Library, the Pentagon, Washington, D.C.

Hilsman's statement is from his article "Orchestrating the Instrumentalities: The Case of Southeast Asia," in *Foreign Policy for the Sixties* (Johns Hopkins University Press, 1965) p. 192.

The Failure of Vietnam

General William Westmoreland's *Report on Operations in South Vietnam, January 1964–June 1968* is available from the Department of Defense.

Paul Kecskemeti's views are presented in "Insurgency as a Strategic Problem," a RAND Corporation memorandum dated February 1967.

Concern over public dissatisfaction with the cost of the war was expressed by Charles Wolf in a RAND Corporation memorandum entitled "Asian Futures," published in May 1968.

Concern with China is expressed by Lt. Col. Don H. Payne in his previously mentioned article; by Guy J. Pauker in "The Future Role of the United States in Asia and the Pacific," published by the RAND Corporation in April 1968; and by Secretary of Defense Laird in 1969 appearing before the House Armed Services Committee, p. 1721.

Concerns with insurrection in Latin America are expressed, for example, by Col. Frank R. Pancake in "Why Military Assistance for Latin America?" published in *Air University Review,* December 1966; by Daniel James, "Another Vietnam in Latin America?" published in *Military Review,* June 1969; and by General Edgardo Jarrín of the Peruvian Army, in "Insurgency in Latin America," also published in *Military Review,* March 1969.

General Taylor's description of where we should not intervene appears on page 41 of *Responsibility and Response.*

Among the many sources of the new techniques of military analysis are an article by Lt. Col. Robert A. Walker, "The Military Analyst in Research War Gaming," in *Military Review,* January 1969; "Systems Analysis, Something Old, Something New," by Capt. Charles Bishop in the U. S. Naval Institute Proceedings, October 1968; and "The Systems Approach and Public Policy", a RAND Corporation memorandum by E. S. Quade, March 1969. Counterinsurgency games are described in a study conducted by ABT Associates in November 1965 titled *Counter-Insurgency Game Design Feasibility and Evaluation Study,* and in an article by Col. William Long in *The Naval War College Review* of May 1969 entitled "Urban Insurgency War Games."

Some of the problems with the new analytical techniques are described by E. S. Quade in "Pitfalls and Limitations," an article appearing in *Systems Analysis and Policy Planning: Applications in Defense,* edited by E. S. Quade, American Elsevier, 1968, and by Yehezkel Dror in a RAND Corporation paper of February 1969 entitled "Some Normative Implications of a Systems View of Policy Making."

Problems of conducting a counterinsurgency operation without alienating the population we are trying to protect are described by General Harold Johnson in *Army,* November 1965 ("We have a very difficult professional problem of not alienating the population by unrestrained use of our force in our attempts to destroy and keep pressure on the armed insurgency.")

As well as Lt. Col. Richard C. Bowman, "National Policy in the War of Wills," in the U. S. Naval Institute Proceedings, April 1965; and Major John S. Pustay, *Counterinsurgency Warfare* (The Free Press, 1965) pp. 157–61.

Major Pustay's comments on the prerequisites for a stable society appear on page 53 of his book *Counterinsurgency Warfare* (Free Press, 1965).

The Command Doctrine for the Military Mission in Iran is quoted in "Promoting Civic Action in Less-Developed Nations: A Concept Realization of the U. S. Military Mission Role," by Alfred D. Kraemer (Human Resources Research Office, July 1968).

The Army's views on Thailand are contained in the *Area Handbook for Thailand,* Department of the Army Pamphlet 550-53, prepared by the Foreign Area Studies Program of American University, September 1968.

The views of Henry Kissinger, President Nixon's Special Assistant for National Security, appear in the January 1969 issue of *Foreign Affairs.*

The testimony of Eugene Rostow and U. Alexis Johnson can be found in "Strategy and Science: Toward a National Security Policy for the 1970s," *Hearings Before the House Committee on Foreign Affairs,* April 27, 1964.

Nicholas Katzenbach's testimony appears in "U.S. Commitments to Foreign Powers," hearings before the Senate Foreign Relations Committee, 1967, especially pp. 72–81.

William Macomber's remarks are included in an addendum to the Committee Report on Senate Resolution 85, 1st Sess. 91st Cong., 1969. This report on the so-called "Commitments Resolution" contains a valuable historical review of the erosion of Congressional power in the conduct of foreign affairs.

For historical background on the long-term development of American foreign policy, see: *Intervention and Revolution,* by Richard J. Barnet (New American Library, 1968); *Containment and Change,* by Carl Oglesby and Richard Schaull (Collier, 1967); *The Roots of American Foreign Policy,* by Gabriel Kolko (Beacon Press, 1969); *The Tragedy of American Diplomacy,* by William A. Williams (Delta Books, 1966); and *Corporations and the Cold War,* edited by David Horowitz (Monthly Review Press, 1970).

THE CAPACITY TO INTERVENE

by Tom Klein

The Growing Need

"Now the rest of the world can try to catch up," proclaimed a double-page ad in *Life* magazine. Beneath a photo of the huge Lockheed C-5A, we learn: "The C-5A Galaxy is more than the world's largest airplane. It's a new kind of defense system. It's like having a military base in nearly every strategic spot on the globe."

To meet the requirements it sees necessary for an interventionist foreign policy, the Defense Department is developing the capacity to "project its forces" anywhere in the world on short notice. The Pentagon foresees no lessening in world tensions and no change in our overseas role after Vietnam, and is now contemplating the possibilities for future interventions. Secretary of Defense Robert S. McNamara summed up its position in his 1968 posture statement when he said, "The ability to respond promptly to clear threats to our national interests and the security of our allies, possibly in more than one place at the same time, can serve both to deter and to prevent such threats from expanding into larger conflicts."

The Pentagon is faced, however, with the practical impossibility of stationing troops everywhere that military confrontations may develop. For this reason, military planners have developed the rapid-deployment strategy. Over the past decade, as the possibilities for limited warfare have increased, so has the emphasis on the rapid-deployment strategy. With the military's current perception of the possibility of two or three more Vietnams, Pentagon strategists, with the enthusiastic support of the Kennedy and Johnson administrations, have been planning for the rapid response that, they insist, will be needed to stop future "threats to our national security."

The Department of Defense has given strong backing to the programs to increase the airlift and sealift capabilities deemed essential for strategic mobility. In fact, the Fast Deployment Logistic Ship Project, the newest development in sealift, was given unprecedented support within the Defense Department: The Secretary of Defense and spokesmen for the Army, Navy, and Marine Corps, ignoring traditional interservice rivalries, all testified before Congressional Committees on the need for a fleet of FDL ships. In addition, the $2.1 billion requested for airlift-sealift programs in fiscal year 1970 represented the largest percentage increase over fiscal year 1969 requests of any major military program in the current defense budget.

The Army is convinced that in the past it has suffered from inadequate airlift and sealift capabilities. Both in World War II and Korea, the two recent land wars, the Army felt hampered by poor strategic mobility. However, the 1958 Lebanon crisis provided a cogent illustration of why the military wanted to improve its airlift and sealift capabilities. Fifteen thousand troops had to be moved quickly to help that Mideast country, as military statements put it, "preserve its independence in the face of violent political agitation throughout the Middle East."

For the show of force to be effective, it had to be mounted quickly. Brigadier General W. R. Desabry, testifying later before Congress in favor of increased transportation spending, explained that the Army believed that "there was no guarantee that this could be done from the United States, for the ability to airlift the needed forces was shrouded in uncertainty." Although the Ready Strategic Army Forces (STRAC) were ready for deployment from the United States, Desabry added, ". . . neither the Air Force nor the Navy had the required lift capabilities." He said that he believed "diplomacy solved the crisis"; however, had the United States wanted more forces deployed, inadequate airlift and sealift capabilities would have been one of the restraining factors.

The 1962 Cuban missile crisis was another situation in which the Army wished that more-adequate transportation had been available. One of the critical problems was, according to Desabry, ". . . the seeds that this crisis bore of worldwide danger precluded the large-scale use of resources already employed elsewhere." And although diplomatic maneuvering ended the crisis, another question remains: would the United States have been more likely to entertain a land invasion of Cuba if the military had had more confidence in its mobility?

The Army also uses the 1965 Dominican crisis as an example, in its requests for increased air- and sealift. Although the deployment of over twenty thousand troops went smoothly, the military has told Congress that the proximity of the Dominican Republic was an important factor in the success of the operation. The military does not envision all future interventions taking place so conveniently near our shores.

Finally, there is Vietnam. The main thrust of the strategic airlift-sealift operation there is to facilitate the regular movement of troops and supplies from the United States to Vietnam; it is not a rapid-deployment operation. However, harbor bottlenecks in Vietnam have held up supply operations. Since July 1965, when the logistic build-up began, some cargo ships have waited for as long as seventy-seven days to unload and depart from the port areas, and the Defense Department has questioned the efficacy of a slow build-up in rapidly developing crises. And Defense officials are aware that a fast deployment of troops to Southeast Asia would have put severe strains on available airlift and sealift capability.

The Kennedy Build-up

There are essentially only two approaches by which a rapid-deployment capability can be attained. The first is to have U.S. forces permanently stationed or pre-positioned at "potential trouble spots" throughout the world. The second and more feasible approach is to maintain a small, ready manpower reserve in the United States, along with transportation capable of deploying the force quickly to any spot on earth.

Although the first alternative might appear to be acceptable because of the rapid-response capability it could give Army forces, it has many limitations. Pre-positioning on land leads to a loss of the flexibility prized so highly by the military, since pre-positioned equipment would be subject to restrictions of the host government. In addition, pre-positioning is useful only if the contingency happens to occur near the equipment. Such equipment has traditionally been placed in Europe and the Far East, because it was assumed that any confrontation would begin in one of those two areas. But with the possibility of limited war breaking out in other places, the military's stocks of equipment are no longer convenient to all the potential trouble spots on the globe.

Another difficulty with pre-positioning was spelled out in a recent Department of Defense fact sheet: "The presence of a large equipment stock with its security and maintenance forces is a propaganda target." As an Air Force official said in a recent interview, "Our troops are resented everywhere." There is also an economic factor involved: one of the reasons for our unfavorable balance of payments is the massive presence of U.S. armed forces overseas. Finally, the Defense Department is faced with the loss of some of the foreign bases it has counted on in the past: France is already lost, and the situation with Libya is uncertain.

The military has used the seaborne pre-positioning of two Fleet Marine Forces, which cruise with the U. S. Navy's Atlantic and Pacific fleets. This Marine Corps program will soon be getting a boost from nine new amphibious assault ships (known as Landing Helicopter Assault Ship, or LHA), which, according to a recent Defense Department news release, will be "faster and more versatile than any modern amphibious warfare ships now in the Fleet." Each of the new ships is designed to land, under battle conditions, two thousand Marines and supporting equipment by helicopter or landing craft. General L. H. Chapman, Commandant of the U. S. Marine Corps, said in a March 1969 magazine article, "It is obvious that we must increasingly rely on going back across oceans; quite likely to land on a hostile shore against a determined enemy . . . ; the future holds not a lessening, but a growing requirement for amphibious or Marine-type landing forces." However, even with the new ships, the seaborne Fleet Marine Forces will be of relatively small size.

Therefore, it is the second approach to the rapid-deployment strategy–reliance on transportation from the United States–which has most interested the Defense Department and the presidental administrations for the past decade. President Kennedy, in his first State of the Union address, stated, ". . . additional air transport mobility . . . will better assure the ability of our conventional forces to respond, with discrimination and speed, to any problem at any spot on the globe at a minute's notice. In particular, it will enable us to meet any deliberate effort to avoid or divert our forces by starting limited wars in widely scattered parts of the world."

Kennedy had help from the Congress. Congressman L. Mendel Rivers, Chairman of the House Armed Services Committee, held hearings before his newly formed Subcommittee on National Military Airlift, and was so impressed by the need for more airlift that he rushed funds through for the immediate modernization of the Military Air Transport Service (MATS).

One of the recommendations of the Rivers subcommittee was that MATS should "increase emphasis on the preparation of limited-war plans." A pamphlet published by this service states, "This same era [late fifties and early sixties] was characterized by the 'brush-fire' war and widely scattered crises. The need quickly grew for fast-reacting, highly mobile forces that offer an effective means to deter, contain, or terminate conflicts which pose a threat to the United States."

By 1963, when the special subcommittee held hearings again, Secretary of Defense McNamara was able to say that airlift capability was being quadrupled. Rivers was enthusiastic about the increased capability. While talking about appropriations, he observed, ". . . one of the difficulties is the failure of many people, even in Congress, to recognize it [MATS] as a combat organization, and we have the feeling that the name has something to do with that." He suggested a new name—to insure that MATS would never again be considered a peacetime airline—and it was soon redesignated the Military Airlift Command (MAC).

As part of the new emphasis on improved strategic airlift, deliveries of the jet C-135s and prop-jet C-130Es were accelerated, and the White House announced the beginning of procurement of the C-141 Starlifters, capable of carrying 129 troops and much of their light equipment. In addition, the Military Airlift Command saw the need to replace propeller-driven C-124s, C-133s, and aircraft in the strategic airlift reserve, by an even newer aircraft.

With the new mobility concepts, much of the equipment that the Army deemed necessary for "maximum combat effectiveness" was unable to fit within the older aircraft. Also, MAC wanted aircraft that would be less constrained by limited range and speed, and by the need for large, paved airfields. By 1964, the requirements for a new aircraft, the C-5A Galaxy, had been developed.

Coupled with the impressive build-up in airlift, the Army took another step to advance the rapid-deployment strategy—the forward pre-positioning of heavy equipment and supplies that could be "married-up" with lightly equipped forces airlifted into the area. General Curtis LeMay, Chief of Staff of the Air Force, was able to report to Rivers' airlift subcommittee that, by fall of 1963, "the Army has something over half a billion dollars invested in pre-positioned equipment." Because land pre-positioning is subject to the constraints mentioned earlier, it was initially increased only in areas where the Army foresaw "potential contingencies." Thus, in West Germany, by 1967, additional equipment for two divisions and some smaller units was in place.

In an attempt to find a more flexible type of pre-positioning, World War II Victory ships were converted into Forward Floating Depots (FFDs), in which equipment could be stored under controlled humidity conditions. The FFDs would be stationed in a U.S.-controlled area, always ready for deployment to a threatened spot, where their equipment could be joined with airlifted troops. By 1965, three FFDs were stationed at Subic Bay, in the Philippine Islands, and the military was seeking more such bases. However, the Defense Department was slow to perceive the potential contribution of sealift, which had always been looked upon as a rather slow means of transportation able only to fulfill the less demanding tasks of long-term support and reinforcement. Most officials thought that the existing military-civil sealift ships such as those in the Merchant Marine and the National Defense Reserve Fleet were adequate for the likely tasks.

The Defense Department's *ad hoc* rapid-deployment measures of the early 1960s were systematized in 1964 with the completion of a study by the Joint Chiefs of Staff's Special Studies Group, entitled "Rapid Deployment of Forces for Limited War." The Special Studies Group, acting on the basis of an assumed "forward defense strategy," concluded that a rapid-deployment capability could be attained most efficiently by a mix of three factors: airlift, sealift, and selective pre-positioning. The group determined that the complementary features of such a combined deployment system would permit supply to several contingency areas from a relatively few forward bases.

The JCS study proposed that rapid deployment could serve as a deterrent to enemy attack: "A demonstrated U.S. ability to move forces rapidly could cause potential enemies to have serious doubts about their chances of military success in remote areas of the world." The study claimed that rapid deployment would provide the capability for halting all threats, and would enable U.S. forces to quickly mount a "show of force in the event of a crisis." One Air Force official described this in an interview as "an advanced form of battleship diplomacy."

In Congressional testimony, military leaders repeatedly justified the heavy cost of rapid deployment by arguing that a quick commitment of forces will mean a smaller commitment in the long run. As General Harold K. Johnson, Chief of Staff of the Army, liked to say, "A brigade in time may save the commitment of nine." One Army official stated in an interview that rapid deployment was actually a "more humanistic approach" to the problem of limited warfare because, he said, it would help the United States to save lives. Military men also state that the rapid-response capability is needed to reassure allies that U.S. armed forces are not deserting them as troops are redeployed back to the United States.

As the Special Studies Group examined the size of the needed rapid-response capability, it became apparent that the cost of meeting the requirement primarily through airlift would be prohibitive. This judgment was made with the knowledge that the C-5A was to become a major part of the airlift fleet. The study demonstrated that airlift was not the complete answer for the lifting of additional equipment to already deployed troops; sealift was more cost-effective. In addition, a study done by the Navy placed renewed emphasis on the potential contribution of sealift.

The Navy study was initiated by the Chief of Naval Operations in 1964 and was entitled "Logistic Support of Land Forces," or Logland. The original concept, as envisioned by the Navy, was to combine high-speed sealift with the Forward Floating Depots. However, further study, plus the awareness that modern shipbuilding technology could provide fast, highly efficient storage ships to complement strategic airlift, led to the development of an entirely new craft, the Fast Deployment Logistic (FDL) Ship.

Logland developed the concept of operating ships loaded with ground-force equipment in selected areas on the periphery of the Eurasian land mass, with other ships maintained in U.S. ports in readiness for quick deployment. The FDLs were to converge on a trouble spot and unload their equipment in time of emergency. At the same time, men would be airlifted from the United States and married-up with the waiting equipment, to become a combat-effective unit. The Navy believed that a substantial number of the FDLs, with a top speed of twenty-five knots, could arrive at trouble spots within two or three days after a deployment decision, and all the ships could be in the area within a few weeks. One limitation of the concept was that the marry-up operation could be accomplished only in a friendly, or at least neutral, environment.

As the emphasis on rapid deployment has grown, so has the Pentagon bureaucracy responsible for its operation. On October 19, 1965, in an appearance before the Special Subcommittee on Military Airlift, General Earle G. Wheeler, Chairman of the Joint Chiefs of Staff, reported that a Joint Transportation Board charged with the continuous review of airlift and sealift requirements had been set up. He added that a "focal point" had been established within the JCS "to concentrate on strategic movement matters."

The establishment of this office has led to further deployment studies. General Wheeler, explaining the need for these studies, told the Rivers subcommittee in 1965:

> I am aware that much has been said about the many studies that have been made regarding strategic mobility. I can assure you much good has come out of the efforts put into these studies. There are many factors that influence our ability to project our power where and when it is needed. These are not purely military or purely international, but some mix of the two. Some of the military factors that must be considered when evaluating strategic mobility are readiness of units, theater reception capabilities, and the type and magnitude of the threat to be countered. Our task is to identify the proper mix of airlift, sealift, and pre-positioning that will provide the proper military response consistent with the military job to be done.

One of the studies subsequently undertaken was the "Strategic Movement Capabilities Plan for 1966 Through 1970," or "Movecap," which considered the forces and equipment to be moved, in the light of existing capabilities to move them, and the readiness of the units. Another key study was initiated at the request of Secretary of Defense McNamara to examine the desirability of a strategic mobility office. In March 1966, the Office of the Special Assistant to the Joint Chiefs of Staff for Strategic Mobility was established to analyze, evaluate, and monitor strategic movement planning and operations. One of the new office's main responsibilities was to be the annual updating of the "Movecap" study. Major General J. C. Sherrill, the first JCS Special Assistant for Strategic Mobility, quickly praised "Movecap" as an exercise that "has indicated several new concepts in strategic mobility."

Deployment Capacity Today

Secretary of Defense McNamara told Congress during a review of airlift and sealift in 1968, ". . . the most demanding contingency which we use for planning our forces is a rapid deployment to Southeast Asia to counter a conventional attack, and a simultaneous reinforcement of our forces in Europe." He went on to say that the military has also examined the requirements for "a more limited contingency." It was determined, he said, after a review of the many possible combinations of airlift, sealift, and pre-positioning, that the most cost-effective force to meet this rapid-response requirement should consist of: six C-5A squadrons, fourteen C-141 squadrons, thirty Fast Deployment Logistic Ships, pre-positioned equipment in Europe and in the Pacific, a Civil Reserve Air Fleet (CRAF) with a cargo capacity equal to 465 DC-8s, and 460 commercial cargo ships. This rapid-response force was also supported by Secretary of Defense Clark Clifford in his 1969 budget statement.

At the end of 1968, the Pentagon had an active strategic airlift force composed of the following: fourteen squadrons of C-141s, thirteen squadrons of C-124s, and three squadrons of C-133s. The procurement of the C-141 Starlifters, the largest operational transport in the Air

Force, was completed in December 1967, and the aircraft are now in the inventory of the Military Airlift Command in numbers envisioned by McNamara. They have been the work horse of the Vietnam supply operation and, by the end of 1968, were producing 75 per cent of the total ton-mile capability of the strategic airlift fleet.

General John P. McConnell, Chief of Staff of the Air Force, told the House Armed Services Committee that the C-5A should enter the Air Force inventory by December 1969. McConnell added: "By the third quarter of FY 73, we will have an all-jet strategic airlift force of C-5As and C-141s, which will, with fewer aircraft, provide greater flexibility and require less maintenance than the mixed force of today."

The Military Airlift Command, now a major division of the U. S. Air Force, directs more than 109,000 men at 419 locations in nearly forty countries. MAC is responsible for several missions that are part of the rapid-response strategy: aerial delivery of combat forces and equipment, logistical resupply of deployed forces, and airdrop of troops and battle equipment. In addition, MAC is in charge of approximately twenty thousand Air Force Reserves, who practice for the airlift jobs they would be called upon to perform during emergencies.

The reserve component of the airlift command is now beginning to train under a new "Associate Unit Concept." General H. E. Estes, Commander of the Military Airlift Command, recently explained the new program: "The C-141 has proved to be so reliable and maintainable that we can, with relative ease, keep it in the air more hours a day than our old piston aircraft. . . . With this level of utilization inherent in the C-141, and promising to be equally attainable in the C-5A, the airplane ceases to be a limiting factor in the production of airlift capability." Therefore, he said, one of the main limiting factors now is manpower to fly these aircraft at their maximum utilization rates in an emergency. Under the "Associate Unit Concept," there will be an associate airlift squadron for each active airlift squadron in the MAC force. These reserve units will train in the C-141s and eventually in the C-5As, but will have no authorized aircraft themselves.

Another responsibility of MAC is the Civil Reserve Air Fleet (CRAF), a backstop force composed of civilian planes which in an emergency would replace military aircraft in the more routine MAC logistics missions. The manner in which this civilian service can be activated has been totally revised in the past few years. Prior to 1963, the airlift capability of CRAF was not available to the Defense Department unless there was a presidentially declared emergency. But as the military became more concerned with limited warfare, the concept of CRAF operation was revised. Now, in a "State I" emergency, determined by the Secretary of Defense, CRAF aircraft can be requisitioned, according to a MAC information kit, "to perform airlift services for DOD [Department of Defense] in support of counterinsurgency activities, localized military emergencies, and similar-type actions." As of August 1968, there were three hundred fifty aircraft (three hundred of them jets) in the International Fleet of CRAF.

Our present airlift capability for the strategic movement of troops and matériel can be measured in terms of a Vietnam operation. In late 1967, MAC moved more than ten thousand troops of the 101st Airborne Division's "Screaming Eagles," along with their 5357 tons of equipment, from Fort Campbell, Kentucky, to Bien Hoa Air Base, Vietnam, in an airlift called "Eagle Thrust." The operation took thirty-one days on an accelerated, but non-emergency, basis. According to information supplied by the Military Airlift Command, had there been a full emergency situation, "Eagle Thrust" could have been accomplished in two and a half days.

In March 1969, twenty-seven hundred soldiers were

transported from the East coast of the United States to Korea. "This 10,000 mile airlift," wrote General Jack Catton, head of the Military Airlift Command, "demonstrated the U.S. national resolve to support its allies and its ability to place its combat forces in the most distant of locations on the shortest notice, equipped and ready to fight."

As Secretary of Defense Clifford said in his fiscal year 1970 budget statement, "We are now well on our way towards the attainment of the airlift portion of the strategic lift objective." However, he went on to note, ". . . unfortunately, this is not the case with respect to sealift." The sealift problem is really divided into two parts, he said; "the long-term adequacy of the Nation's total sealift resources, particularly the U. S. Merchant Marine," and "the immediate availability of suitable shipping" for rapid-deployment operations. Clifford added that the condition of the Merchant Marine is a national problem, while the need for a rapid-response fleet is of more-immediate concern to the military. He made clear that the existing Defense Department-controlled sealift force, consisting of fifteen Victory ships, six aircraft ferries (converted cargo ships), three Forward Floating Depots, two Navy roll-on/roll-off ships, and one new privately owned roll-on/roll-off ship on long-term charter to the Navy was considered "inadequate, both quantitatively and qualitatively". This fleet is not considered extremely useful for rapid deployment, because it is fully engaged in point-to-point cargo operations during peacetime and would have to discharge its cargo and return to ports before taking part in a military deployment. In addition, most of the ships lack capabilities that the Defense Department considers desirable for its rapid-response fleet: the ability to store and maintain wheeled and tracked vehicles for prolonged periods; the ability to transport, in a ready-to-fly condition, the helicopters now being used extensively by Army forces; and the ability to unload cargo rapidly with no assistance in undeveloped port areas. The current limitations on rapid deployment help to explain why the DOD placed such a high priority on the Fast Deployment Logistic Ship fleet.

The Military Sea Transportation Service (MSTS) has the basic mission of providing the sealift necessary for the support of military strategy throughout the world. This command is geared to respond rapidly to emergency sealift requirements primarily with the fleet of Navy-owned ships and, if the situation is serious enough, with U.S. merchant ships. As of January 1969, the MSTS-controlled fleet consisted of: a government-owned fleet of 152 vessels, 144 reactivated ships from the National Defense Reserve Fleet (composed largely of World War II cargo ships sitting in the Hudson River for years), and 209 vessels under charter from the U.S. commercial fleet. The numbers are impressive; however, the Navy is quick to point out that the ships are overage and in poor condition. In addition, the Navy, concerned with the threat of limited warfare, is interested in finding a method for utilizing commercial ships during a contingency that is not a declared national emergency. It is seeking a maritime equivalent to the Air Force's Civil Reserve Air Fleet and is now working with the maritime industry on a similar concept called the "Respond" program, to augment military shipping with commercial sealift.

The Navy has not staged many global operations or exercises to demonstrate its present sealift capability. The most significant exercise involving sealift took place in early 1964 and was called "Quick Release." It involved the three Forward Floating Depots stationed in Subic Bay and a brigade of the 25th Infantry Division. Although the main purpose of the operation was to test the feasibility of storing equipment under controlled humidity conditions, it also offered a chance for the military to examine the "marry-up" concept. The troops were airlifted from Hawaii to Okinawa and joined with their equipment. The exercise was judged a success; no major breakdowns occurred and the equipment was in good to excellent condition. Since the equipment had been stored for over a year and a half, "Quick Release" assured the military that prolonged storage of Army matériel on board ships was feasible, an important factor in the Fast Deployment Logistic Ships program.

C-5A–The Fastest with the Mostest

Two new pieces of equipment are considered vital to the growing fast-deployment capability: the huge C-5A jet cargo transport, which will soon be in the inventory of the Military Airlift Command, and the Navy's Fast Deployment Logistic Ship, which is still on the drawing board because of continued Congressional denial of construction funds.

Secretary of the Air Force Robert C. Seamans told the Senate Armed Services Committee in 1969 that an effective airlift posture should have the ability to airlift the troops with their equipment; airlift all the necessary heavy equipment, including weapons and vehicles; organize the arriving forces into effective units; and provide sustaining support.

The C-5A was designed to fulfill these requirements. Speaking at the March 2, 1968, rollout of the C-5A at Lockheed's Marietta, Georgia, plant, President Johnson explained the role of the plane this way: "For the first time, our fighting men will be able to travel with their equipment to any spot on the globe where we might be forced to stand–and they will travel rapidly and efficiently. . . . So it is much more than a rollout of a great aircraft that you are seeing here today. We are observing a long leap forward in the effective military might of America."

The C-5A can transport the weapons and equipment needed by an Army division–including tanks, armored personnel carriers, and helicopters. The payload/range capability of the C-5A is three times greater than that of the older airlift aircraft, including the C-141. Despite its size, the C-5A can operate on small, primitive airfields–an important factor in rapid deployment to an undeveloped area.

The importance of the C-5A to the Military Airlift Command is enhanced by its easy loading capability. The aircraft has full-width openings equipped with their own mechanical ramps, which enable trucks, tanks, and other vehicles to drive aboard. In addition, the entire cargo floor can be lowered to truck-bed height for easy loading. The military envisions the C-5A landing in areas where ground facilities might not be available, and this equipment gives the C-5A the ability to load and unload at great speeds without the aid of elaborate terminal loading facilities.

Former Secretary of the Air Force Harold Brown spoke highly of the C-5A's potential in a speech at the Air Force Association Convention on April 5, 1968: "For the first time, we will be able to airlift a regular infantry division anywhere in the world using approximately 500 C-141 flights, primarily for troops, and 270 C-5A flights to lift the equipment. With our programmed airlift force, we could take the first brigade of such a division from the mid-United States to the Far East in less than five days and the entire division in about ten days." The "Eagle Thrust" operation described above needed 391 aircraft missions; 115 C-5A missions would have done the same job in less time.

In his 1968 speech, President Johnson said, "This aircraft that we roll out here today is a signal; it is a signal that responsible men shall never abandon the road of responsibility. We shall march it proudly. . . ." If, as the defense establishment insists, responsibility is measured by our military power, then our overwhelming airlift capability is truly such a signal.

FDL—a Port on Any Beach

The sealift counterpart to the Air Force C-5A is the Navy's Fast Deployment Logistic Ship (FDL). The Navy, in conjunction with the Army, has determined that the FDL must meet the following criteria: Where ports are available, the ships must have a short unloading and turnaround time. (This means a ship in which wheeled and tracked vehicles can move on and off under their own power.) For other contingencies, the ships must be able to unload on beaches.

If the FDL is built, the Navy will have a non-combatant vessel with distinctive features to meet Army requirements. The ships will have storage parking lanes to accommodate helicopters and the large quantities of wheeled and tracked vehicles of a typical Army division. These storage areas will have environmental controls to help preserve Army equipment and supplies for periods of up to three years. For a rapid unloading over beaches, there will be special amphibious craft and cargo helicopters operating from the FDL flight deck. Twelve of the FDLs will be required to transport the matériel of an infantry division, consisting of over twelve thousand vehicles, fifteen days of initial supplies, and back-up goods, all weighing about 130,000 tons. Finally, the FDLs will have a range of over eight thousand miles at a sustained speed of more than twenty-four knots.

This endurance, plus the relatively long self-sustaining capability of the ships, means that FDLs will be able to cruise near potential trouble spots for long periods of time. And, with their high speed, the ships will be able to get to troubled areas quickly. In a chart supplied by Army Chief of Staff Johnson to the House Armed Services Committee, FDL sailing times from the United States to various "key strategic areas" were given as follows: to Thailand (from the West coast)–12.5 days; to Chile (from the West coast)–8.5 days; to Venezuela (from the East coast)–3.1 days; to Benelux (from the East coast) –6.0 days. The military also realize that ships pre-positioned closer to these "key strategic areas" would give more-advantageous sailing times.

There is disagreement within the military on just how the FDLs would be utilized. At issue is whether the FDLs would be used in a "light" deployment, similar to those in the Dominican Republic and Lebanon, or whether they would be used only in larger deployments, for example to Europe to fight a conventional war. This question came up during hearings before the House Armed Services Committee in 1967, when Congressman Nedzi of Michigan told Secretary of Defense McNamara, "I think the concern here, Mr. Secretary, is if you have such a force [of FDLs], the temptation to expand our commitments is going to be there, and what a commitment is is somewhat subjective. . . ." McNamara replied:

> I think his point deserves an answer. His point is that this greater mobility given to us by the FDL may be used to expand our existing political commitments.
>
> I would say if that capability is used to expand them, in the sense of supporting an administration recommendation to the Congress for undertaking some additional political commitments, then the Congress has the opportunity at that point to say yes or no to the commitments. . . .
>
> The Dominican Republic . . . was really quite a small military operation. . . . What I am saying is the small actions don't require and wouldn't benefit significantly from the FDL program. The FDL program is a large program, and it would be used in connection with relatively large actions. . . .

I am simply saying the FDL does not give us an increased small-operation capability. . . .

One of the Pentagon's military leaders had a different assessment. During the same hearings, Army Chief of Staff Johnson told a questioner about the planned use of the FDL:

It would be used *any place* that our Government requires forces to be deployed. It could be used in either of two ways. One, to reinforce forces that currently are deployed in forward areas, specifically Europe and Korea. And second, it could be used in places where we might want to introduce forces. And an example of that, of course, is the type of action that we had in Lebanon in 1958. (emphasis added)

McNamara's definition of a small military operation—one that would not involve the FDLs—was the 1965 intervention in the Dominican Republic, where twenty thousand troops were deployed. General Johnson, on the other hand, cited Lebanon—where fifteen thousand troops were sent ashore—as a type of deployment in which the FDLs would be valuable.

Johnson's view of the projected use of the FDLs seems to be the more accurate one. Assistant Secretary of Defense Paul Ignatius told the Senate Merchant Marine and Fisheries Subcommittee soon after, that the FDLs were programmed "to deploy their loads into the relatively unprepared and undeveloped areas characteristic of many potential contingency areas." It is clear from Ignatius' statement, plus Johnson's chart listing FDL sailing times to such "key strategic areas" as Thailand, Korea, Iraq, Benelux, Liberia, India, Venezuela, and Chile, that the FDL would be used not only for a massive deployment to Europe or Korea, but also in more-limited interventions.

The Navy's goal for the FDL was spelled out by Rear Admiral Nathan Sonenshein, the FDL Project Manager, in a 1967 presentation on the new ships: "We want to reduce the response time of these ships to a minimum, so that the effect of this capability will be comparable with that of maintaining large forward deployed forces, yet at greatly reduced cost and difficulty." He added that the ships "may move in irregular patterns in ocean areas near expected trouble spots, where their presence may be unknown. . . ."

Testifying before the Senate Armed Services Committee, Paul Nitze, Deputy Secretary of Defense, said, "The thought was, in the event of a crisis, we would be able to pre-position the ships close to the point where it looked as though the crisis might be arising. You would move these ships and unload your equipment prior to the time of hostilities breaking out." Yet, by reducing the response times, and locating them—sometimes secretly—near trouble spots, the FDL ships themselves could become the cause of a crisis. And if a crisis does arise, the American public might be the last to hear of it. In his 1967 presentation outlining the potential of the FDLs, Sonenshein made this remarkable statement:

> Because of the freedom of the seas and the extended endurance envisioned for them, FDLs could steam *without public knowledge,* if necessary, to an advantageous position for rapid deployment. The combination of good intelligence and FDL ships can indeed make a very substantial contribution to our rapid-deployment capability. (emphasis added)

If ships are to be sent without public knowledge, it must be assumed that this means without the consent of Congress. One Pentagon official, asked in an interview about the possibility for covert FDL deployments, replied, "That sort of thing is inherent in the FDL concept."

There is even another role envisioned for the FDLs.

During hearings before the House Armed Services Committee, General Johnson was asked whether the military had considered a mission for the vessel in a nuclear war. He replied:

> I would say "yes." . . .
>
> I think that we tend to lose sight of the fact that in a nuclear exchange there is still going to be some kind of activity going on with regard to the general-purpose forces. You are not going to have, as we visualize it, at least as I visualize it, a total and complete devastation. You are going to have severe and significant damage, but something is going to survive. And whatever survives must be supported.

Criticism from Congress and the Merchant Marine

Some Congressmen have been sharp critics of the deployment programs in recent years, but their criticisms have had only limited effect on the rapid-deployment program. In fact, only the newest components of it have even been debated. C-5As already are approved for construction. After Congressional criticism of rising costs, the Defense Department announced in November 1969 that the C-5A force would be held to the eighty-one aircraft already approved by the Congress, rather than growing to the original target of one hundred twenty. At no time has Congress challenged the military's assumptions behind the initial purchase of these planes; there have only been protests aimed at the cost and the contracting procedures, as indicated by the following exchange on the Senate floor between Senator Symington and Senator Proxmire:

Mr. Symington: I appreciate this dialogue with the Senator from Wisconsin about the C-5A, because I know he is not against the C-5A as such; he is merely questioning the number of C-5As that should be built. Is that correct?

Mr. Proxmire: That is correct.

Only Senator Fulbright offered a wise caveat, when he said, ". . . the C-5A does not itself represent a commitment to anybody, but it represents a significant new facility for the making of commitments in the hands of the executive."

The C-5A has been called by Senator William Proxmire, Chairman of the Joint Subcommittee on Economy in Government, "one of the greatest fiscal disasters in the history of federal procurement." He was complaining about a cost overrun of more than $2 billion on the initial contract with Lockheed Aircraft Company for the construction of fifty-eight C-5As. By now it is difficult even to determine the original price estimates for the jets. The figures given by the Air Force have ranged from $2.5 billion to $3.4 billion. In March 1968, Air Force officials told Congress that they expected no serious price problems with the C-5A; Major General D. L. Crow, Air Force Budget Director, said, "As a matter of fact, the cost history of this program is probably the best cost history we have ever had on any program." A. E. Fitzgerald, the cost expert subsequently fired by the Air Force, later told Proxmire's subcommittee that official Air Force studies actually showed that the production costs of 120 C-5As would be $5.3 billion.

There have also been internal Defense Department studies questioning the cost-effectiveness of the C-5A fleet. These studies concluded that the C-5A was so costly to build and operate that it could be justified only if it was used in the first ten days of a conflict; thereafter, the smaller C-141s and sea transport could do the job far more cheaply. However, the Army's ability to mobilize men and equipment is so limited that it probably could not fill more than half the planned fleet of 120 C-5As in this ten-day period. Also, the study found that the rise in the cost of the C-5A made it no longer an economical replacement for the C-141. Nevertheless, the program is going ahead, albeit toward a reduced goal of eighty-one aircraft.

Unlike the case of the C-5A, debate has surrounded the FDL ever since the Department of Defense introduced the program. As early as 1966, the maritime industry had already begun a major attack on the FDLs; it wanted the FDL construction money to go instead into new commercial ships which civilian operators would make available to the Department of Defense during crises.

One of the maritime industry's arguments was summarized by John Blandford, Chief Counsel for the House Armed Services Committee, in 1967, when he said:

> . . . once the world in a sense settles down to where we only have two trouble spots instead of 52, and we have got 30 of these ships . . . sitting in Norfolk someplace with equipment . . . and some future Secretary comes along, who is very cost conscious, and we have seen some people who are cost conscious, and they say: "Look, we put $1,332,587,647.22 into this program. Now it is a crime not to use these ships. So we will put them into the MSTS and use them to carry cargo to supply our overseas commitments."
>
> This is what bothers the privately owned lines, because you can't commit a future Secretary, and we can't commit a future Congress. Once they are built, they are going to be there always, as a sort of sword of Damocles hanging over the privately owned lines, and it is as simple as that.

General Johnson did not agree with Blandford's assessment:

I think your premise is wrong, Mr. Blandford; that is, that the time is coming when we are going to have just two trouble spots in the world. All the studies we have done indicate that in the years since 1945 the number of trouble spots has increased, rather than decreased, and this is occasioned largely by the enormous number of new nations that have appeared, particularly in Africa.

By early 1967, Congressional criticism of the FDL program began in earnest, directed both against the developing role of the United States as world policeman and the potential effect of the program on the U. S. Merchant Marine. In July, Representative Robert Leggett, a member of the House Armed Services Committee, challenged the FDL in a letter to President Johnson, which said in part: "I am satisfied that the United States needs more of a capability to get out of encounters easily rather than get in. . . . If the ships were used once capriciously or ill-timed, thereafter our fleet would be persona non grata all over the world."

The Defense Department has operated a strong lobbying effort behind the FDL, with congressmen getting high-level briefings from Pentagon and corporation officials. An internal Navy memo on the lobbying activities reports that, within a few weeks, Admiral Sonenshein briefed Senator Tydings; Dan Houghton, the president of Lockheed, talked with Senator Russell; and Roger Lewis, president of General Dynamics, met with Senators Kennedy and Burke. (Both Lockheed and General Dynamics were involved in the contract-definition phase of the FDL program.) The memo itself, dated January 31, 1967, provides a rare insight into the extensive lobbying activities of the Pentagon. Under a section entitled "Specific Adverse Indication," the following was said about visits to two congressmen and some unions:

Congressman Garmatz has expressed opposition to the FDL on the basis that the program will be detrimental to the Merchant Marine. He is attacking the concept of the FDL vs Merchant Marine rather than the military necessity. Since he does not understand the "instantaneous response" requirement, a briefing is in order and will be scheduled.

The Maritime Unions are opposed to the program, as it appears to them to be a threat to the Merchant Marine. Arrangements are being made to brief the Union executives and the people who write speeches and press releases.

Representative Lennon (North Carolina) opposes the FDL program and recommends instead that the money be applied to amphibious ships and the merchant marine. Representative Lennon has heard only one side of the story. Briefing required.

The criticism that most worried the military came from Senator Richard Russell, then the powerful chairman of the Senate Armed Services Committee. Throughout 1967, Russell attacked the FDL, saying at one point that it "suggests we are going to be drawn into war in new places." Later, on the Senate floor, he charged, ". . . they [the FDLs] would have been constantly deployed in forward areas throughout the world," and stated that his committee had disapproved the program in part because it "was concerned about the psychological effect" of the FDLs at home and abroad. "Some nations would consider this facility for intervention anywhere, anytime, as an intimidation," Russell said, adding that with the suggested positioning of the FDLs, it would have been even easier for the United States to "police the entire world or impose a Pax Americana."

Russell's criticism, for all its validity, smacks of political rhetoric. He offered no such arguments against the C-5A Galaxies being constructed in Lockheed's plant in Marietta, Georgia. Insiders in Washington believe that Russell turned against the FDL program when he perceived a threat from the Pentagon to keep the C-5A contract out of Georgia if he did not go along with the FDLs. Not to be blackmailed (and certain of President Johnson's support for the C-5A contract), Russell responded by opposing the FDLs.

The Senate, following Russell's direction, has repeatedly refused to authorize the FDL program. Smarting from this defeat—one of the rare times that body has rejected outright a weapons system—McNamara took his case to the House Armed Services Committee. On April 13, 1967, he made this defense of the FDL:

> It is not now, nor has it ever been, my intention to propel the United States into a role as world policeman. I think it is entirely legitimate for the Senate to raise this issue. However, I disagree that approval of the FDL program would bring about such a result.
>
> We now have many treaty commitments which may well involve us in combat . . . ; the question is whether we will be able to take action to support these commitments effectively or ineffectively. . . .
>
> We have not taken on any new commitments because of the FDL program nor do we contemplate doing so. Congress retains full authority to ratify or veto new commitments should they ever be considered.

McNamara also told the House that the total force would not be routinely deployed far from the United States. Twelve or thirteen would, however, be placed at Pacific bases, he said, with the rest based in U.S. waters. "Hence, none of them would be routinely cruising the high seas looking for trouble," he claimed, adding that he was "willing to defer the forward basing of the FDLs pending thorough Congressional review of the concept and its relationship to meeting present treaty commitments."

McNamara's assurances did not alter the key rationale for the FDL fleet—its ability to deploy to a potential crisis area in time of trouble. This was made clear during the same hearings, when Representative Alton Lennon of North Carolina had this exchange with Secretary of the Navy Paul Nitze:

> And so the intent is to deploy in the oceans of the world, free or not free oceans, these so-called, well, we won't call them floating warehouses, but they are in a sense a floating military warehouse, to be subject to call if and when hostilities break out anywhere. Is that the philosophy of this concept?

Nitze replied, "I think it is a simplified description of this, but is not wrong."

One of the harshest attacks on the FDL came from Representative John Dow of Michigan, who told his colleagues on May 9, 1967, that he was disturbed because none of them had asked, "Should the United States prepare itself to crush all rebellions of underprivileged men in all quarters of the globe?" Dow charged that the decision to build the FDLs had been "generated by the Defense Establishment, and not by Congress." He then asked, "How can we allow technicians of the shipbuilding craft to guide the juggernaut and lay down the policies of our Nation and the destiny of the world?"

When the Department of Defense returned again in 1968 with its request for thirty FDLs, it was met with another barrage of criticism from Congress. Senator Russell, speaking on the FDLs shortly before the program was again rejected, said, "I don't think we can give any demonstration of greater readiness to intervene. We intervene everywhere. The minute fighting breaks out all over the world, we are there."

The Navy tried again in 1969 with a reduced program of fifteen FDLs. By this time, Senator John Stennis of Mississippi had assumed the chairmanship of the Senate Armed Services Committee, and he had a direct interest in the FDL program. In anticipation of Congressional approval of the FDL, the winner of the design competition for the new ships, Litton Industry's Ingalls Shipbuilding Corporation, had begun work in Pascagoula, Mississippi, on what was to be the most highly mechanized shipyard in the world. Nevertheless, the Senate committee continued its denial of FDL funds. The Navy announced in May 1969 that the Ingalls Shipbuilding Corporation had been awarded a $114 million contract for the construction of a Landing Helicopter Assault Ship (LHA). The contract has an ultimate potential, according to the announcement, of slightly over $1 billion, for the construction of nine LHAs. Navy officials deny that Litton received the new contract to offset the loss of the FDL.

The following material was added to this article in March, 1970:

The FDL program was omitted from the defense budget that the Nixon administration presented to Congress in early 1970. Request for air- and sealift was $1.428 billion, down from the preceding year's figure of $2.1 billion. But as the *Armed Forces Journal* noted, ". . . this does not tell the whole story. Rather than depend on government-owned vessels to meet military sealift requirements, as McNamara era theorists proposed to do, the Nixon administration apparently intends to rely instead on the nation's domestic flag fleet, the country's 'fourth arm of defense,' to be the real sealift partner in the airlift/sealift team."

Contained in the budget request for the Maritime Administration is initial funding of $200 million for a ten-year program of ship construction. The new program calls for construction of about thirty specially designed ships per year to provide sufficient shipping capability by 1983 "to meet the nation's projected emergency military and civilian requirements." The objectives of the decade-long plan, according to budget documents, ". . . are based on shipping capability needed by the nation for defense in times of crisis and participation in essential international trade in times of peace."

This move by the Nixon administration solves the problem of opposition of the domestic maritime industry to the FDL plan. The government funds ships owned by private enterprise, which in turn leases the ships to the government to serve the military. A total of 309 ships will be added to the maritime fleet by 1983 "to meet the maximum requirements currently foreseen under conditions of limited war. . . ."

The air- and sealift situation in the spring of 1970 was assessed by *Armed Forces Management.* In its annual defense forecast issue, it concluded, ". . . the Nixon administration, under pressure for an austere budget, is seeking to maintain mobility forces generally at the presently established level for the immediate future with a build-up planned for the mid-1970's. Although admitting sealift is now inadequate, Defense will try to hold the line with aging available ships until the proposed national maritime program and the long-term charter program produce the vessels required to meet any planned contingency."

NOTES

The Growing Need

Sec. McNamara's statement supporting the need for air- and sea-lift is from p. 192 of the *1968 Hearings Before the House Subcommittee on Department of Defense Appropriations* (hereinafter cited as House Defense Subcommittee), Part 1.

The Army's views on the inadequacy of airlift/sealift in past operations can be found on pp. 364–67 of the *1968 House Defense Subcommittee Hearings,* Part 6. Desabry's statement comes from p. 365 of the same hearings. The limitations of our airlift/sealift capability are also discussed by General Johnson on pp. 578–79 of the *1967 Military Posture Hearings Before the House Armed Services Committee.*

The Vietnam situation is described by Secretary of the Navy Ignatius on p. 1093 of the *1968 Hearings Before the Senate Subcommittee on Department of Defense Appropriations* (hereinafter cited as Senate Defense Subcommittee), Part 1.

The Kennedy Build-up

The two approaches to rapid deployment are discussed extensively by Sec. McNamara on p. 192 of the *1968 House Defense Subcommittee Hearings,* Part 1. The problems with pre-positioning on land are discussed on p. 362 of the *1968 House Defense Subcommittee Hearings,* Part 6; on p. 1092 of the *1968 Senate Defense Subcommittee Hearings,* Part 3; and in an article in the June 1968 issue of *Army* entitled "The Army and the Elusive FDL." The statement on equipment serving as a propaganda target is included in a fact sheet put out by the Dep. Sec. of Defense in 1967 (copies available in the Navy Speech Bureau). The balance-of-payments problem is discussed in Sec. Clifford's posture statement entitled "The 1970 Defense Budget and Defense Program for Fiscal Years 1970–74," pp. 37–40.

Much of the information on the Fleet Marines comes from a Department of Defense news release entitled "Litton Industries Wins LHA Ship Construction Award," dated May 1, 1969. Additional information is in an article in the June 1969 issue of *Armed Forces Management* entitled "Navy Begins Construction of Marine 'Dream Ship,'" p. 59; and in a study by J. I. Coffey for the Institute for Strategic Studies entitled "Technology and Strategic Mobility," p. 17. For Chapman's statement, see "Hostile Shores Must Still Be Taken," in the March 1969 *Armed Forces Management*, p. 36.

The Congressional views on MATS can be found in the *Report of the 1960 Special Subcommittee on Military Airlift.* The statement on brush-fire wars appears in "The Military Airlift Command (MAC)," a pamphlet included in a Military Airlift Command Information Kit. (This packet is updated to January 1969 and is available from the Air Force Office of Information.) McNamara's statement on the increased airlift capability is on p. 5969 of the *1963 Special Subcommittee on Military Airlift Hearings.* Rivers' statement on the change of name can be found on p. 6032 of the same hearings.

Sources on the modernization of the airlift fleet include: p. 381 of the *1968 House Defense Subcommittee Hearings,* Part 6; p. 2093 of the *1969 Military Authorization Hearings Before the Senate Armed Services Committee;* and p. 12 of "Airlift–the Key to Strategy," an article in the September *1966 Supplement to the Air Force Policy Letter for Commanders.*

For an extensive discussion of the build-up in pre-positioned equipment and the rationale for the FFDs, see pp. 361–63 of the *1968 House Defense Subcommittee Hearings,* Part 6. General LeMay's statement can be found on p. 6054 of the *1965 Special Subcommittee on Military Airlift Hearings.* The reasons for the slow emergence of sealift appear on p. 193 of the *1968 House Defense Subcommittee Hearings,* Part 1.

The information on the JCS and Logland studies comes from many sources: "The FDL Ship Program–Description, Questions, and Answers," a paper released by the Navy on November 14, 1966 (available from the Navy Speech Bureau); "Presentation on the Fast Deployment Logistic Ship Program," a February 1967 presentation by Rear Admiral Sonenshein (available from the Navy Speech Bureau); "Aircraft Development–Its Role in Flexible Military Response," an article in the January–February 1969 issue of *Air University Review,* p. 23; "NSIA/Navy Proceedings of Navy

Briefing to Industry on Fast Deployment Logistic Ship Program," transcript of a National Security Industrial Association meeting held on December 15, 1965 (available from the Navy Speech Bureau or NSIA); pp. 192–94 of the *1968 House Defense Subcommittee Hearings,* Part 1; and an article in the February 1967 issue of *Armed Forces Management* entitled "Navy's Fast Deployment Ships Designed for U. S. Military-Economic Needs," pp. 38–40. General Johnson's statement on the value of a timely commitment can be found, among many other places, on p. 581 of the *1968 Senate Defense Subcommittee Hearings,* Part 2.

General Wheeler's prepared statement on the Joint Transportation Board is on pp. 6790–93 of the *1965 Special Subcommittee on Military Airlift Hearings.* The Office of Strategic Mobility is discussed in "Why Defense's 'Mr. Transportation' Is a Key in Military Planning," an article in the September 1966 *Armed Forces Management,* pp. 57–61.

Deployment Capacity Today

McNamara's statement can be found on p. 193 of the *1968 House Defense Subcommittee Hearings,* Part 1. The cost-effective force is described in the same place. Clifford's suggested force is outlined on p. 57 of the *1969 Senate Armed Services Committee Hearings.*

The information on the strategic airlift fleet comes from General McConnell's 1969 presentation to the House Armed Services Committee, pp. 53–63 (available from the Committee); and from pp. 316–18 of the *1968 Senate Defense Subcommittee Hearings,* Part 1.

Material on the Military Airlift Command can be found in four pamphlets from the MAC Information Kit: "The Military Airlift Command (MAC)," "Military Airlift Command and the Air Force Reserve," "MAC's Reserve Associate Unit Program," and "MAC and the Civil Reserve Air Fleet." Additional sources are "How Workable Is the Associate Unit Concept," an article in the May 1969 *Armed Forces Management* (General Estes' statement is on p. 55); and pp. 6728–42 of the *1965 Special Subcommittee on Military Airlift Hearings,* which contain an extensive discussion on the change in the CRAF concept.

"Eagle Thrust" is described in two pamphlets in the MAC Information Kit—"Military Airlift Command (MAC)" and "Global Exercises and Operations"—and in "Thrust of the Screaming Eagles," an article in the April 1968 issue of *Airman.*

Clifford's discussion on sealift can be found on pp. 60–62 of the *1969 Hearings of the Senate Armed Services Committee.*

Information on MSTS is on pp. 1076–78 of the *1968 Senate Defense Subcommittee Hearings,* Part 3, and on p. 2776 of the *1969 Hearings of the House Armed Services Committee.*

"Quick Release" is described on pp. 385–86 of the *1968 House Defense Subcommittee Hearings,* Part 6, and on p. 17 of Coffey's paper for the Institute for Strategic Studies.

C-5A—The Fastest with the Mostest

Seaman's testimony on the four components of airlift and the description of the C-5A can be found on p. 2001 of the *1969 Military Authorization Hearings Before the Senate Armed Services Committee.* The C-5A is also described in a 1969 fact sheet from the Air Force Deputy Chief of Staff for Plans and Operations and in a pamphlet from Lockheed Aircraft Corporation entitled "C-5A."

Excerpts from Air Force Secretary Brown's 1968 speech to the Air Force Association can be found on p. 24 of the Summer 1968 issue of *Defense Management Journal,* in an article entitled "The Impact of the C-5 on Airlift of the 70s."

FDL—a Port on Any Beach

FDL criteria are described in the *1967 Military Posture Hearings Before the House Armed Services Committee,* p. 582. Additional information on the FDL comes from "The Fast Deployment Ship Project," an October 1966 booklet published by the Naval Material Command (available from the Ships Acquisitions Public Affairs Officer of NMC); and from "The Fast Deployment Logistic Ship," a booklet published by Litton Industries (available from the Manager of Customer Liaison at Litton Systems Advanced Marine Technology Division).

The chart of sailing times appears on p. 581 of the *1967 Military Posture Hearings Before the House Armed Services Committee.*

The discussion between Cong. Nedzi and Sec. McNamara appears on p. 1074 of the *1967 Military Posture Hearings Before the House Armed Services Committee*. General Johnson's contradiction of Secretary McNamara can be found on pp. 627–28 of the same hearings. On pp. 644–45, Johnson reiterated that the FDLs would have been used in Lebanon.

Ass. Sec. Ignatius' remark can be found on p. 2 of the transcript of his statement to the Merchant Marine and Fisheries Subcommittee on April 13, 1967.

Admiral Sonenshein's statements are from his February 1967 FDL presentation, available from the Navy Speech Bureau.

Nitze's statement is on p. 666 of the *1967 Joint Senate Armed Services Committee and Senate Defense Subcommittee Hearings.*

Sonenshein's remarkable statement is from p. 9 of his February 1967 presentation.

General Johnson's statement on nuclear war appears on p. 666 of the *1967 Military Posture Hearings Before the House Armed Services Committee.*

Criticism from Congress and the Merchant Marine

The cutback in C-5A procurement is reported in the New York *Times,* November 15, 1969. Senate debate on the costs and uses of the C-5A can be found in the *Congressional Record,* September 9, 1969, pp. S10305–44.

For Sen. Proxmire's statement on the C-5A, see the *Congressional Record* for August 13, 1969, p. S9972. Proxmire's speech (on pp. S9972–81) presents one of the most complete histories available on the procurement scandal.

The $2.5 billion figure is quoted in the January 17, 1969, New York *Times*. The $3.4 billion figure is reported in *The Wall Street Journal* of the same day. The statement by Major General Crow is in the November 25, 1968, *Wall Street Journal*. A. E. Fitzgerald's figure is reported in *The Wall Street Journal* of January 17, 1969.

The internal study of the C-5A is reported in the Washington *Post,* August 31, 1969.

A description of the attack planned against the FDL program is in the December 28, 1966, Syracuse *Herald Journal*. The arguments of the maritime industry can be found on pp. 1079–1161 of the *1967 Military Posture Hearings Before the House Armed Services*

Committee. The Navy's point of view on the issue of FDL vs. Merchant Marine is explained by Ass. Sec. Ignatius in his April 13, 1967, appearance before the Merchant Marine and Fisheries Subcommittee. The exchange between Chief Counsel Blandford and General Johnson appears on pp. 609–10 of the *1967 Military Posture Hearings Before the House Armed Services Committee.*

Cong. Leggett's letter to Pres. Johnson is dated January 9, 1967. (Copies are available in the Plans & Programs Division of the Navy Office of Information.)

The internal memo of January 31, 1967, is entitled "FDL Public Affairs." A copy can be found in the appendix to the Report of the National Security Summer Research Project, in the *Congressional Record,* November 6, 1969, pp. E9417–23.

See the *Congressional Record* for March 21, 1967, pp. 7511–12, for Russell's comments on the FDL.

Sec. McNamara's statement to the House committee is in the form of a letter to Rep. Rivers in response to a request for additional information. It appears on pp. 1076–77 of the *1967 Military Posture Hearings Before the House Armed Services Committee.* The exchange between Rep. Lennon and Secretary Nitze can be found on p. 627 of the same hearings.

See p. H12009 of the *Congressional Record* of May 9, 1967, for Rep. Dow's speech.

Sen. Russell's statement on the U.S. quick-intervention policy is on p. 558 of the *1968 Senate Defense Subcommittee Hearings,* Part 2.

The Navy's fifteen-ship program for FY 1970 is explained in the *1969 Military Authorization Hearings Before the Senate Armed Services Committee* on pp. 292–93, 559–60, and 648–49.

The information on the new Litton shipyard comes from the Defense Department news release on May 1, 1969, and from "The Shipyard of the Future," a booklet published by Litton's Ingalls Shipbuilding Corporation. Denials from the Navy about a connection between the two contracts come from an exchange between Rep. Hardy and Admiral Collwell that appears on p. 9477 of the *1968 Military Posture Hearings Before the House Armed Services Committee* and from a July 8, 1969, interview with an officer in the Naval Material Command. (The officer added that Litton received both the LHA and the FDL contracts, in part, because of the number of ex-Assistant Secretaries of Defense who now work for the corporation and "know what the Department of Defense wants.")

Information on the Nixon program for subsidies to the maritime industry was taken from the *Armed Forces Journal,* Feb. 7, 1970, p. 28.

Assessment of 1970 air- and sealift capabilities and the Nixon administration's plans for the seventies appears in the April 1970 issue of *Armed Forces Management.*

III. ARMS AND INDUSTRY

Defense spending bears little relation to the actual defense needs of the country. As an editorial in *Fortune* magazine observed, "At a staggering cost, the military has repeatedly bought weapons and deployed forces in ways that have added only marginally to national security . . . ; the interplay between the services and their suppliers generates pressures to maintain high levels of defense spending, almost regardless of the external threat. The natural desire of military men to have ever-more-sophisticated and effective weaponry coincides with the desire of the contractors to supply it."

Evoking the mystique of modern science, industry has taken advantage of the desire of each military service to remain on the frontier of advanced technology, persuading them that they need newer, more-sophisticated devices to meet foreign "threats" and the competition from their sister services. Costs become irrelevant, as technical performance and sophistication bring prestige and promotion to the defense bureaucracy. At the same time, the Defense Department takes care of the industry, insuring that each segment receives its share of military business. The result of this symbiotic relationship, which David Sims outlines in detail in his paper, is a permanent war economy and the ever-present likelihood of new military involvements as the Defense Department "exercises" its forces.

Even weapons systems that appear to have met their demise rise up phoenixlike to haunt the taxpayer. Such is the case with the manned bomber that Mary McCarthy documents in her study. The paper by Nancy Lipton and Leonard Rodberg on the missile race makes clear how the operation of the defense industry, particularly the aerospace industry, is predicated upon continuing technological change, making weapons procurement a never-ending process. The research and development process is supported by Defense Department funds, producing a constant stream of ideas and intense, continuing pressure to purchase the weapons of the future. Marc Kramer's brief survey gives examples of this phenomenon.

No place on earth is safe from the energy and technological genius of what Secretary Laird calls the "military-industrial team." As Sam Baker and Kerry Gruson suggest in their paper, a committed complex has already begun to develop a vested interest in American domination of the ocean bottom.

This series of studies suggests that the solution to the arms race and high military budgets does not lie in disarmament talks. Only when the real source of the problem–the defense establishment and its associated industries–are dismantled or converted to the production of useful civilian goods, will it be possible to talk of disarmament, or of peace for this troubled land.

SPOON-FEEDING THE MILITARY—HOW NEW WEAPONS COME TO BE

by David E. Sims

"WE JUST do what the government asks; we build what they want," explained a vice-president of the General Electric Company at a college symposium on the military-industrial complex. A typical industry advertisement in *Air Force and Space Digest* announces: "You state the requirement . . . we meet the need." The defense industry would like the country to believe that it provides a public service without wielding substantial power of its own. Inquiry into the actual operation of the industry leads to a quite different conclusion.

The Defense Industry

The defense industry is composed of over twenty thousand firms, dealing directly and indirectly with the government and providing items and services ranging from sophisticated weaponry to the smallest general-supply goods, at a cost to the Department of Defense of roughly $40 billion a year. Released through prime-contract awards, this money goes to a relatively small number of firms; the one hundred largest contractors win about two thirds of the total, and the top twenty-five roughly half.

The most concentrated part of this industry is involved

in producing new weapons systems: missiles, aircraft, electronics, ordnance, and shipbuilding—the most advanced products of this country's technology. In fiscal year 1969, the weapons industries received in excess of $24 billion for new weapons and their components, in addition to the bulk of $7.7 billion in awards for military research and development. A handful of firms received the majority of this business. A statistical breakdown of the weapons market for fiscal year 1967 presented at a Senate Judiciary Subcommittee hearing, showed that in twelve of the top weapons categories there were eight firms receiving 99 per cent of the business, and with four receiving more than 90 per cent. The majority of the weapons contracts ($16.9 billion in 1968) went to the aerospace industry, where, in 1967 for instance, ten firms received 62 per cent of the military business, and five firms 45 per cent. The remainder went to shipbuilders, small-weapons and ammunition manufacturers, and non-aerospace electronics companies. Murray Weidenbaum, Assistant Secretary of the Treasury, has noted that weapons sellers are, by any economic definition, in oligopolistic situations, and that the degree of concentration in the military market is probably higher than in American industry generally.

Many defense firms rely heavily on defense business; seven of the top ten companies did more than 50 per cent of their business with the Defense Department between 1960 and 1967. These companies were all aerospace firms; within the aerospace industry itself, the reliance on the military is very great. For instance, total sales of aerospace products in 1969 are estimated as follows:

DOD	$16,700
NASA and other government	3,690
Non-government	5,600
Total sales	$25,990 (millions)

The individual aerospace companies are large but not mammoth, as compared to such corporate giants as General Motors and Ford. As Dr. Weidenbaum said, "the medium-size corporations—those with assets over $250 million but under $1 billion—receive the largest share of defense contracts." On the average, half of these firms' fixed capital is leased from the government, and a very large proportion of their costs are for personnel rather than machinery, factories, or other fixed assets.

In 1966, for the nation as a whole, out of every one hundred industrial workers, 2.9 were scientists and engineers. Defense firms employ a much higher proportion of engineers, scientists, and technicians, reflecting the technological sophistication of their products. Of the ten manufacturing industries with the highest proportion of engineers and scientists, ordnance and missiles was first, with 24.5 per one hundred; communications equipment was second, with 16.6 per one hundred; and aircraft and parts was fifth, with 12.1 per one hundred. Recently, the proportion of scientists and engineers within defense industries has been increasing. For example, in ordnance and missiles the number of 1966 was 47 per cent more than in 1961, while, over the same period, the number of production workers increased only 10 per cent and non-production workers remained constant. In the aerospace industry there were 106,300 engineers and scientists working in research and development in 1968, 27 per cent of the total, making aerospace the largest single employer of R&D engineers and scientists in the nation.

Companies such as General Motors and General Electric are primarily oriented toward civilian production, but still do a substantial amount of defense business. Other defense contractors, such as Ling-Temco-Vought and Litton Industries, have become multiproduct conglomerates with particular divisions concentrating solely on defense. Such firms may have activities covering a diverse range of defense products, making it difficult to classify them in any specific area.

The subcontracting system, by which prime contractors buy system components from other firms, adds to the proliferation of economic ties stemming from defense business. Subcontracts account for roughly half the price of the average prime contract, and these awards, administered completely by the prime company, go mostly to small businesses, not to other large defense companies. Little information is available on subcontracting, for since 1963 the government has not even asked for over-all subcontracting data.

Because of the structure of the defense market, a profitable return is almost automatic. The 1947 Procurement Act stipulated advertised price competition (in which the seller bids a price to include his desired profit margin) as the preferred method of contracting, but included in the regulations sixteen exceptions when negotiation could take the place of competitive bidding. These exceptions have become the rule, and price competition is almost completely absent. Admiral Rickover has declared:

> There is no real price competition for most military equipment. There is sometimes competition "to get in," that is, to get the initial award of a particular item. However, there is usually little or no competition in the pricing of individual contracts, and the Government must negotiate with a supplier to establish prices.

Sole source selection (a negotiating situation with only one possible weapons supplier) was the basis for 58 per cent of military prime contracts in 1968, and formally advertised competitive bidding for only 11.5 per cent of total procurement dollars. Such proportions have held for years. In most cases, rates of profit are determined by negotiation between the contractor and the government agency, and thus can often be assumed even before production starts. And, as Admiral Rickover pointed out, "The Department of Defense's own data from its profit review system also indicates that contractors generally do realize the profit included in negotiated contracts."

There is considerable evidence that defense industries enjoy handsome rates of return from this process. If profits are measured as a percentage of sales, then they have been low as compared with other industries, but as several critics have recently pointed out, a more accurate measure of profit is the return on net investment. The following table, presented to the Subcommittee on Antitrust and Monopoly in the summer of 1968, shows that the rate of return on investment has been clearly above the national average, even while the rate of percentage of sales has been lower:

	Average of sample of defense firms		*Average of sample of industrial firms*	
	1952–55	*1962–65*	*1952–55*	*1962–65*
Profit margin on sales (%)	3.0	2.6	4.5	4.6
Capital turnover per year	x6.1	x6.8	x2.9	x2.3
Return on net worth (%)	18.6	17.5	13.0	10.6

Besides a comfortable profit situation, there are numerous advantages defense contractors enjoy that result, as a recent Senate subcommittee report on defense procurement summarized, "in a vast subsidy for the defense industry, particularly the larger contractors." One is the Defense Department's policy of providing government-owned property and federal working capital to defense contractors. The value of government property controlled by defense firms averages half their total capital assets; in 1968, the total value of this government-owned property controlled by industry was $13.3 billion. And the Defense Department's policy of granting interest-free progress payments to a contractor during the execution of a contract relieves the company of using its own funds to meet production costs. These payments, which reimburse the firm up to 90 per cent of incurred cost at specific intervals, are "not necessarily related to progress in the sense of work completed."

Another advantage derives from the Defense Department's patent policy. In this case, "the government permits contractors to obtain exclusive patent rights, free of charge, on inventions produced in the performance of government contracts. . . . The contractor, in other words, obtains a monopoly which he can exploit for his own private gain in the commercial market for inventions paid for by public moneys." As noted by Admiral Rickover in the Subcommittee on Economy in Government hearings, one half of these patents are owned by the same large corporations that obtain the most defense contracts. In a similar manner, non-patentable technological ideas and problem solutions discovered while executing a defense contract can be used later for a commercial product.

The larger firms are in the secure position of knowing that the government will not forget them. Behind this is an informal policy that large defense firms must be kept financially healthy and technologically proficient, on the grounds that they represent a necessary part of our security. It is widely believed that that attitude underlay the decision to award the contract for the TFX fighter plane to General Dynamics, which was in deep financial trouble at the time. In fact, there is a clear tendency for all large defense firms automatically to receive a share of military business. An official of North American Rockwell told us he did not think this resulted from conscious planning on the Defense Department's part, but was simply characteristic of the market. As he explained, the government's demand for weapons keeps most of the available industrial capacity occupied, and when there is some idle capacity, the government is quick to use it. As he put it, "Everyone feeds at the trough, even though it's not planned that way." Similarly, if a company has idle industrial capacity resulting from a program cancellation, there is a tendency to use it some other way. A good example of this arose after the Congressional rejection of the FDL (Fast Deployment Logistics) ships, for which a division of Litton Industries had done the development work and, hoping to produce the ships, had begun building extensive shipyard facilities. Several months after the rejection, the Navy announced that Litton had been awarded the contract for the LHA amphibious assault ship, with a potential follow-up valued at over $1 billion.

There is no mechanism in the Pentagon for basing future contract awards on the supplier's past performance, and frequently firms can prosper in spite of poor contracting records. A study prepared in 1968 by Richard Stubbings, an official in the Budget Bureau, disclosed a series of performance inadequacies in high-risk electronics components for aircraft and missiles. Attempting to connect a firm's performance with its profits and continued government business, Stubbings was forced to conclude "that the current special partnership which exists between government and the aerospace industry not only results in a very high incidence of delivered electronics systems with degraded performance, but there is no effective mechanism in existing contractual arrangements to reward or penalize contractor performance." He gave a historical sketch of the profits and performance of two large aerospace contractors, identified as North American and General Dynamics, respectively, in a Washington *Post* article of January 26, 1969:

> Contractor X, whose volume is 98% government, produced one highly successful military aircraft in the mid 1950's,

then became involved in numerous highly complex electronics programs reaching 50% of total sales volume over the last decade, with the following box score on six military hardware programs: one met systems specifications, one cancelled for technical reasons; four programs with actual MTBF (Mean Time Between Failure) 25% of system specifications. A look at contractor X's profits over this period shows the remarkable fact that average profits were 40% above those of the aerospace industry and 50% above those of all U.S. industries. Only in the last two years does X show a return below that of the aerospace industry, but it still remains above the all-industry average. The correlation of performance with profits is absent in this case.

Contractor Y had an even poorer performance record. Of 7 weapons systems with complex electronics developed over the period, not a single program measured up to expectations. Electronics reliability was the key deficiency in every case, with actual costs 2–3 times original estimates—reflecting overruns, schedule delays, and modification efforts to improve low system performance. This company also ventured into the development of commercial aircraft in the late 1950's which proved abortive and resulted in major losses in 1960–61. The company today does 100% government work. With this dismal performance record, and despite the absence of profits in 1960–61, Company Y shows an average return over the 10 year period above that of all U.S. industries and just below the aerospace industry average. Again, one must conclude that performance has little correlation with profit.

In the face of all this, one can see that in the defense market the modern corporation has a head start in achieving its goals. With the limited competition, generous subsidies, and stable market structure, the defense market is a comfortable place to do business, despite industry protestations to the contrary.

Defense firms are satisfied with their present economic positions. They frequently complain about low profits and high risk, but their behavior in the past, and perspective on the future, tell a completely different story. In the 1950s, the rapid growth of Defense Department expenditures brought a concomitant rise in the fortunes of the weapons manufacturers and established certain firms as leaders in the market. Testimony in Senate Judiciary hearings have shown that the resulting entrenchment was striking: twenty-one of the top twenty-five firms in 1966 had also been in the top twenty-five a decade earlier. Murray Weidenbaum pointed out that this low turnover was due, on the one hand, to protection from upstart entry into the market, because of the high level of scientific and engineering capabilities required to compete, and to exit barriers, on the other, which "can be inferred from the many unsuccessful attempts these companies have experienced in penetrating commercial markets." Furthermore, no large defense firm has folded, and few have significantly reduced their military business in the past decade.

Significantly, the large defense firms see no change in their position in the future. Bernard Nossiter, staff writer for the Washington *Post,* reported on interviews with the heads of some of the largest aerospace firms in two articles published in the fall of 1968. These dealt with the plans and expectations of the aerospace giants, and at the same time recorded the attitudes of the men in charge. For instance, Edward J. LeFevre, a vice-president for General Dynamics, explained: "Basically, we're a big systems builder for military weapons. Over 90 per cent of our business is military. We're in that business to stay." And James J. Ling, head of the Ling-Temco-Vought conglomerate, stated, "Our future planning is based on visible contracts," enabling the planners of LTV's aerospace division to estimate that total military sales will reach $1,070 million in 1973, compared to $475 million in 1968. Other companies, while not quite as optimistic, were all looking toward a bright future.

The end of the Vietnam War, while it may bring a slight reduction in total military expenditures, will not necessarily affect the big weapons companies. Only $2 billion of the aerospace industry's armed military business is related to Vietnam: instead, the enormous expense of the war has forced many programs for new, sophisticated aircraft, missiles, and electronics components to the sidelines, with the normal replacement of strategic and tactical weapons systems also largely deferred.

Aviation Week analyzed trends in Defense Department R&D spending and noted that the development of concepts and designs of new weapons has been slowed because of Vietnam, but the same journal showed that future R&D will be concentrated in space technology, missiles, and avionics. Vietnam has been "too practical." As the end of hostilities approaches, there are already clear indications of increased spending for new weapons systems, with the Safeguard ABM system, Poseidon and Minuteman III missiles, F-14 and F-15 fighters, and others all entering production this year.

Some defense firms, such as United Aircraft and Boeing, have always had considerable civilian work, but the majority of the large weapons manufacturers have shown an inability to develop inroads into civilian markets. One such venture by General Dynamics with commercial aircraft in 1959 almost destroyed the company, rescue coming at the last minute in the form of the TFX contract. More recently, the concept of applying aerospace "systems approaches" and engineering versatility to city and social problems has become fashionable.

Starting in 1965, there have been a growing number of proposals worked out, first by government officials and economists, and later by industry as well. A key government study, led by Gardner Ackley, former chairman of the President's Council of Economic Advisers, examined the economic impact of defense and of potential disarmament steps, and asserted that the new disciplines used in evolving weapons programs could be employed in solving the social problems of mass transit, education, and urban renewal. As Bernard Nossiter remarked, the document was reassuring: "It suggested that the great military contractors easily could and would convert their electronic swords into social plowshares. It implied that the Nation, therefore, need not worry about an industrial group with a vested interest in arms." At present, industry has taken up this banner of conversion and is vigorously waving it in speeches, pamphlets, and study groups, to show that they are concerned, and that people need not worry about their interest in weapons.

However, the Washington *Post*'s inquiry disclosed that the aerospace industry does not in fact have the desire or the ability to pursue these ends. Some industry executives think it may be possible to enter the civilian market on a big scale, "but even the most sanguine think that day is far off. As a result, they have invested little of their time, and less of their stockholders' money, pursuing this track." Nossiter's report goes on to say:

> The large defense contractors see no need to chase commercial chimeras; they expect and are planning for bigger and better arms business once Vietnam is out of the way. More importantly, the industry wonders whether the techniques required to build an electronically guided, supersonic, missile-equipped jet plane can be used to rebuild ghettos or cleanse the air.

Each large contractor may have tentative plans to expand into commercial areas; but, as Nossiter concludes, "None of this, however, detracts from the central theme: the great aerospace firms have a strong appetite for military business. They look forward to expanding, not contracting, their sales in this sphere."

In sum, the position of the big defense companies in the weapons market is comfortable, and even if they wanted to, they would find it difficult to go elsewhere. They like their elevated status in the society, can make money there, and therefore can be counted on to fight for a continuing market, and to enlarge it if possible. Knowing what is at stake for them makes it easier to see the reasons for the vigorous engineering marketing efforts of the large weapons industries and the resulting influence on and identification with military decisions. For, as we shall see, to insure contracts requires an all-out effort to be involved with the military decision process itself.

Military Contracting

The large weapons firm aims at winning contracts for the production of aircraft, missiles, ships, and their components. This is where the money is—in the actual production of hardware rather than the R&D contracts. As described to us by a marketing representative at North American, the "pot of gold" is the hardware contract, and all marketing efforts are oriented toward winning it. Not only are the large profits realized from hardware, but it is essential for the corporation to have, at all times, ongoing major production contracts to fully utilize capital and personnel and to maintain the necessary capacity to win and carry out new contracts. Also, winning a large hardware contract puts a company in a virtual monopoly position if improvements for, or additions to, the particular system are decided upon—and, more and more, the Pentagon is keeping weapons systems deployed for longer periods by "modernizing" them. The Minuteman missile, first tested in 1961, has gone through three major stages, with several models in each stage, and has had over twenty thousand engineering modifications while being produced and deployed.

It would seem, then, that marketing efforts should be concentrated toward winning the hardware contract at the time of contracting, but this is not the case. Every weapons system that reaches procurement has gone through a long planning, development, and testing process, studded with reviews, changes, and modifications. Because of the sophisticated nature of the technology and competition among the firms, industry efforts must be pushed back into these planning and development stages to gain information and to establish foothold contracts in new programs. As an executive assistant for one of General Dynamics' vice-presidents stated it, "You have to get in on the ground floor or forget it."

The marketplace, where alternative products are presented to the customer by competing firms, occurs in these early stages, where the requirements are evolved for which systems are to be built. As Murray Weidenbaum put the question at a Senate subcommittee hearing, "To what extent is the major competition for military business at the wrong end? At the present time, typically, the key competition is for the relatively small development contract, and the winner of that virtually automatically gets large, so-called follow-on, procurement contracts." And the competition among firms to win the development contracts, to have their ideas heard and considered, is, of course, intense.

When a new system is being considered for development, there will normally be only two or three firms with the technological capability and the available capacity to meet its requirements. Thus it is natural that an intense competition (or, as Admiral Rickover prefers to call it, a rivalry) between a couple of firms will ensue. When this occurs, firms go all out to win. As Frederic Scherer, one of the authors of *The Weapons Acquisition Process,* an authoritative study performed at Harvard University, states, ". . . firms are frequently compelled to make overly optimistic technical promises, to divert top technical talent from research and development work to selling activities, to hoard scarce technical talent, and to diversify at government expense into fields often served more effectively by existing specialists." They are compelled to make these moves in order to keep up with the efforts of their rivals. They cannot afford to passively follow the strict rules of contracting; they must go beneath the formal structure to learn at an early stage what is being considered and to try to swing these considerations to their advantage. For instance, one Washington sales representative for a large defense firm told us, "If you wait around until the RFP [Request for Proposal] comes out, you're dead." And an official at North American stated, ". . . any company which would go by all the rules would have no ideas about what the government wants and would be developing things which would be completely out of line."

The prime consideration in awarding a production contract is the technological performance of the eventual weapon. As Peck and Scherer note in *The Weapons Acquisition Process,* "In deciding the winner . . . , greatest weight has usually been assigned to the attractiveness of technical proposals and the availability of suitable human and physical resources. . . ." In *Defense-Space Market Research,* prepared by businessmen from weapons firms and research organizations, there is a description of the defense market that asserts, ". . . it is a market in which scientific achievement may be the major requirement. The intensity of the customer's demand may be far less a function of his available income than of the products or systems available through technological advance." Also, standard policy governing military R&D demands that everything possible be done to move forward in every area of possible technological advance.

The Industry's Marketing Efforts

As the Pentagon plans years ahead, industry must also plan. Facing a market characterized by long product lead times, rapidly changing military requirements, and an advancing state of the technical art, the large defense firms must devote a considerable proportion of their resources to planning, product design, and "market research" (that is, to information gathering). *Defense-Space Market Research* states:

> The time from the inception of a new weapons system idea until the time the weapons system initially goes off the line may be from six to eight years. Thus, the necessity for planning is increased (over non-defense companies). As a consequence, the importance and necessity of market research and broader aspects of planning are greatly increased for firms in the defense-space market. It also means that if a firm has failed to plan ahead and it begins the product development cycle two or three years late, it is two or three years behind its competition. As a consequence, its competitive situation will have become seriously deteriorated.

Three marketing/planning organs, closely interrelated and sometimes combined, are identifiable in most firms. There is a long-range requirements analysis office, a larger engineering office dealing in advanced programs, and, most important, a sales/marketing organization. Some corporations which are divided into relatively autonomous product divisions prefer to have these groups contained within each division, but others maintain them at the top of the entire corporate structure.

The future-requirements analysis group, composed of engineers, social scientists, and management specialists, attempts to analyze in broad terms the future of the military market, trying to foresee political, economic, and technological influences on forthcoming weapons procurements. Their work parallels much of the work on military threat projects that the Defense Department undertakes. Indeed, they frequently prepare such projections under contract with the Defense Department. Lockheed, Boeing, and General Electric are among the firms that have, through this means, provided the forecasts on which their own later manufacturing contracts are based.

The primary purpose of these advanced planning groups is to provide industry with a knowledge of general strategic issues paralleling that of the military, and, what is more important, with the negotiating advantage of being sure of their ground, of being able to say, "We have worked on this problem, too." These groups also help to convince stockholders of the company's orientation toward future developments. A North American official described it as mostly window dressing, yet something that has become more or less essential in the business.

Much larger and more important is the advanced engineering group, sometimes autonomous, sometimes part of the marketing department, and sometimes part of a larger engineering office. Located at company headquarters, this department studies new areas that the top management thinks are worth while, and prepares detailed technical studies that can become either Unsolicited Proposals or responses to RFPs. Using advanced technological information and systems-analysis techniques, these talented engineers develop solutions not only to specific technical problems, but to the broad design of new weapons systems as well. This work is closely co-ordinated with concurrent R&D contracts being carried out within the company–gleaning technical information and a knowledge of future government requirements from them. The work must be done on a timely basis, and considerable flexibility is necessary to enable crash work to be done on an important study when it must be geared to the issuing date of an RFP. A firm need not invest much of its own money in this work, since the costs of successful Unsolicited Proposals are reimbursable, and funds for independent research and development (IR&D) can be included in current contract overhead costs.

The sales/marketing organization, under various titles, such as "Program Planning" or "Government Relations," is usually composed of a central office and a small army of field men stationed all over the country, who form the real backbone of the marketing effort. They work in Washington, near Air Force bases, government laboratories, and missile test sites, and can be found in all the country's major defense industries; in effect, they exist wherever decisions involving new weapons are made. Their tasks are threefold: to open and maintain channels of communication with the military, to glean as much information as possible concerning new weapons, and to sell their products and ideas. These sales representatives are closely linked to their firms' advanced engineering offices, for it is their task to let the engineering staff know what the government is planning, what its requirements will be, and when proposals will be necessary. Likewise, they must depend on "Advanced Engineering" for the technical arguments and proposals that provide them with their negotiating leverage.

The Washington office of the marketing organization is usually the largest in this network. Here each marketing representative has responsibility for a particular office in the Defense Department, or a particular weapons system of interest to the company. For example, the Pratt & Whitney Division of United Aircraft has a man for AMSA (Advanced Manned Strategic Aircraft), another for the F-15, and so on, while the sales staff of North American's Aerospace Division concentrates on particular offices in the Pentagon, maintaining the flexibility to put one or more representatives on a particularly hot program.

The governing principle for the Washington efforts, as well as for marketing around the country, is to increase military contacts on all levels, at every planning stage, and in every service. In establishing ties with personnel in the Pentagon working on particular programs or systems, the salesman finds that there is only a small group of middle-level program planners and managers who are fully informed, and it is to these people he directs himself. However, it is only for big systems, and then only at crucial moments, that he will go to this level. As the military sales chief of one of the largest contractors said to us, "If it is a technology thing, we don't go too far up the totem pole." A considerable effort is directed toward the service planning and requirements offices and to those service arms that manage their respective research and development centers and field centers. At this level of contact, industry salesmen nurture relations with the service project officers, each of whom deals with a particular weapon from its development through production. (The Army alone has some three thousand of these officers.)

Marketing representatives also establish contacts at the funding and engineering requirements offices of the Office of the Secretary of Defense, often teaming up with a particular service to argue for a weapon that a service wants. While much of the marketing effort is aimed at the lower, engineering-oriented echelons, salesmen are not reluctant to go as high up as necessary–to the flag-rank officers and the civilians who manage research and development and make the long-range plans of the Services.

Marketing Practice

At all levels of contact with the military, sales representatives emphasize a primarily personal approach. The importance of the informal, personal tack is recognized throughout the business, and is the backbone of the entire sales effort. Not only are industry's marketing connections with the military built on personal relationships, but so are those at the engineering and managerial levels. This does not mean that the whole enterprise rests on friendships between industry and government people; it is more a realization that tactful, cooperative measures will build respect, and, through this, mutual understanding of each other's problems. This soft-sell stance builds the "teamwork" they feel is so necessary for the smooth functioning of the defense establishment.

Defense firms are well aware of this need when they recruit their sales personnel, but personal appeal is not the only requirement for a sales representative. Of equal importance is a sound technical understanding, preferably based on engineering training. For, as one representative remarked, ". . . the day of the back-slapping, cigar-smoking, cocktail-sipping, glossy-brochure-selling syndrome is gone. The marketing process is highly technical and sophisticated." Defense firms need people who can hold their own in technical discussions. As another representative put it, "We aim to be represented by technical-professional people who also have a flair for personal relations. We try to bring our people's technical talent into mesh with government people's."

Because of the Pentagon policy of rotation of military personnel every two or three years, there is a limitation to the value of close personal ties. Thus, the marketing effort is aimed as much at particular offices as at individuals, in an attempt to establish the company's name and reputation. As described by a salesman at LTV, the head of a military planning office will frequently be sufficiently won over that, on leaving, he will recommend the company and its representative to his successor.

In Washington, with its formal atmosphere and with the political overtones that attach to any act, there is a limit to what personal rapport can accomplish, and the numerous social functions arranged in the capital by the various industrial associations to foster industry-military relations are not too productive. However, the marketing effort is also directed toward the bases, test ranges, and R&D complexes throughout the country, where weapons programs are conceived and guided. Major defense firms have one-or-two-man marketing offices at all the important sites. Because most base towns are fairly small, these field men are in close social contact with military and civilian engineers and managers. According to a sales representative who served in one of these small towns, everyone goes to the same clubs to play bingo and cards, to golf together, and to enjoy an informality and camaraderie not possible in Washington. As he put it, ". . . it's like being in camp together." Out of these contacts come a wealth of information and warm mutual relationship between the salesman and his customers.

One reason the personal approach is so successful is the defense firms' use of former military officers to create and maintain ties with the Defense Department. In 1959, there were 721 retired officers employed by the hundred largest defense contractors; by 1969, that number had risen above 2072, and those were only officers of the rank of colonel or Navy captain and above. Not only do these former military men have ties of friendship with officers still in the armed forces, but they, as one colonel put it several years ago, ". . . exercise overpowering influence upon the high rankers left behind who could not be promoted to grades they now hold until those who retired had gotten out of the way." The case of a former Chief of Naval Operations, uncovered by a special investigating subcommittee of the House Armed Services Committee in 1959, is an example of the extremes of this practice. Admiral William Fechteler, a former CNO who went to work for General Electric after retiring, told the subcommittee that his role with the company was that of a "convenient, glorified messenger boy" who arranged for company executives to meet important admirals. His GE pay came to $38,500 in 1958, and he was still receiving his military retirement pay of $1014 per month. Military regulations prohibit retired officers from selling weapons for a defense contractor, but as an industry source quoted in the *Congressional Quarterly* said, "At least 90 per cent of the retired officers hired for top-level positions by the defense contractors ignore that regulation."

At the Pentagon, as well as at the service planning offices around the country, the primary method of formal contact is through "briefings." By this mechanism, a marketing representative will arrange for his company's engineering staff to present the right military people with the company's Unsolicited Proposals. Often, depending on the prior familiarity of participants, other, related problems will be discussed, and the briefing will become an informal cross-fertilization. In fact, the content of the proposal may be less important than the succeeding discussion. To a Washington representative for Pratt & Whitney, briefings were primarily mechanisms for "establishing a dialogue." And one salesman stressed the give-and-take atmosphere of such meetings: "We get together with development planning people in military services and swap information around, coming up with something through an iterative process."

One of the main tasks of the marketing representative is to secure timely information about upcoming weapons systems, or, as one representative put it, "finding out what's coming down the pike." As he described it, the representative monitors the activities of a program by keeping track of who the officials are that are concerned with the program, the stages of development it must go through, inner Defense Department politics affecting it (Is it stuck somewhere? Who are its major proponents and detractors?), prospects for an RFP going out, and the date of issue. This information serves as technical backup for proposal preparation and as a basis on which to plan bid strategies and future discussions with the military. For if a firm can know very early the date of issue and the technical specifications of an RFP, it can enter the negotiations with a substantial advantage over its rivals.

It may seem surprising that government officials readily provide this kind of information, but there is usually good rapport between industry representatives and their military counterparts. The industry representatives usually have information the military men would like to know, and, realizing this, the salesmen are ready to enter fully into this "I'll help you if you help me" situation. The guide *Defense-Space Market Research* counsels marketing personnel, ". . . it is always advisable to be in a position to contribute as well as receive information. Often a certain amount of cross-fertilization between projects and between Services can materially assist the military planner, who may have less opportunity than the astute market researcher to become familiar with a broad range of command and service projects. It is not unusual that the industrial market planner can provide the military planner budgetary estimates for projects in the planning stage which are more realistic than any such estimate developed by a military planner who may not be as well grounded in the technological base required for the project."

The masses of information that a defense firm needs

do not come only from the marketing field men. A vigorous effort is made to use every possible contact with the government to find out what are its future plans. Thus, company personnel involved in development and production work on current contracts are asked to report anything they learn that might be useful to the central marketing office, which interprets it and sends it on to the advanced planning department. Because of the close relations between military and industry planners during the execution of an R&D project, there is a potential by this means for the acquisition of valuable information. An example of how important this can be was described to us by a representative of LTV Aerospace: Grumman Aircraft was able to win the development contract for the F-14 (a new Navy fighter) because, from its work on the F-111, it knew, before LTV, that the Navy would not be receiving its planned version of that plane and would be needing another fighter. It was able to prepare for this by finding out very early what the F-14's essential requirements would be, and preparing proposals that would convince the Navy that, from its experience with the F-111, it could best meet these requirements.

Influence of the Marketing Effort on Military Planning

Even though much of the marketing effort is aimed at collective information and establishing contacts, the sum of all these efforts is to maintain a steady market for new armaments.

Close contacts between marketing personnel and military planners are established at all levels. These relationships provide fertile ground for selling weapons by direct influence or, as it is called in the business, by "creating a need." To what extent do marketing representatives consciously do this? Are defense firms simply passive responders to governmentally determined military requirements, or do they actively influence the nature of these requirements? To paraphrase Bernard Nossiter, to what extent are industry's expectations of military business self-fulfilling?

Peter Schenck, an official of the Raytheon Corporation and former president of the Air Force Association, described the process as follows: "The day is past when the military requirement for a major weapons system is set up by the military and passed on to industry to build the hardware. Today it is more likely that the military requirement is the result of joint participation of military and industrial personnel, and it is not unusual for industry's contribution to be a key factor. Indeed, there are highly placed military men who sincerely feel that industry currently is setting the pace in the research and development of new weapons systems."

Marketing representatives themselves admit that they attempt to influence military requirements. When working to win a specific contract, a field man will do more than simply try to find out all the relevant information about a forthcoming request for proposals. In his discussions with military planners, he not only asks questions but, depending on the level of rapport with the official, may also seek to influence the request itself. The industry marketeer knows very well what requirements and specifications would be most easily met by his company, and it would save precious time, as well as give his firm a definite advantage, if a request were to include these requirements. One representative for North American, commenting on the briefings that precede an RFP, said, "The words used in your presentation at a briefing hopefully end up in a request. This depends on how well your liaison with the other guys is and whether they owe you a favor. Your ultimate goal is actually to write the RFP, and this happens more often than you might think."

Also, one of the most useful strategies used by industry in winning contracts is what could be called the "better product approach." As described by a civilian in the Naval Material Command, a firm will go to the military when they know a weapon is under consideration with a design that contains more features than the initial plans. If the military listens, then when the Specific Operational Requirement (SOR) comes out, that firm will be, in effect, in a sole-source situation. And even after a request goes out, if a firm can come up with a design containing many extra features, that design may have an advantage over others. In most cases, such a proposal will be enthusiastically received. When questioned about this, an official at LTV said, "Certainly, in R&D, your technology can affect requirements. Several companies may come up with a good design, but what makes you better is what else you might come out with, what added component you have, what possible break-through you stimulate." In effect, defense contractors can determine the form of a weapon the military wants.

But industry influence goes far beyond this. Defense firms take advantage of their technological knowledge to put themselves in the strategic position of being able to say to the military, "You know that we know more than you about the feasibility of this project. Our engineers have been working on this for months. You have to listen to us." Industry has the initiative in the new and more-complex military technologies. There are now engineering departments within some military agencies, but industry rules in the area of advanced technology, where it enjoys considerable sales leverage. A member of Pratt & Whitney's marketing office boasted, "We have the technical superiority and are on the offensive. We spoon-feed them. We ultimately try to load them with our own ideas and designs, but in such a way that, when they walk away from the conference table, they are convinced it was their idea all along."

Bernard Nossiter quoted the president of North American Rockwell's Aerospace and Systems Group as saying, "A new system usually starts with a couple of military and industry people getting together to discuss common problems. By far the largest part of the business comes from requirements established by the Defense Department or NASA. But it isn't a case of industry here" (gesturing with one arm outstretched to the ground) "and the government here" (pointing with the other to the air). "They are interacting continuously at the engineering level." And these engineers are sympathetic with each other; they are apt to be enthusiastic about technical solutions and are eager to cooperate with industry engineers. As one former Pentagon official quoted in *Fortune* observes, "The contractor's engineers and the government's engineers get all excited and oversell each other."

A mathematician in the Systems Analysis Office of the Pentagon, when asked about the source of new ideas, replied that there is really no question of a division between industry and the military. At the highest levels of concept formulation and requirements discussion, "the interface is perfect"; the dialogue is smooth. For example, he pointed out, there are advanced planning studies prepared by each Service every two years that, although developed within the Services, are discussed continuously with the associated industries, which submit their own interpretations of future problems. Papers giving cost estimates are kept from industry eyes (so as not to jeopardize future bidding negotiations), but military planners are open and eager to discuss their problems and ideas with industry representatives.

Within the military, various groups are always pushing for particular new weapons systems. A Service that is arguing for a program must sell it to the Office of the

Secretary of Defense. It must convince those who hold the purse strings that what it wants is far superior to present weaponry and industry can be a powerful ally in this effort. With its vaunted technical expertise, it can present, in conjunction with a Service, a convincing picture of a weapon's versatility, reliability, and ability to confront whatever technological marvels the enemy may spring on us. And because proposed new weapons are initially only paper designs, the military's confidence in them depends on those in the best position to interpret them–the industry engineers and analysts.

Historically, each Service has tended to lean toward the same firms in its contracting, and there have grown up Service company alliances that aid in the bargaining process. Since the weapons funding must be approved by Congress, the Services have been known to ask defense firms to help push a particular program through the legislature. A good example of this is the Navy's lobbying effort for the Fast Deployment Logistics Ship. Aware that there were certain Congressmen critical of the program, the Navy called on the presidents of General Dynamics and Lockheed (both of which were involved in the contract-definition phase) to brief skeptical senators.

Because the need for a particular weapon depends on a technical analysis of the "threat" and because an appropriate response also rests on a technological interpretation, a firm frequently finds itself in a position to influence much more than just the form of a proposed weapon. It can also provide the "threat analysis" that justifies the need for the new weapon. And since the rationale behind a particular weapon is the result of discussion among differing factions within the Pentagon, industry finds that it, too, has a good chance to be heard. As Richard L. Garwin, writing in *International Science and Technology,* remarked, "Unfortunately, the threat on which it is easiest to obtain both consensus and support is typically one which requires a considerable increase in spending."

Military Receptiveness to the Advances of Industry

The efforts of defense firms to sell in the defense market, and their consequent attempts to influence the military customer, would be of little avail if military planners were not receptive to their approaches. Since the channels of communication are built largely on personal ties and a spirit of cooperation, industry would not find a very responsive audience without a contribution to the rapport from the military. When a defense firm's representative claims to have a better solution or a new concept, his military counterpart will weigh his proposals according to his own concepts of military need and his personal values. Industry efforts can succeed only so far as these concepts and values mesh with those of industry. Fortunately for the defense firm, military planners and the Services they represent have goals that coincide all too perfectly with what industry wants—more weapons, and the more-sophisticated and expensive, the better.

Take career officers in the Navy, Army, and Air Force. It is they—the project officers, the procurement functionaries, the engineering-oriented officers in the planning offices, and the top generals and admirals—that the defense firms must deal with. From his service academy on, the career officer is told to put aside personal goals and to work for the security of the nation. A civilian in Naval Material Command said that the naval officer, as a result of his Annapolis training, is mainly motivated "to serve the fleet, to get the *best* support material possible for the fleet, regardless of cost." Another civilian, in the Systems Analysis Office, put it a little differently and much more bluntly: "The ranking officer's main goal is the status or glamour of his Service, *not* the defense of the nation or even the welfare of the people under him. It is new weapons which produce the glamour, and the success of the Service is, in the military officer's eyes, measured by the size of the budget and the increased control it brings over the business of defending the nation."

The professional officer's training enables him to appreciate the merits of better weapons and of technological solutions to military problems. At all the service academies, an engineering curriculum is stressed; and those officers who end up in weapons planning and development offices receive further engineering education to enable them to cope with the increasing complexity of weapons systems. This is exactly what defense firms want, for they are able to marshal their engineering talent to present designs that are magnificent in their technological complexity and are most apt to be appreciated; they are able to press their ideas on the level they know best, and can exploit the engineering camaraderie to achieve the necessary rapport at planning sessions.

The professional officer also has his career in mind. As part of the most stratified, status-conscious organization in the country, he is forced to measure his personal achievement by his mobility through the ranks. To advance in rank, any officer must show his dedication to his Service; for the officer involved with the planning and development of new weapons, advancement will depend on his success in winning for his Service the weapon he has helped design or develop. Nossiter quotes an official in the Pentagon as saying, "Each [military] guy has his own piece—tactical, antisubmarine, strategic. Each guy gets where he is by pushing his own particular thing." Industry, realizing this, is ready to team up with these military planners, to help them argue their particular "thing." The military planner, in turn, is eager to listen.

The professional officer must also think beyond his

military career. The long-standing Pentagon policy of optional retirement with half pay after twenty years' service produces many retired officers in their forties, who still have twenty years of effective work-life left. While still in the Service, these officers begin to consider their future employment possibilities, and one of their choice options is a job with a defense firm. Such industry positions often seem to be rewards offered by a weapons firm for acceptance of the firm's viewpoint in acquisition and planning matters. It was recently disclosed, for instance, that four officers intimately concerned with the development and production of the Minuteman guidance system recently retired to assume high-ranking positions with the guidance contractor–North American Rockwell.

There are no exact figures on the number of retired officers working for weapons manufacturers, but Senator Stephen Young of Ohio said he was aware of at least thirty-six hundred officers who, immediately following retirement, became associated with defense companies. In a March 24, 1968, speech on the Senate floor, Young said, "It is with a feeling of sadness that I report it is taken for granted in Washington . . . that when an officer of our Armed Forces . . . retires following twenty years or somewhat more of active service to receive the generous retirement pay for the remainder of his life . . . [he] immediately announces that he is now a vice-president or technical adviser or is occupying some extremely high-salaried official position of a well-known corporation thriving on so-called defense contracts." The salaries officers can expect are often much higher than the pay schedules of their previous military commissions, and are certainly higher than other non-defense offers the officer might be fortunate enough to find.

The officer who is still in the service but is approaching retirement must view a defense job as one of his better alternatives, and even the most ethical soldier would find it difficult to refuse to help a company in the face of such an immediate potential reward. And his help need not be obviously collusive. Working, as the officer does, in close contact with industry representatives, he has a chance to show that he is willing to fight for the company's proposals. That is enough.

The Defense Department employs a large number of civilian engineers, analysts, and managerial personnel who are part of the weapons-planning process. The Office of the Director of Defense Research and Engineering, attached to the Office of the Secretary of Defense, manages the $8 billion R&D budget and is primarily staffed by technically trained civilians. Each Service has offices that manage the R&D contracts with industry. In addition, each Service has its own in-house R&D laboratories (with a total budget of $2.2 million for 1970), where civilian engineers are employed to help design and develop new weapons systems. Some of these people make their careers in government service, but many others have been previously employed in private industry or will hold future jobs in the private sector. Industry engineers, because of their experience in advanced weapons technology, are needed by the government; and for the same reason, government engineers considering other work find their best and sometimes only opportunities with weapons manufacturers. Those government engineers previously employed by defense firms can be expected to maintain ties with their past employers, and those hoping for future jobs will avoid jeopardizing their chances for future employment in industry.

A civilian in the Systems Analysis Office thought this to be particularly true with people in DDR&E. "It is almost criminal the way the people there shift back and forth between industry and DOD jobs," he remarked in an interview. An official in DDR&E estimated that one third of the professional civilian staff stay with the office only two or three years. As he explained it, civil service pay scales do not attract many people with career intentions, but scientists and engineers in private industry can be attracted for a short time span because of personal reasons or because they feel they need experience in government.

The same situation exists with the top Defence Department civilian managers. For these jobs, four or eight years is often the maximum span of service, and top people are frequently picked from the ranks of defense firms and defense-oriented research organizations. In the Nixon administration, the most obvious example is the Deputy Secretary of Defense, David Packard, cofounder and chief stockholder of the Hewlett-Packard Company, an electronics and computer-systems firm, which in 1968 had one hundred million dollars worth of business with the Defense Department, other government agencies, and private defense contractors. Daniel Fink, presently with General Electric's Missiles and Space Division, was from 1963 to 1968 Deputy Director of Defense Research and Engineering; before that, he was an executive of Allied Research Associates, a research firm with a considerable portion of its work in contracts from NASA and the Air Force. Many other examples could be cited.

Certainly many of these appointments are made on a basis of competency only, but this does not mean that the employees will be free of biases, not to mention pecuniary motivation. Admiral Rickover has said, "It is too much to expect that they will break all connections with their company; that they will, for the short time they are in government, adopt a government viewpoint." Even if conflict of interest somehow does not arise, the defense industry roots of many of the top officials in the Pentagon insure a sympathy with industry proposals and a viewpoint conducive to the interests of industry. As Admiral Rickover again points out, "The real problem is that during a lifetime of working in a given field he [the businessman] will have acquired a viewpoint that is in consonance with the philosophy and practice of his previous organization. How could he have become an official of the company otherwise? If he hadn't believed in its philosophy, how could he have been successful in his work? How then can you expect that when he enters Government service he will ipso facto change his faith?"

Conclusion

Holding together the private and public sectors of the weapons-development process is the common philosophy that there is a partnership between government and industry, that in order to get the job—"national security"—done, there must be a cooperative effort, which, above all else, is a patriotic endeavor. This constantly evoked image grew out of the Second World War, when such a partnership, coincidental with a total wartime economy, helped win the war. It has been the banner waved at testimonials and conferences for two decades. This belief in the importance of cooperation between business and the military is self-reinforcing, assuring each person involved that what he is doing is right and even noble. Today it enables Secretary of Defense Melvin Laird to reject the idea that there is a military-industrial complex, preferring instead to view it as a "military-industrial-labor team which is a tremendous asset to our nation and a fundamental source of our national strength."

The result of this "teamwork" has been ever-rising defense spending, a continuing danger of further costly interventions, and military dominance of American institutions, industry, and technology. One begins to wonder whether freedom and democracy can survive such a collaboration.

NOTES

This paper was based, to a large extent, on interviews conducted in the summer of 1969 with industry and government officials in Washington. These interviews were carried out with a prior understanding that the interviewees would not be identified. Quotes in this paper that are not specifically identified come from these interviews. Defense firms that granted interviews were General Dynamics, North American Rockwell, Ling-Temco-Vought, Boeing, and the Pratt & Whitney Division of United Aircraft. On the government side, officials were interviewed in the Systems Analysis Office (OSD), the Office of the Director of Defense Research and Engineering, and the Naval Material Command. Also, interviews were conducted with officers of the National Security Industrial Association and the Aerospace Industries Association.

Three other sources were heavily used: Bernard Nossiter's articles on the aerospace firms in the Washington *Post,* Admiral Rickover's testimony before the House Currency and Banking Committee and the Joint Economic Committee (Subcommittee on Economy in Government), and papers by Dr. Murray Weidenbaum, Assistant Secretary of the Treasury and former professor of economics at Washington University.

The *Fortune* editorial quote is in the August 1969 issue, p. 62.

The Defense Industry

Statistical information on the defense market and the prime contractors can be found in many places. The Department of Defense annually publishes lists of contractors in *Military Prime Contract Awards and Subcontract Payments.* Monthly information on contract awards can be found in the periodical *Defense Industry Bulletin. Hearings Before the Subcommittee on Antitrust and Monopoly, Senate Judiciary Committee,* entitled "Competition in Defense Procurement" (1968), contain a vast amount of information on the characteristics of the defense market. For a breakdown of the defense budget, see the annual statement by the Secretary of Defense before the Senate and House Armed Services committees.

The statistical breakdown of the weapons market is from "Competition in Defense Procurement hearings," *op. cit.*, p. 21, data presented by Murray Weidenbaum.

Figures on concentration in the aerospace business are compiled from the 1967 list of one hundred prime contractors. Dr. Weidenbaum's conclusions on concentration are from *Competition in Defense Procurement Hearings, op. cit.*, pp. 20–21. Aerospace total sales are from *Aerospace Facts and Figures 1969*, published by the Aerospace Industries Association of America, p. 9. Dr. Weidenbaum's quote can be found in *Competition in Defense Procurement, op. cit.*, p. 16.

Employment figures are from *Scientific and Technical Personnel in Industry, 1961–1966*, published by the U. S. Department of Labor, Bureau of Labor Statistics, pp. 11 and 12, and also from Aerospace Facts and Figures, *op. cit.*, p. 84.

For comment on the goals of the modern corporation, see Bruchey, S., "The Inadequacy of Profit Maximization as a Model of Business Behavior" (*Business History Review*, no. 4, 1960, pp. 495–97); Donaldson, G., "Financial goals: Management vs. Stockholders" (*Harvard Business Review*, May–June 1963, pp. 116–29), and "Personal Values and Corporate Strategy" (*Harvard Business Review*, March–April 1965, pp. 107–18).

Admiral Rickover's first statement is from *Hearings Before the House Committee on Banking and Currency* on H. R. 15683, *To Renew the Defense Production Act of 1950, as Amended*, April 1968, p. 64. Figures on defense buying practices are from a report, of the Subcommittee on Economy in Government of the Joint Economic Committee, on the *Economics of Military Procurement* (released in May 1969), p. 4. Rickover's second statement can be found in the Committee on Banking and Currency's hearings, *op. cit.*, p. 76. Figures were presented by Rickover at the hearing to prove his point.

Descriptions of military contracting procedures can be found in the hearings cited above. For more detail, see *The Military Market in the United States*, written by Murray Weidenbaum for the American Marketing Association, 1963. An article by Richard Kaufman in *The New York Times Magazine* (June 22, 1969, p. 10) contains many critical insights into the contracting structure.

The table on defense versus non-defense industry profits, compiled by Dr. Weidenbaum from a sample of defense firms that do more than three fourths of their business with the military, is from the "Competition in Defense Procurement" hearings, *op. cit.*, p. 22.

The statement on subsidy to defense industries is part of the

Economics of Military Procurement summary report, *op. cit.*, pp. 4–9.

For a thorough discussion of the TFX controversy, see *The TFX Decision–McNamara and the Military,* by Robert J. Art (Boston: Little, Brown & Company, 1968).

The Stubbings Report can be found in the *Congressional Record,* February 7, 1969, pp. S1450–55. Other examples of poor contractor performance are numerous. Cost overruns are the most notorious, and the Subcommittee on Economy in Government hearings, *op. cit.* (Nov. 1968 and Jan. 1969) give detailed instances of these overruns and the continued contracting successes of the offending contractors.

The reference to Dr. Weidenbaum and defense-firm entrenchment is from the *Competition in Defense Procurement* hearings, *op. cit.,* p. 18.

The Bernard Nossiter articles are in the Washington *Post:* "Arms Firms See Postwar Spurt," December 8, 1968, and "Defense Firms Leery of Civilian Work," Monday, December 9.

The two *Aviation Week and Space Technology* articles are "Vietnam Stalls Defense Research Effort" (March 10, 1969, pp. 41–44) and "Transition Period to Spur New Policies, Technologies for Aerospace" (March 10, 1969, pp. 32–33). Other optimistic articles along this line can be found in *Air Force and Space Digest, Ordnance,* and *Armed Forces Management.*

The literature on defense industry conversion is voluminous. Volume 2 of *Selected Readings in Employment and Manpower,* prepared by the Subcommittee on Employment and Manpower, Senate Committee on Labor and Public Welfare (88th Cong., 2d Sess.) is the best single source. The Ackley report, "The Economic Impact of Defense and Disarmament," is available from the Government Printing Office. For a good example of the aerospace industry's effort to show its social concern and interest in conversion to civilian markets, see a pamphlet entitled "Aerospace Technology: Creating Social Progress," published by the Aerospace Industries Association.

Military Contracting

For a detailed description of the Defense, Army, Navy, and Air Force contracting processes, see *Insights into the Changing Government Marketplace,* by Anton B. Schmalz, published by the North American Rockwell Corporation.

Dr. Weidenbaum's statement on competition is from the "Competition in Defense Procurement" hearings, *op. cit.*, p. 29. *The Weapons Acquisition Process* (Harvard University) is a two-volume study; the first volume, *An Economic Analysis*, was written by Merton J. Peck and Frederic M. Scherer, and the second, *Economic Incentives*, by Prof. Scherer alone. The quote on industry efforts to win contracts is from the abstract of the second volume.

Defense-Space Market Research was edited by J. Fred Weston, and published by the MIT Press, 1964; the quote is from p. 16.

The Industry's Marketing Efforts

The defense firms' marketing organizations described here are based on interviews in Washington. The *Defense-Space Market Research* quote on information trading is from p. 18. See *Insights into the Changing Government Marketplace* (*supra*) as well as the annual Air Force Almanac issue of *Air Force and Space Digest* for descriptions of the service R&D organizations.

Marketing Practice

The number of officers employed by defense firms was disclosed by Sen. Proxmire in a Senate speech, available from his office. Col. Nesbit's statement is referred to in *The Military Establishment*, by John M. Swomley, Jr. (Boston: Beacon Press, 1964) p. 106. The case of William Fechteler is also discussed in Swomley's book, p. 107. The *Congressional Quarterly* quote is from the May 24 special issue on the military-industrial complex, p. 6. (*Congressional Quarterly*, p. 1160).

The section from *Defense-Space Market Research* on information trading is on p. 86.

Influence of the Marketing Effort on Military Planning

A good example of the efforts of one industry to make a weapon more attractive, and the military's enthusiasm for their efforts, is found in Robert Art's *The TFX Decision, supra;* Chapter Five discusses how the source-selection boards and the military were enamored with Boeing's plan for reverse thrusters, overhead air scoops, and use of the new metal titanium, while McNamara thought these added attractions were too risky. McNamara overruled the military decision and awarded General Dynamics and Grumman the contract.

Schenck's quote is taken from the *Congressional Quarterly, op. cit.*, p. 1164 (p. 10 of the special report).

Nossiter's quotes from North American's group president are found in the first Washington *Post* article of December 8, 1968 (*supra*).

Fortune's quote from the Pentagon official is in their August 1969 issue, p. 62.

For a discussion of the powerful connections between defense industries and the Congress, as well as the contributions of members of Congress to pressures for increased military expenditures, see the *Congressional Quarterly*, special report of May 24, 1968 (*supra*). Garwin's quote is from his article in *International Science and Technology*, October 1968, entitled "Strengthening Military Technology," p. 23.

Military Receptiveness to the Advances of Industry

Whether the military officer is concerned with getting the best possible support for the men on the line, or is more concerned with the glamour provided by sophisticated weapons, can be inferred from the record of weapons performance in combat. Many of the weapons produced for Vietnam have been too advanced to be effective, and too complex to be reliable. A secret Pentagon report leaked to the Washington *Post* (June 28, 1969, "Pentagon Report Criticizes Air Force on Electronic Gadgets") asserts that the Air Force is wasting billions of dollars on electronic gadgets that have reduced the effectiveness of tactical fighters and bombers. The Air Force has tried to automate navigation and bombing with the use of in-board computers and fire-control systems that offer enormous possibilities—if they work. But the report, as described in the *Post,* asserts that the performance of American tactical aircraft has been reduced by these innovations. The report compared ten modern systems with one World War II bombing device: "The older instrument was reliable at the target more than 75% of the time. Of the ten modern systems, five were reliable between 50% and 75% of the time and five less than 50%."

The quote of the Pentagon official is in the first of Nossiter's articles, *op. cit.* Information on the Air Force officers now working for North American Rockwell is on p. 503 of the hearings of the Joint Economic Committee, *The Military Budget and National Economic Priorities* (Government Printing Office, 1969).

Senator Young's speech is found in the Congressional Record, March 24, 1968, pp. S3043–44.

For other examples of the shuttling of personnel between government and industry, see Richard Barnet's *The Economy of Death* (Atheneum, 1969), pp. 108–10.

Rickover's statement is on p. 69 of the Banking and Currency hearings, *op. cit.* In his testimony before the *Economics of Military Procurement* hearings, *op. cit.*, he gives good examples of DOD sympathies with industry. Replying to Sen. Proxmire's request for observations on the procurement process, he listed the following examples:

> Recently, a Department of Defense official refused to approve one of my contracts—a $50 million contract—because he thought the contractor should get a higher profit than the latter had previously agreed to accept.
>
> Another Department of Defense procurement official told me I had no business negotiating a profit lower than that suggested by Department of Defense procurement regulations.
>
> In still another case, I found that one supplier was charging the Government $8 an hour for design work while he charged commercial customers only $6 an hour for the same work. The Department of Defense decided that this procedure was proper under "generally accepted accounting principles." At my request the General Accounting looked into this contract and concluded that the Department of Defense had been overcharged $5 million.
>
> Another case: For several years the Navy paid more than the Atomic Energy Commission for the same work at two Atomic Energy Commission-owned laboratories. I first pointed this out in 1964, but the DOD did not correct the situation until 4 years later.
>
> Another case: I found a major defense contractor not complying with the requirements of the Truth-in-Negotiations Act 6 years after its enactment. During those 6 years he had received about $1.2 billion in defense contracts.
>
> Another case: DOD procurement regulations do not have accounting principles for fixed-price contracts even though three-fourths of defense procurements are in this category.
>
> Another case: Department of Defense officials claim they have "no evidence of excessive profits," yet they have no knowledge of the profits being made on more than 50 percent of their contracts.

Sen. Proxmire's response to these disclosures was: "This is shocking; this is really shocking."

Rickover's reply: "What is so shocking about it, sir? It has been going on for many years."

Rickover's observation on the businessman's philosophy is from the House Banking and Currency hearings, *op. cit.*, p. 69.

THE MANNED BOMBER—A MYSTIQUE IN SEARCH OF A MISSION

by Mary McCarthy

The Rise of the Strategic Bomber

BEFORE the Second World War, the United States had depended on its Navy to protect its interests abroad and to defend its shores. To the consternation of both the Navy and the Army, the experience of World War II and the invention of the atomic bomb seemed to indicate that air power would be the key to postwar security. The pressure to "bring the boys home" led to rapid demobilization and a shift to a nearly total reliance on the glamorous new airborne technology to preserve America's newly established worldwide interests.

The Strategic Air Command was established in 1946, consisting initially of only nine bombardment groups, including three of jet aircraft and just one unit capable of delivering nuclear weapons. Powerful pressures soon developed to expand this force, and in 1948 the President's Air Policy Commission, headed by Thomas K. Finletter, called for a seventy-group Air Force by 1950. This goal, echoing Air Force plans set in motion even before the close of the war, received immediate support in the Congress, which quickly appropriated the necessary funds. But the Truman administration, facing heavy pressure to keep the budget in check, was forced to cut the funds, and in 1949 requested appropriations for only forty-eight groups. Nevertheless, SAC alone had by then grown to fourteen groups, and the Air Force had clearly won pre-eminence among the Armed Services.

It was not until the outbreak of the Korean War that the lid was removed from military expenditures. The build-up was then very rapid. Aircraft procurement, which had averaged $900 million per year from 1946 through 1950, leaped to one billion dollars a month for the first two years of the Korean War. Total national security expenditures increased from $13.0 billion in fiscal 1950 to $50.4 billion in fiscal 1953. In 1951, for the first time, the Defense Department departed from tradition by giving more funds to the Air Force than to the Army or the Navy. In recognition of the central role of air power in our military policy, this practice has been followed by every succeeding administration. By 1960, the Air Force was taking 46 per cent of the military budget, with SAC alone getting 20 percent (just 3 per cent less than the entire Army).

From the late forties until today, the core of U.S. strategic planning has been its superiority in nuclear weapons. This advantage has been thought to provide protection against any major or minor Soviet military action. Before 1960, bombers were the only available delivery system for nuclear weapons, and the modernization of SAC became the top-priority defense goal. The following is a brief outline of the progress of that program:

1946–The bomber force consisted of B-17s and B-29s, left over from the Second World War.

1948–SAC organized its first air refueling squadrons, to increase the range of the bomber force. The B-50 and the B-36 were introduced into the force. The B-50 was only an advanced version of the B-29. The B-36, however, approached the status of a true intercontinental bomber–a significant goal, if SAC was to be able to operate from the continental United States.

1950–The B-29s and the B-50s were downgraded to medium-bomber status as the number of B-36s increased. By 1955, they had all been phased out.

1951–The all-jet B-47 began to replace the B-29 and the B-50. More than seven hundred of them remained in the force until the mid-sixties, when they were phased out.

1954–The last B-29 was phased out.

1955–The last B-50 was phased out, and the first B-52 was introduced into the force. The advanced models of this bomber, of which 646 are operational, provide the bulk of the present SAC fleet.

1960–The supersonic B-58 medium bomber was introduced. (Only eighty were ever operational, and they are now being phased out.)

1965–Plans to introduce the FB-111 swing-wing bomber were announced.

The introduction of the B-52 led to a major controversy that foreshadowed the sharp clashes that would develop in the sixties over the successor to that aircraft. After the 1955 Moscow air show, when the Soviets flew what appeared to be a large number of long-range bombers, the Air Force mounted a campaign for more bombers. The Senate Armed Services Committee appointed a special subcommittee, chaired by a former Secretary of the Air Force, Senator Stuart Symington, to investigate the status of American air power. The Air Force, through General Curtis LeMay, then commander of SAC, warned that the United States would lose its supremacy in strategic air power by 1960. The Congress voted $800 million in additional funds for aircraft procurement, but the Eisenhower administration refused to increase the rate of B-52 production. By the beginning of the sixties, when the "bomber gap" was expected, the United States found itself with more than a four-to-one advantage in intercontinental bombers. (It later turned out that the Russians had only three prototypes of their new bomber, which they repeatedly flew over Moscow during the air show. With the craft circling beyond the horizon before reappearing over Red Square, observers on the ground were led to the mistaken belief that the bombers were already in mass production. This would not be the last time that the Russians would exaggerate their weapons inventory and produce an overreaction on this side of the Atlantic.)

But 1960 did mark a turning point in the fortunes of bomber proponents. The threat came, not from an enemy bomber defense, but from a competing means of delivering nuclear weapons—the ballistic missile. The first sign of trouble appeared when President Eisenhower decided against procurement of the B-70, a new, high-altitude bomber with a cruising speed three times the speed of sound. The Administration argued that it would be an unnecessary addition to the Atlas, Titan, Polaris, and Minuteman missile programs.

With the incentive of John Kennedy's pledge to expand America's armed strength, the Air Force launched a renewed campaign to save the B-70. But the new Administration adopted the Eisenhower position and refused to approve production. Secretary of Defense McNamara argued that the proposed plane, capable only of high-level flight, was inflexible and vulnerable, with a mission that could be carried out more effectively by a missile. Failing to gain acceptance as a bomber, the B-70 became a classic case of a weapons system in search of a mission. The Air Force tried in 1962 to resurrect it as a reconnaissance-strike aircraft. McNamara remained stubbornly opposed to the aircraft, on the grounds that it was technically infeasible for a high-altitude craft to fill such a role. Two prototypes were finally produced before the entire program was canceled, after a total cost of $1.5

billion. (One crashed during the filming of a public relations film for North American Aviation, its producer.)

A second blow to the manned bomber was delivered by McNamara in 1961, when he announced that B-52 production would end the following year. General LeMay, then Air Force Chief of Staff, took his opposition to Congress and persuaded them to provide $525 million for future procurement, but the Administration refused to spend the funds, and no new B-52s were purchased. The size of the bomber force steadily declined as the B-47s were phased out. Then, in December of 1965, McNamara announced that the B-58s and the older B-52s would be replaced by fourteen squadrons of the new FB-111, reducing the total bomber force from 680 to 465 units. Since the FB-111 was a fighter-bomber, not in the heavy B-52 class, this decision also foreshadowed a reduction in the intercontinental bomber force. No new bomber was in sight, and it seemed that the days of SAC were numbered.

Enter AMSA

Suddenly, after nearly ten years in the back of the bus, the strategic manned bomber reappeared in the forefront of Defense Department planning. During hearings on military procurement, Secretary of the Air Force Robert Seamans called the full-scale development of a replacement for the B-52 "our most urgent requirement."

Preliminary design studies for a new bomber were initially funded in 1962, after the B-70 program was finally buried. The guidance to the designers seemed to have been to come up with a manned bomber regardless of its mission. As Secretary of the Air Force Zuckert testified in 1963, ". . . if the B-70 proves to be a blind alley for any reason, we have to explore all the other methods because we have to come up with a manned system, in our opinion." Proposals were made for a "Dromedary"—a long-endurance, large, slow aircraft designed to fly for up to forty-eight hours and to serve as a flying missile-launching platform—and for a low-altitude penetrator. Since fiscal year 1965, the Air Force had tried to convince the Secretary of Defense to initiate systems-engineering development for the Advanced Massed Strategic Aircraft, or AMSA, intended for both high- and low-altitude flight at supersonic and subsonic speeds. But Secretary McNamara and, later, Secretary of Defense Clifford resisted Air Force and Congressional pressures for the manned bomber, arguing that what will be needed to assure the effectiveness of the United States strategic bomber force in the presence of advanced Soviet air defense "is not so much a new aircraft, but rather new penetration aids and weapons."

The dispute within the Pentagon over the need for another bomber can be explained, in part, as a difference in judgment regarding future developments in Soviet air defenses. The only expected improvement in Soviet defenses is the possible introduction of a new high-performance fighter-intercepter, the Foxbat. However, the Air Force wants insurance against any possible threat. In his 1969 defense-posture statement, Secretary Clifford described such a possible threat to the bomber force as a large airborne warning and control system and an interceptor force with a good "look-down, shoot-down" capability, coupled with an extensive, low-altitude surface-to-air missile system that could destroy a very sizable number of our bombers before they could reach their targets. AMSA is intended to provide assurance against this unexpected threat.

The difference in judgment within the Pentagon was resolved when, in November 1968, Secretary Clifford accepted the Air Force position and approved a $77.2 million program allowing AMSA development to enter the competitive design phase. Secretary of Defense Melvin Laird later increased the budget request to $100.2 million in order to shorten the design phase and permit the beginning of a full-scale engineering development in fiscal year 1970. It was with Secretary Laird's decision that AMSA became "our most urgent requirement." His revision would advance the date of a production decision, now expected in 1971 or 1972, and move the date of an initial operating capability from 1978 to 1977. According to present plans, five prototype craft would be built by 1973, and final production decision would be made at that time.

The AMSA design combines the characteristics of the B-52 and the FB-111. It is designed to carry one hundred thousand pounds of bombs and missiles (more than the B-52) and to have a range of six thousand nautical miles with one refueling. Its variable-sweep wings will permit it to fly at high or low speeds at high or low altitudes. AMSA will be capable of supersonic flight and of carrying conventional bombs, nuclear bombs, or combinations of bombs and the new stand-off missiles—the Short Range Attack Missile (SRAM) and the Subsonic Cruise Armed Decoy (SCAD). The Air Force projects an initial order of 240 planes. It estimates the cost of one AMSA to be between $25 million and $30 million, with the total system estimated by the Air Force to cost $12.6 billion, including $1.9 billion for research and development, $7.2 billion for production, and $3.5 billion to operate the system for a ten-year period. Given the Pentagon's poor record in cost estimation, it is safe to assume that the cost of the system will be far greater than $12.6 billion. Senator John Stennis, chairman of the Senate Armed Services Committee, estimated that it would increase by 25 per cent through the effect of inflation alone, and suggested that there may be additional cost increases through "other unknowns" related to the complex technology of AMSA. As he said, "It will be an expensive weapon, and I think that all weapons will be expensive hereafter . . . ; they require more and more electronics; they are required to do more and more things. They have to take advantage of the technology that is available in order to be a modern weapon. So the prices will go up on all weapons."

Senator William Proxmire, Chairman of the Joint Economic Committee's Subcommittee on Economy in Government, called the Air Force estimate on the per-unit cost of AMSA "the biggest underestimate of a long list of underestimates in the Pentagon." The Senator predicts a more expensive system delivered at a later date than the Air Force expects: ". . . the history of both costs and delivery dates for major weapons systems is such that they routinely are delivered two or three years late and at costs which greatly exceed estimates. In my judgment, then, we are talking about a fleet of 240 planes which will be delivered a decade from now at a cost of at least $24 billion."

Whatever the cost, this aircraft will be an advanced and versatile weapon. But the important question is not whether it will improve the bomber force, but rather of what use is an improved force, and is it desirable at a time when, with the Russians, we are negotiating to bring the strategic arms race to a halt?

The Obsolete Deterrent

Deterrence of nuclear war is the primary purpose of our strategic weaponry, and any judgment of AMSA must [illegible]ade in light of this strategy. There are two questions [illegible]ed, then: First, in a missile age does a bomber [illegible]ugh to our deterrent capacity to justify its cost? (Even without the new, more expensive AMSA, it is now costing us $2 billion each year to maintain our bomber force.) And if one were to conclude that bombers do still have a deterrent role, will the replacement of the B-52 by the AMSA add significantly to this capacity?

According to our announced strategy of deterrence, we must design our forces to convince all potential enemies that we have the strength to absorb even a massive, surprise attack and still strike back, destroying their homeland. It is commonly assumed that the promise of four hundred warheads (or less than one tenth of the total number of U.S. warheads) delivered on target is adequate to deter the Soviet Union from attacking this country. (An attack of this size would kill 30 per cent of the Soviet people and destroy 76 per cent of their industrial capacity.) This capacity is known in Pentagonese as an "assured destruction capability."

To contribute to our retaliatory or assured-destruction capability, a weapon must be able to survive an attack and to penetrate enemy defenses. On both counts, the bomber fares badly when compared to the missile: A bomber is far more vulnerable to enemy attack, since it can be destroyed by a blast one sixtieth that required to knock out a Minuteman. Bombers are maintained on the ground in groups of fifteen or more, so that one warhead can destroy many of them; missiles, on the contrary, are spaced in such a way that one warhead is necessary to destroy each one of them, while Polaris submarines are considered virtually invulnerable under the sea. Steps can be taken to improve the survivability of the bomber force, such as increasing the percentage of the force kept on fifteen-minute alert or deploying the over-the-horizon radar presently being developed by the Defense Department. However, at the same time, the Soviets' deployment of Polaris-type submarines, which can circumvent these measures, is presenting an unexpected threat to the co tinued usefulness of the U.S. bomber force. (One justification given for the Safeguard ABM system is its ability to provide early warning of an attack on our air bases from these submarines.)

The portion of the bomber force surviving an ICBM attack will then have to face sophisticated Soviet air defenses. The Air Force expects that all bombers, even those with a low-level flight capability, will have to depend on penetration aids, particularly supersonic stand-off missiles (which can reduce aircraft flight time below that required for the delivery of free-fall bombs). Two of these missiles, the Hound Dog and SRAM, have already been developed, while the development of a third, the SCAD, has just been initiated. The Hound Dog, which became operational in 1960 and is now carried by the B-52s, was originally designed with a range of several hundred miles for strikes against vulnerable airfield-type targets. SRAM, with its small size and short range, is designed primarily to be launched in large numbers to destroy air defenses. SCAD is designed as a nuclear-armed decoy that will appear as a large bomber on an enemy radar.

While these missiles may solve the problem of bomber penetration, there is doubt about their over-all usefulness. During a discussion of the Skybolt missile program, which was canceled in 1962, Secretary McNamara commented that such a stand-off missile combined "the disadvantages of the bomber with those of the missile. It would have the bomber's disadvantages of being soft and concentrated and relatively vulnerable on the ground and the bomber's slow time to target. But it would not have the bomber's advantageous payload and accuracy, nor would it have the advantages usually associated with a manned system." Although missile technology has advanced since the days ... ill-fated Skybolt, the SRAM program, too, has run ... problems and cost overruns. The Air Force ... ncern about delays in the SRAM capacity to avoid or suppress enemy defenses. Such a demand for the standoff missile is an implicit admission of the strategic obsolescence of the manned bomber. As McNamara suggested in 1963, ". . . the alternative is not manned bombers, on the one hand, in the traditional sense (as a launch platform for a free-fall bomb), versus missiles on the other. The alternatives are missiles launched from the sea, missiles launched from the land, or missiles launched from the air, and of these three modes of launch, the missiles launched from the air are, by far, the most complex missiles, likely to be the most expensive and unreliable, and certainly would require the most advanced development." Air Force experience with the Skybolt and SRAM programs tends to bear out McNamara's doubts.

In 1962, Defense Department estimates indicated that two hundred fifty hardened and dispersed Minuteman missiles or six Polaris submarines could be purchased for the price of one wing of B-52s with Skybolt missiles and tankers. McNamara decided to reduce the size of the SAC force because, in his judgment, manned bombers could fill only "a supplemental role" in the assured-destruction mission and, unless missile effectiveness fell to much less than was actually expected, the B-52 would remain too costly an alternative. Of course, the supersonic, highly sophisticated AMSA will be an even more expensive alternative than the B-52. However, such comparisons were not even made this year in presenting the AMSA budget request.

Proponents of a "mixed force" of missiles and bombers insist that, while the bomber has some disadvantages, the flexibility of a manned system offers valuable options unavailable with an all-missile force. The argument runs somewhat along these lines: If an attack is expected, missiles must be fired, which assures that the holocaust has begun, or they must remain in their silos until the attack has begun and a number of them are destroyed. Bombers, on the other hand, can be launched prior to attack and maintained safely in the air until ordered to return or to proceed to target. Bombers can be retargeted or recalled, but once missiles are on their way, there is no turning back.

There are several objections to this argument: First, it is not the case that bombers *can* be launched while missiles *must* remain on the ground–rather, the vulnerable bombers *must* be launched, while missiles can survive in relative safety on the ground or under the sea. Second, if an attack is not in progress, the bombers must be brought back to their bases for refueling and to rest the crews. They then become vulnerable again. Further, launching the bomber force could be provocative to the enemy–hardly a boost to the prevention of nuclear war. Third, a missile's flight time is just thirty minutes; while AMSA would require five or six hours of flight, including one to two hours after release from the "fail-safe point." Because of its much greater speed, a missile is then actually more flexible than a bomber. It can be retargeted before launch and, even after the latest time at which a bomber's mission could be altered, could still reach a new target before a bomber. (It should be realized that a modern jet bomber is actually little more than a "manned missile." At the speeds at which these craft must move to avoid air defenses, their crews cannot survey the ground and search for "juicy," exposed targets. They must be pretargeted and must use radar and other means to home in on these preset targets.)

Further, arguments of bomber proponents in favor of a mixed force are, first, that it insures against unforeseeable technological break-throughs in enemy forces, but Minuteman III and Poseidon will soon carry MIRV warheads to assure ABM penetration, and superhard silos are now being developed to house the Minuteman III and any future generation of ICBMs.

The argument that a mixed force requires the Soviets to mix their defenses is equally weak. If the Soviets were to build more or better defenses to counter AMSA, eventually we would have to build another, even more expensive, bomber to counter the defenses we have forced them to build. And is it to our advantage to have an even larger portion of the Soviet budget going to its armed services, strengthening the very forces that oppose a relaxation of tensions?

It should be noted that a new bomber is not needed, if the goal is to make the Soviet Union spend money on air defenses. In addition to our long-range bomber force, we have nearly three thousand nuclear-armed tactical aircraft based in Europe and on aircraft carriers and capable of striking far inside the Soviet Union. Further, our present bomber force includes 255 B-52Gs and -Hs capable of low-altitude penetration, and it will soon contain at least seventy-six FB-111 bombers capable of high-altitude supersonic flight. Together, then, these aircraft will have the same capabilities as the AMSA and will require the Soviets, if they so choose, to defend against the same combination of high- and low-level, supersonic and subsonic attack. AMSA would not change the threat they face, only combine it in a single craft.

"Damage limitation," or the reduction of damage to the United States in the event of nuclear war, is the second announced purpose of U.S. strategic planning. It can include both defensive and offensive measures—defenses to prevent enemy missiles and planes from reaching our shores, and offensive forces to destroy enemy forces before they can be put to use. Bombers seem to have a very small role in damage-limiting, since surprise would be a crucial element in a first strike. Missiles require only minutes to reach their targets; bombers require hours. By the time the bomber force could arrive, the enemy forces would long since have been launched.

The Soviet long-range bomber fleet consists of only one hundred fifty bombers, many of them propeller driven, compared to our six hundred-plus jet-powered B-52s, FB-111s, and B-58s. Its small size, and the Soviets' repeated statements emphasizing that missiles have rendered the manned bomber obsolete, suggest that they are not impressed with the advantages of the bomber as a deterrent weapon. Our present missile force consists of one thousand hardened and dispersed ICBMs and 656 missiles in forty-one Polaris submarines. The Defense Department plans to equip many of these missiles with MIRVs, increasing the total number of warheads in the U.S. arsenal to over ten thousand. The addition of a bomber to this force will add little to the Soviets' reluctance to attack the United States.

Those who believe, on the contrary, that bombers are an essential part of our deterrent force also argue that the B-52 will not be able to fill this role for very much longer. Proponents of AMSA maintain, as General LeMay put it, that "our strategic bombers are going to the trash pile with age." While this might be where they belong, it is simply not true. The new FB-111 strategic bomber has just been introduced into the SAC force, and Air Force studies indicate that, with some modification, the B-52 could be kept in the inventory until at least 1980. Indeed, Secretary of Defense Laird has said, ". . . the structural life of the newest model B-52s will last, under projected usage, until sometime in the early 1980s with appropriate modifications."

If the B-52s should age faster than expected or are needed beyond the eighties, more could be built at far less cost than is involved in developing a new AMSA. One authority has estimated the cost of modifying the

B-52s to increase their lifetime at about $120,000 per plane, while reopening the B-52 production lines to produce new aircraft, if that were necessary, would cost about $16 million per plane, or one third the currently estimated cost of AMSA.

In summary, AMSA, in its primary, deterrent role, will add little to our existing missile force, and any advantage a manned system might provide will be more than offset by its slow speed and poor penetration capability. Any remaining need for a bomber might justify the maintenance of the present bomber force, but not the production of a new bomber. Nevertheless, there is evidence that the Defense Department intends to go ahead with the new bomber, even if there is an arms control agreement with the Soviet Union. They envision an agreement that would limit the number of long-range bombers, but would permit the replacement of one type with another—for instance, the replacement of a B-52 with an AMSA. Even in a situation in which there can be no build-up of strategic forces, either offensive or defensive, on either side, the new manned bomber flies on.

The Sources of Irrationality

Since the mid-fifties, it has been impossible for any nation to acquire the capacity to launch a successful first strike. As early as 1958, then Secretary of the Air Force Donald E. Quarles noted, ". . . the build-up of atomic power in the hands of the two opposed alliances of nations makes total war an unthinkable catastrophe for both sides. Neither side can hope by a mere margin of superiority in airplanes or other means of delivery of atomic weapons to escape the catastrophe of such a war. Beyond a certain point, this prospect is not the result of *relative* strength of the two opposed forces. It is the *absolute* power in the hands of each, and in the substantial invulnerability of the power to interdiction."

One would expect this stalemate to lead to a plateau in the postwar military program. Although intelligence reports indicated in 1961 that no missile gap existed—and that, if anything, the United States had a substantial lead over the Soviet Union (a "missile gap in reverse")—the Defense Department proceeded to build one thousand Minuteman missiles and forty-one Polaris submarines.

It is evident that the concept of deterrence is not the actual basis of military planning. The weakness of the case for AMSA suggests that deployment of this system provides yet another example of exaggerated fears, institutional biases, and political pressures substituting for sound military planning.

Many military and Congressional leaders still cling to the obsolete notion of winning a nuclear war. For example, General LeMay, former head of SAC and Air Force Chief of Staff, argued for new strategic weapons on the grounds that a war fought from "a base of nuclear superiority, maximum options, a traditional balance of friendly offensive and defensive forces, and with quick-strike retaliation would leave the United States sorely wounded, but viable and victorious."

However illusory his expectations, his desire to maintain a superior nuclear force with manned bombers is echoed by many politicians. As Senator Thomas Curtis recently put it, "How do you win the peace after the missiles have been fired and after a large part of your civilization has been destroyed? I submit that the side that still has manned bombers left after a nuclear exchange, after the missiles are gone and the holes are empty, that side will still retain a nuclear-power status and will control the peace and the world—or what is left of it."

Beyond such apocalyptic visions, a favorite practice of the opposition party has been to vigorously attack the party in power for supposedly allowing our military superiority to deteriorate. The automatic response of the party under attack is to claim it has greatly improved and/or increased our arms, and to promise more in the future. This reflex has fostered a political climate in which more and better weapons becomes a political necessity for any administration. The voter is conditioned to this argument and, generally dependent on the expertise and experience of the nation's leader, concludes that new weaponry is essential to his security and expects candidates to support it.

The pressure for superiority is complemented by the commitment of the Air Force man to his own Service. It is not easy for those who have spent their lives flying and commanding bomber fleets to accept a diminishing role for American air power. SAC fears the loss of the manned bomber, for it would then become an all-missile, earthbound command. Air Force Chief of Staff General Thomas F. White expressed their longing for a simpler age when he said, during the B-70 debate, "It is the philosophy even more than the overt decision to cut back the B-70 that bothers me, because I feel that war is an art and will always be an art. It cannot be reduced to a mathematical equation, which is the kind of philosophical approach that I see just over the horizon. . . . It is the tendency to downgrade the value of the man in the future." Such sentiments, coupled to the instinct for self-preservation of the Air Force bureaucracy, can easily lead to weapons policies that lack any sound justification. As one aerospace industry journal candidly admitted, ". . . if AMSA is built, it will probably be our last strategic bomber. Once the present generation of Air Force commanders is gone, the top-level manpower will no longer be there to produce the sort of pressure that has kept AMSA alive for so long."

The proponents of such new systems are aided by the Pentagon practice of estimating the "greater-than-expected threat." If the real threat does not help push your system toward production, this practice provides a convenient means of inventing a suitable danger to justify the new weapon. And, if the threatening force was not going to exist in the first place, the enemy will probably build it eventually to offset your new system, justifying your original fears. Thus, the only limit to the threat is the technical potential of your own research and development effort.

Another factor is the incentive in the military establishment to be on the frontier of advanced technology. This incentive seems to be a consequence of both the bureaucratic drive for prestige and the attraction of what Dr. J. Robert Oppenheimer called "the technically sweet, that is, a kind of aesthetic pressure to develop the most advanced tools merely because one is able to do so." The AMSA will represent a substantial technical advancement over existing military aircraft, and it is natural for men who have worked on the program to be anxious to see it come to fruition. This internal constituency adds to the pressures to produce the unnecessary best.

The ill effects of such irrational factors are seldom offset by rigorous public debate. Until the Vietnam War, the military was regarded with such respect by the American people that their expertise went unchallenged, and to criticize the military was considered politically costly. The honor of the military has been an issue throughout the bomber debate. During the 1968 hearings, Assistant Secretary of Defense Alain Enthoven encountered Congressional hostility to his apparent downgrading of the military:

The Chairman (L. Mendel Rivers): How do you account for the fact that the Secretary of the Air Force and the Joint Chiefs of Staff have recommended an AMSA? They are just not realistic?

Dr. Enthoven: No, Mr. Chairman, it is a question of differing judgments as to the likelihood of various uncertain future events.

The Chairman: How are the Joint Chiefs getting out on a thing like this? Their judgments ought to be good for something. Do they ever win a decision? . . .

The Chairman: It is incidental their advice isn't heeded, isn't it?

Dr. Enthoven: But their advice is heeded. I have the greatest respect for their advice, and I know that the Secretary of Defense does.

Since the beginning of the sixties, the influence of civilian strategists in the Pentagon has been a source of aggravation to bomber supporters in the military departments and on Capitol Hill. General LeMay, in his book *America Is in Danger,* warns, ". . . one of the major reasons our system of national defense is in such a deplorable state is that an anti-military bias throughout the land prevents the military from becoming a true American profession. This bias heaps hundreds of amateur administrators on top of the professionals, and continually subjects the professionals to barriers to progress in the name of civilian control." The bias expressed here is clear; a civilian's judgment is amateur and anti-military and, therefore, incorrect. This prejudice, common among officials and voters alike, is clearly an obstacle to any reasonable debate, and an addition to the momentum of our internal arms race.

LeMay's complaint certainly does not apply to Congress, which has consistently supported the Air Force position over the recommendations of the Secretary of Defense. Of the $1.8 billion appropriated for the B-70 program between 1954 and 1962, only $1.2 billion was used by the Defense Department. Between 1965 and 1968, Congress appropriated almost three times the amount requested in the budget for AMSA development. Through a combination of a glorification of the military, a distorted view of the Soviet threat, a lack of information, and political self-interest, the Congress has acted as a rubber stamp for major military positions.

One other factor underlies the continual pressure for a new manned bomber for the Air Force. The aerospace industry has worked closely with the Air Force in developing the design concepts for a new supersonic bomber, and it wants the billions of dollars of new business that the AMSA represents. The Air Force has been frank in viewing AMSA as a boost for the entire aerospace industry. Because of diminishing sales of large transports, Boeing Aircraft, one of the prime contenders for the B-1 contract, had to lay off more than eleven thousand workers during the first nine months of 1969, and other firms see a similar prospect ahead in the 1970s.

This quite natural desire for new business is reinforced by their interest in the technological "spin-off" from this Air Force-sponsored development project. Breakthroughs that can be applied in commercial aviation are more welcome if the government pays for them. This factor may have played an important role in the support for the B-70. As aviation technology advanced, the cost of research and development became too great for private industry, and government subsidies became the rule. When President Kennedy offered to pay only 75 per cent of the development costs of the SST, the aviation industries balked. To design a huge supersonic plane required a quantum jump in airframe and engine technology, and the industries, in an effort to get the SST by the back door, threw their full weight behind the Air Force campaign for B-70 development, which involved many of the same design problems. When the B-70 program failed to get off the ground, both the industry and the Air Force began to justify the B-70 by emphasizing the SST as a commercial spin-off. This partnership kept the B-70 alive for years, and it is spurring interst in AMSA today.

Conclusion

The inadequacy of the strategic arguments for many weapons programs, including the B-70 and the AMSA programs, strongly suggests that extrastrategic considerations and pressures have played a significant role in these decisions. Confusion over strategic objectives, fierce service loyalty, the political risks in cutting back weapons programs, and economic self-interest have helped to push military inventories and budgets upward. The result is not a policy of deterrence, parity, or sufficiency, but rather one of maintaining a maximum number of options through the support of a mixed force—that is, the Defense Department builds as many weapons systems for as many roles as the over-all budget permits. This policy permits the Secretary of Defense to partially satisfy all parties, reduces vulnerability during election years, and provides the public with the illusion that its security is wisely tended to by the experts. It has produced a weapons constituency that enjoys political influence far out of proportion to its contribution to the national life, and has led to an extraordinary misallocation of resources. Now the bitter taste of the Vietnam War has prompted many members of the Congress and the public to take a critical look at the defense establishment. Clearly, strategic arms is the first area in which the present disequilibrium between unreal and reasonable defense policies should be examined and corrected.

NOTES

The Rise of the Strategic Bomber

The most generally useful source on changing attitudes toward the role of strategic bombers is the various hearings held over the years by the House and Senate Armed Services committees (hereafter termed HASC and SASC, respectively). Good descriptions of the pre-missile development of the Air Force may be found in *A History of the United States Air Force,* Alfred Goldberg, ed. (D. Van Nostrand Company, Inc., 1957), and *The Compact History of the United States Air Force,* by Lt. Col. Carroll V. Glines, Jr. (Hawthorne Books, Inc., 1963).

Enter AMSA

An extensive debate on AMSA took place in the Senate in the fall of 1969, and much useful material appears in the *Congressional Record* of September 12, 13, and 15, 1969, pp. S10533–38, S10572–89, and S10630–53. Air Force Secretary Seaman's discussion of the need for a new manned bomber appears in SASC 1969, p. 972. Secretary Zuckert's testimony on the need to come up with a manned bomber, first given in 1963, appears in the *Congressional Record* of December 16, 1969, p. S10634. Secretary of Defense Clifford's dissent on the need for a new bomber appears on p. 34 of SASC 1969, while his discussion of Soviet air defense capabilities appears on p. 30. Secretary of Defense Laird's discussion of his request for increased funding for AMSA appears on p. 100.

Air Force estimates of the cost and eventual size of the AMSA program appear in *The Defense Marketing Survey* and in *Aerospace Daily* for November 10, 1969. Sen. Stennis' remarks on the cost increase of AMSA appear in the *Congressional Record* of September 15, 1969, p. S10587. Sen. Proxmire's comments on the estimated cost of the program appear in the hearings of the Subcommittee on Economy in Government, Joint Economic Committee, 1969, p. 541, and in the *New Republic* of May 31, 1969, p. 18.

The Obsolete Deterrent

The vulnerability of bombers is discussed by Ralph Lapp in the *New Republic,* June 21, 1969, p. 18, and by Jeremy J. Stone in "Containing the Arms Race: Some Specific Proposals" (MIT Press, 1966), p. 82. Sec. McNamara's discussion of the disadvantages of the stand-off missile appears in HASC 1963, p. 312.

The statement by the Air Force that all bombers will eventually need a high-speed stand-off missile to penetrate the enemy air defenses, appears in SASC 1969, p. 1056. Sec. McNamara's analysis of the relative value of such stand-off missiles appears in SASC 1963, p. 76.

General LeMay's criticism of our aging B-52 force appears in his book *America Is in Danger* (Funk & Wagnall's, 1968), p. 56. Sec. Laird's statement on the projected life of the B-52 appears in the *Congressional Record* of September 15, 1969, p. S10584. Air Force studies on the potential longevity of the B-52 are recorded in HASC 1968, p. 8720. The New York *Times* of November 4, 1969, p. 69, reported that Defense Department officials are discussing a strategic arms agreement with the Soviet Union that would permit us to replace the B-52 with AMSA.

The Sources of Irrationality

Sec. Quarles's statement is quoted in HASC 1968, p. 8502.

General LeMay's argument for new strategic weapons appears on p. 62 of his book. Sen. Curtis' vision of the aftermath of a nuclear war appears in the *Congressional Record* of September 16, 1969, p. S10632.

General White's defense of the manned bomber appears in the *Hearings on Defense Appropriations Before the House Committee on Appropriations,* 1961, Part III, p. 435. The possibility that AMSA will be our last strategic bomber was expressed in a 1969 issue of *Space/Aeronautics Magazine.*

Robert Oppenheimer's statement is quoted by Robert Rothstein in the *New Republic* of March 22, 1969, p. 21. Mendel Rivers' questioning of Alain Enthoven appears in HASC 1968, p. 8871. General LeMay's critique of the downgrading of military professionals appears on p. 22 of his book *America Is in Danger.*

A description of Boeing Aircraft's declining fortunes during 1969 appears in the October 7, 1969, issue of the Washington *Post.*

H. L. Nieburg, *In the Name of Science* (Quadrangle Books, 1966), documents the relationship between the B-70 program and the SST on pp. 324–33.

THE MISSILE RACE—THE CONTEST WITH OURSELVES

by Nancy Lipton and Leonard S. Rodberg

A VARIETY of early initiatives were necessary before the Air Force missile program could get underway. Immediately after the war, with the formation of the RAND Corporation, the Air Force acquired the capacity to carry out scientific studies of the weapons of the future. As early as 1946, RAND was investigating the potential of orbiting satellites–which RAND then called "world-circling space ships." However, the Air Force was dominated by the "bomber generals" of World War II and advised by leading scientists who looked upon an intercontinental ballistic missile as a pipe dream. The Air Force insisted, instead, on pouring funds into the construction of a fleet of nearly two thousand intercontinental bombers, the last of which came off the production line after the first squadron of ICBMs was already operational. Those who looked beyond the manned bomber could envision only a limited extension of it–the pilotless aircraft–and hundreds of millions of dollars went into developing the air-breathing Snark and a missile-launched pilotless craft, the Navaho, before these foredoomed programs were mercifully halted.

However, in the early fifties a combination of new technical developments and hard-driving leadership moved the missile program forward to first priority among the country's military activities. One reason for the low priority of the ballistic missile had been the relatively low explosive yield of the atomic bombs available in the late forties, and the consequent need for exceptionally high accuracy if the missile was to be an effective delivery system. The AEC's "Mike" shot, held in the mid-Pacific in November 1952, proved that a thermonuclear, or hydrogen, bomb could be constructed with a very high explosive yield, equivalent to millions of tons of TNT. From that point on, the ballistic missile became an inevitability. The "Shrimp" shot of March 1954 confirmed a breakthrough in reducing the size and weight of these weapons, so that the size and thrust required of the ballistic missile came within the range of attainable rocket technology. By 1958, when the Soviet-American moratorium on nuclear testing went into effect, we had tested warheads sufficiently small and light to be carried on all our current long-range missiles. The hundreds of tests conducted since the end of moratorium in 1961 and the signing of a partial test-ban treaty in 1963 have refined these devices and fractionally increased their explosive yield. But such refinements have not altered the basic fact that, by the late fifties, this country had warheads and missile-delivery systems that could, at the press of a button, wipe out any city on earth.

The Rise of the ICBM

The three men most closely identified with the start of the Air Force's ICBM program were Trevor Gardner, John von Neumann, and Bernard A. Schriever. Almost immediately after taking office in 1953 as Assistant Secretary of the Air Force for Research and Development, Gardner began pushing for the accelerated development of the ICBM. He convened the Teapot Committee—more formally, the Strategic Missiles Evaluation Committee—

chaired by mathematician John von Neumann. This group examined strategic weapons technology six to eight years ahead and, for the first time, predicted that the necessary warhead, guidance, and propulsion technology could be in hand to make long-range missiles technically feasible by the end of the decade. The next year, a second Von Neumann committee urged an immediate start on a high-priority program to develop and produce the Atlas missile, a liquid-fueled ballistic missile with a nine-thousand-mile range.

The recommended goal of developing and flight-testing the Atlas missile by 1958, with a significant operational force to be in place by 1960, was approved by the Air Force and, soon after, by President Eisenhower. No project involving such great technical uncertainty and such a wide range of necessary innovation had been undertaken since the Manhattan Project, which developed the atom bomb during World War II. Expertise had to be drawn together from a variety of scientific and engineering specialties, advances had to be made across a broad front of new technologies, and these had to be fitted together into a complex system involving both the missile and its associated launch sites. It was to meet these needs—and especially to integrate all parts of the program to achieve the agreed goal on time—that the Air Force (and the Navy as well, although that is a separate story) developed the "systems" techniques now widely touted for solving the problems of our cities.

To cut through normal bureaucratic sluggishness, one man—General Bernard A. Schriever—was put in over-all charge of all Air Force ballistic missile development, with broad decision-making authority and direct access to the civilian chiefs of the Air Force. Programs to develop propulsion systems, guidance and control techniques, nose cones, missile airframes, and test facilities were initiated at Air Force research labs and with industrial firms across the country. Technical direction and systems engineering for the program were provided through new and still-controversial mechanisms that placed non-governmental technical experts in charge of much of the program. Through the Ramo-Wooldridge Corporation, its subsidiary the Space Technology Laboratories, and, later, the Aerospace Corporation—all created for the sole purpose of serving these technical management and advisory functions—the Air Force was provided with technical advice and with over-all technical direction for the program.

Operating with a presidentially approved top national priority, the Atlas development program met its goal, with the first successful flight test at the end of 1957 and the first operational missiles in the hands of the Strategic Air Command by late 1959 (in time for Khrushchev to see them when he visited this country that year).

The Navy entered the strategic missile field in 1956 with the start of its highly successful program to develop the solid-fueled, submarine-launched Polaris missile and the nuclear-powered submarine to carry it. Spurred by the Navy's success in entering what had until then been its exclusive domain, the Air Force began the development of the solid-fueled Minuteman in 1958. Using the same management structure that was then pursuing the Atlas program, the Air Force carried through the construction of large, solid-fueled missile boosters and successfully test-fired the first Minuteman in February of 1961. Buoyed by this success, the new Kennedy administration ordered a speed-up in the Minuteman program. By December 1962, the first Minuteman squadron became operational, and it soon stood as the backbone of the land-based deterrent force, with a total of one thousand of these instant-firing missiles in place.

Soon after the Atlas program was started, the Air Force had received permission to begin a parallel program to develop the Titan missile, also an intercontinental ballistic missile and a liquid-fueled vehicle like the Atlas, but involving substantially different design features. The justifications given for this expensive addition to the Air Force program included a concern that some unforeseen technical problem might develop in the Atlas project, making a substitute missile capacity essential to give the United States a deterrent, and a desire to broaden the base of the aerospace industry. Of course, by this time funds were available in large quantities for missile development, and the Air Force took advantage of the sense of urgency that had by this time developed within the government to initiate this large, new program. As it turned out, of course, the Atlas program achieved all its objectives, and, in fact, it alone gave the United States a substantial advantage over the Soviet Union at the very time—in the early 1960s—when it was feared that there would be a large "missile gap" in favor of the Soviet Union. And the very expensive Titan (each operational missile costing nearly ten times as much as a Minuteman missile) did not become operational until 1963—after the Minuteman, which was begun later. Today all the Atlas missiles have been deactivated, and only fifty-four Titan missiles remain in service.

As this brief history suggests, the effort to develop a long-range ballistic missile was a challenge to technology and management and an opportunity to implement the new systems techniques then becoming fashionable among weapons specialists. A well-oiled machine—the military-industrial aerospace "team"—was created in the fifties and performed magnificently when asked to produce a wholly new weapon in a remarkably short time. New research and development centers in both government and industry were created, and the number of scientists and engineers engaged in aerospace R&D was more than doubled.

However, the technical, industrial, and management base set up during the fifties led inexorably to the kind of accelerated arms race that we experienced in the sixties and that threatens now to spiral to even higher levels in the seventies. The technological juggernaut created then continues to lumber forward, producing ever-more-sophisticated and deadly weapons which, through the twisted logic of the arms race, now seem to be justified chiefly by the very prospect of their existence.

The Search for Certainty

As early as 1958, Senator John Kennedy had seen the "missile gap" as a potent political issue. Kennedy drew on the advice of his friend, columnist Joseph Alsop, who projected that by 1961 this country would have only seventy ICBMs against the Soviet Union's five hundred, and that by 1964 the gap would be even greater, with one hundred thirty American missiles pitted against a Soviet arsenal of two thousand ICBMs. Kennedy declared, ". . . the deterrent ratio during 1960–64 will in all likelihood be weighted very heavily against us. . . . [Soviet] missile power will be the shield from behind which they will slowly advance . . . ; the periphery of the Free World will slowly be nibbled away." This projection of American inferiority was the fuel for the Democratic presidential race of 1960.

Immediately upon taking office, the Kennedy administration discovered that, far from being at a disadvantage with respect to the Soviet Union, we had a chance to achieve a substantial early lead. In his special message to Congress in March 1961, Kennedy announced his decision to accelerate the production of Minuteman and Polaris missiles. Plans were set in motion for the eventual construction of one thousand Minuteman launchers, while the Polaris fleet grew to its current level of forty-one boats carrying a total of 656 missiles.

How can this massive missile build-up be understood? According to Jerome Wiesner, President Kennedy's Science Adviser, Secretary McNamara justified asking for such a large number of ICBMs by arguing, ". . . it is the smallest number I can propose without getting murdered by the Congress." With the Air Force asking, according to some reports, for as many as three thousand Minuteman missiles, McNamara apparently felt that the influence of the generals upon the Congress was too great for him to resist them successfully.

Years later, Secretary McNamara was to admit that, when he joined the Defense Department, the Soviet Union actually had a very small arsenal of ICBMs, and the decision to extend our forces was a "conservative hedge." In a speech delivered in 1967, he said: "In the course of hedging against what was then only a theoretically possible Soviet build-up, we took decisions which have resulted in our current superiority in numbers of warheads and deliverable megatons. But the blunt fact remains that if we had had more accurate information about planned Soviet strategic forces, we simply would not have needed to build as large a nuclear arsenal as we have today."

Thus, according to McNamara, the decision to increase our forces was based, not on information about the actual growth of the Soviet arsenal, but on hypothetical estimates of a "theoretically possible Soviet build-up." Whether the missile gap was the result of deliberate political manipulation or inaccurate estimates or both, it had become a formalized part of U.S. strategic planning. Today it lives under the name of the "greater than expected threat."

The "greater than expected threat" is based upon the enemy's use of all his *potential productive capacity,* even though he must substantially increase his defense budget to exploit this capacity. In spite of the obvious air of unreality surrounding this estimate, it is used in planning our major strategic forces. Alain Enthoven, former Assistant Secretary of Defense for Systems Analysis, explained how the greater than expected threat is arrived at: "We begin with the National Intelligence Estimate [the intelligence community's agreed prediction of *likely* military developments]. We then use a planning and analytic device called the greater than expected threat. What we do is to develop a substantially larger threat than the National Intelligence Estimate shows. This is developed by consulting various of the experts around the Government . . . and approved by the Joint Chiefs of Staff." Other officials have noted an important advantage of the greater than expected threat as a planning device: It is relatively easy to obtain the agreement of the Joint Chiefs of Staff to this intentionally inflated projection, and so a good deal of internal wrangling is avoided. (Of course, the taxpayer pays the bill for this artificial harmony!)

This device can readily justify the development of advanced weapons systems for which an immediate military need is not apparent. As explained by a former Secretary of Defense, "while the foregoing threat is both quantitatively and qualitatively far greater than that projected in the latest intelligence estimates, we cannot foreclose the possibility that all of these developments may occur, and occur simultaneously. Accordingly, we must take timely action now to place ourselves in a position where we can move forward promptly to meet any or all of these threats should they actually materialize." We then have a rationale for simultaneously developing weapons in every area of strategic warfare. For, if we must assume that the enemy is capable of such prodigious efforts, then surely we must match him. We introduce new, larger missiles carrying multiple warheads, since he may install an ABM defense; we install an ABM system, since he may install multiple warheads; we purchase a new manned bomber, since he may expand his air defense; and we expand our air defense, since he may produce a new manned bomber. And our worst fears then turn into self-fulfilling prophesies, as we force *him* to respond to the "greater than expected threat" we have presented to him.

Behind the quantitative exaggerations of the greater than expected threat lies the oft-stated assumption of American military planners that we need absolute certainty of our ability to destroy a large portion of the Soviet Union in a nuclear war. In the words of Secretary Clifford, we need "the ability to inflict at all times and *under all foreseeable conditions* an unacceptable degree of damage upon any single aggressor, or a combination of aggressors." (emphasis added) In the case of the Soviet Union, such an "assured destruction capability" has meant, in quantitative terms, our ability to destroy, in a second strike, more than two fifths of the Soviet population and about three quarters of their industrial capacity.

The quest for certainty leads us to build ever larger, more destructive forces. In the words of the Defense Department's research chief, ". . . any uncertainty in our knowledge about the Soviet Union's strategic forces which could attack our strategic forces . . . will of necessity cause a concomitant increase in our assured forces to cover that uncertainty."

While we have used our supposed ignorance of Soviet capabilities to justify the across-the-board growth of our own strategic forces, some of our civilian leaders have sought to avoid a corresponding escalation by the Soviet Union. This was the reasoning that led Secretary McNamara to adopt a policy of advertising our own retaliatory strength. Yet, many military planners do not subscribe to the logic that says that reciprocal certainty works in the cause of stability, and stability works in the cause of peace. For example, a frequent argument used to defend a weapons system is that it will "throw the Russians off." Air Force Chief of Staff General John P. McConnell argued that even though the Soviets could penetrate any ABM system we might deploy, the ABM should be built because it would "augment our offensive forces by introducing uncertainty into the enemy's planning, compounding their targeting problems and causing them to divert resources from other essential tasks." What might appear to most as escalatory and dangerous brinksmanship is in fact a widely held position among military planners. It can be summed up by the statement made by Army Chief of Staff General Harold Johnson: "The more uncertainty we can create, the greater likelihood there is of avoiding a nuclear exchange."

But the missile escalation of the early 1960s cannot be explained by Kennedy's political reasoning, or the Defense Department's strategic unreasoning, alone. We must also recognize the influence of the mystique of technological progress within the defense establishment, where feasibility is equated with obligation, where if we can build it, we must. Conceivable developments that others might choose to ignore for reasons of cost or consequence are seen, instead, as challenges to the vision of the armed services and their allied industrial technologists.

Weapons that are rationalized publicly by the need to meet potential threats, are in fact conceptualized and developed long before those threats are perceived. In fact, as McNamara's explanation of the missile build-up made clear, the military justification of a weapon is often an *ex post facto,* even unforeseen, consequence of what was a technical/political decision. The only ceiling on weapons development then becomes technological imagination.

Since World War II, we have been significantly ahead of the Soviet Union in strategic weapons technology. Our development of both propeller-driven and jet-powered intercontinental bombers occurred significantly before theirs; we had warning radars installed long before they did; we had a militarily significant ICBM force in place several years before they did; the ABM system they began installing in 1966 used technology equivalent to that in the Nike-Zeus system, which we had rejected in 1962; they still do not have an operational solid-fueled missile; they are only now beginning to deploy a sea-based missile comparable with our Polaris; and so on. Indeed, the Defense Department's research chief has asserted that, across the board, we have a "margin of technical superiority" such that "there are no areas at present where we know Soviet technology to be significantly ahead of U.S. work."

One consequence has been that, since the Cold War began, we have used our own superior technology to drive the arms race forward. The same technical experts who develop our weapons also serve on the government panels that forecast Soviet developments, and they naturally predict that the Soviets will make the same moves we are planning. Even though the Soviets invariably lag far behind these predictions, our own programs go forward as if the forecasts were accurate. The result has been, as Jerome Wiesner put it, that ". . . we are running an arms race with ourselves."

Keeping up with the State of the Art—at Any Cost

Through the dynamic of technology, missile follows missile in an inexorable flow of "generations"—the very term suggests the expectation that today's version will have "descendants"—each generation said to be a logical progression from earlier efforts, and each justified by reference to some anticipated or imagined threat.

This can be illustrated best with the Minuteman system, for which there have been three public generations: Minuteman I, the original weapon to be deployed; Minuteman

II, a more accurate version with more carrying capacity; and Minuteman III, with a multiple-warhead capacity. Each was claimed to have important advantages over previous models, and each was justified by the need to counter anticipated advances in Soviet weapons.

In actual fact, developments in the Minuteman program have been cumulative, with over eight thousand changes made in the system since the first. As General Schriever has noted, "We did not develop just one missile, or just one family of missiles, but a series of missile systems, each of which was more advanced than the one before."

One Pentagon official has testified that the designations Minuteman I, II, and III were actually arbitrary afterthoughts in the conduct of the program. Officials working on the Minuteman system had never even heard of Minuteman II until they received a notice from the Pentagon ordering them to re-estimate the costs of a system designated Minuteman II. And the multiple-warhead system, or MIRV (multiple independently targeted re-entry vehicle), was originally associated with Minuteman II, not Minuteman III as publicly advertised now.

Changes were introduced into the system to improve its accuracy, carrying capacity, and range, and to make use of the latest technical advances. In this high-technology industry, maintaining a position on the "leading edge" of technology and incorporating the latest "state of the art" improvements into a weapon lend prestige to the government office responsible for the system and bring new contracts to the firms supplying the hardware. Of course, the introduction of new, untried technology to achieve improved performance invariably raises the chance that the design will fail or will prove to be unreliable after installation. But failure only brings more money until success is achieved. And performance can be directly measured when the new component is delivered, while its unreliability only shows up through later experience in the field—after the bills have been paid.

From the start, there were misgivings about the reliability of the Minuteman program. Doubts existed within the military itself, and Air Force Secretary Zuckert observed that one reason for extending the number of Minuteman tests was to increase the crews' confidence in the system.

In 1966, the Air Force reported severe reliability problems with the Minuteman II guidance and control system. The difficulties were not detected in production or test firings, but appeared only when the missiles were placed in the operational silos. Repeatedly, test flights of the Minuteman from their silos failed, once as late as August 1968.

The Washington *Post* reported that the guidance and control systems—the "brains" of the weapon—were breaking down four times as rapidly as specified. In 1967, the Air Force decided that it had to buy four hundred additional sets in order to keep enough missiles in operating condition. Far from suffering for its failure, the manufacturer, North American Rockwell, earned a handsome profit from the additional four hundred million dollar sale that resulted.

The missile program has operated in a climate that emphasized performance over cost. Historian Schwiebert observed that, to insure prompt approval of missile-site construction programs, ". . . detailed line-item scrutiny of the construction program during the fund-apportionment process was waived. The Air Force was given wide latitude in determining design criteria and standards, in designating construction agencies for specialized missile requirements, and in shortening facility completion dates, even though higher costs might be involved."

More-recent testimony has indicated that the program continues to operate in such a "cost-free" environment.

The original estimates on the cost of research, development, and deployment of the Minuteman II and III (as explained earlier, it is not easy to separate them) totaled about $5.5 billion, but the estimated cost is now, according to Defense Department figures, more than $3 billion higher.

Cost studies performed on Minuteman II for the Air Force demonstrated repeatedly the potential for reducing costs and at least blunting the cost growth of the project. A consulting firm was engaged by the Air Force in 1963 to survey Minuteman system contractors, including North American Rockwell's Autonetics Division, which produced the guidance and control system. Their report recommended a cost-reduction program, but after submission to the Minuteman Program Director, ". . . all tasks in our proposal which dealt with cost reduction were deleted." Moreover, the study noted engineering cost overruns and recommended a survey of the contractor's cost position, but the contractor refused to supply the necessary information and denied access to the plant. The Air Force waited two years before beginning any formal cost-control program, but even then did not back up the program with concrete action that might have reduced costs.

Initial cost estimates for new developments are invariably low, making it easier to sell the program to senior officials and the Congress. The inevitable cost increases can always be made up through later appropriations, since funds are only allocated for such projects one year at a time, and the momentum generated once a program is underway insures that it will not be cut off solely because of cost increases.

The original contract for development of Minuteman II guidance and control systems, negotiated in June 1963, provided for $170 million. Five months later, the contractor's estimates had risen to $252 million, and a year later they reached $320 million.

For reasons that are never completely clear, later versions of a weapons system or component always cost more than the earlier one. Usually the later model is more "sophisticated" and, hence, more complex, as with the guidance and control system, which for Minuteman I cost $401,000, while for Minuteman II its cost was $1.6 million. Even unchanged parts such as cable assemblies increased in cost, from $14,700 for Minuteman I to $19,800 for Minuteman II.

The hundreds of design changes each year on Minuteman offer contractors an opportunity to offset past, present, and even expected financial difficulties. Such changes are, in fact, customarily referred to as "contract nourishment." Testimony has revealed that the Pentagon does not have information on costs as they relate to the over eight thousand changes made in the Minuteman program. The military receives only a generalized bill for modifications, with no breakdown of items.

Clearly, cost has not been an issue in missile development. The control of cost increases and imposition of cost-reduction efforts have not been a standard part of contracting. Neither civilian nor military personnel involved in missile programming have a defined responsibility in the area of costs like the responsibility that is clearly laid out for them in the area of technical performance or scheduling. There exists within the Department of Defense a climate wherein cost growth is, in one expert's words, "socially acceptable."

MIRV—the Instant Multiplier

While the Air Force could claim for Minuteman II only a moderate quantitative advance over the first-generation Minuteman (improved accuracy and a lengthened casing for propellant, making possible increased range and payload), Minuteman III has been hailed as a major event in missile history. This latest model embodies a new third stage, aptly termed a "space bus," for it can deposit a number of individual warheads successively along different trajectories, aimed at widely separated targets. Hence one missile, carrying several of these multiple independently targeted re-entry vehicles, or MIRVs, can do the work of many.

The MIRV system for Minuteman III will carry three individual H-bombs of about 170 kilotons each, and will, almost overnight, constitute a tripling of our land-based delivery capacity. The Air Force plans to replace every Minuteman I and II by Minuteman III by 1974, at which point the Minuteman force will consist of a thousand Minuteman III, adding two thousand warheads to the original force of one thousand. (Similarly, the thirty-one nuclear submarines to be armed with Poseidon missiles, each carrying fourteen separate warheads, will raise the U.S. sea-based nuclear capability to include nearly five thousand separate warheads.) This massive force will be targeted on the Soviet Union, which, as one relevant comparison, has only seven cities with metropolitan areas exceeding one million in population.

Flight testing of the MIRV system began in August 1968; two years later, the Air Force is beginning to deploy them on operational missiles. Although MIRV was still in the testing stage in mid-1969, the Pentagon awarded contracts to produce them for deployment. General Electric's contract for the MIRV re-entry system was, in fact, awarded on the same day that President Nixon stated that a moratorium on MIRV testing might become part of an arms control agreement with the Soviet Union. It is widely believed that the Joint Chiefs of Staff have sought to delay the arms talks with the Soviets until MIRV testing can be completed. At the same time, the Pentagon has, by awarding the production contracts, indicated to the Soviet Union that it believes MIRV is already a deployable system.

According to recent Defense Department figures, the current estimated cost of the MIRV (Poseidon plus Minuteman III) program is $8.6 billion. (This figure does not include the cost of the warheads—more than a billion dollars—which is borne by the Atomic Energy Commission.) What has justified such a massive and costly program?

The original public rationale offered for MIRV pointed to the need to overcome a Soviet ABM system by exhausting its supply of interceptor missiles. MIRV was proposed as the most effective, least destabilizing (that is, least likely to cause an accelerated arms race) among the available methods for responding to such missile defense.

At the time of the decision to deploy Poseidon, Minuteman III, and the MIRV system (1965–67), it was believed that the Russians were building an ABM system around Moscow, as well as an extensive radar/interceptor network across northern Russia which might be the forerunner of an ABM system. It is now known that the ABM system around Moscow was never completed. Apparently, the Russians had intended to install about one hundred anti-missile missiles at this site, but they halted construction after installing sixty-four, and have never completed work there. Even if they had, the system would have been quite ineffective. It used technology similar to that in the Nike-Zeus system, which the United States decided not to deploy back in 1962 because of its inability to operate in the face of even the simplest forms of penetration aids (decoys, dispersed aluminum foil, etc.).

The network across northern Russia—called by them the Blue Belt and by us the Tallinn system—was originally thought by some (primarily Pentagon military officials) to be an ABM system, and by others (primarily civilian intelligence specialists) to be an air-defense system, presumably installed in the expectation that our high-flying but ill-fated B-70 bomber would actually be deployed. It is now agreed within the "intelligence community" that this system is in fact an advanced air-defense system, designed to intercept high-altitude bombers.

Why, then, was MIRV approved? Research chief Foster has described it as a response to the greater than expected threat: "Our current effort to get a MIRV capability on our missiles is not reacting to a Soviet capability, so much as it is moving ahead again to make sure that, whatever they do of the possible things that we imagine they might do, we will be prepared." Underlying such paranoiac projections, though, is the insistent pressure for deployment arising from the mere presence of newer, more-sophisticated missile technology, with the expectation in the Air Force and its associated industries that, if the technology can be developed successfully, then it will be deployed. It is only natural for each missile generation to be followed by its more potent and effective progeny.

However, while this can help us understand the internal processes that led to MIRV, this multibillion-dollar program could not have been justified publicly without a more substantive rationale—nor would it, probably, have been approved at the highest civilian levels of the Pentagon without an appropriate justification. In this case, the need to respond to a Russian ABM system, even before it existed, was enough to secure approval for the program. The "assured destruction" principle, under which we needed *absolute* assurance that we could destroy a substantial portion of the Russian population, and most of their industry, was sufficient. The insistence on complete assurance of an extraordinarily high level of destruction produced a built-in compulsion to respond to any build-up of Soviet defenses. Here it led us to add to our nuclear deterrent more than five thousand warheads, in response to what eventually became a grand total of sixty-four obsolete ABM interceptors!

However, even this compulsion cannot explain why the program has continued after learning that the Russians never completed their Moscow ABM and that the Tallinn system has no anti-missile capacity. Indeed, if MIRV as a penetration aid should at some point be deemed vital, the lead time to deploy it—twelve to eighteen months—is considerably shorter than the five to seven years it would take the Soviets to build a thick city defense. Thus, we could afford to wait. As one Pentagon official told the Washington *Post,* "If they tell us they are not going to defend their cities, we'll lose a lot of interest in MIRV. Since its purpose is to penetrate Russian cities' defenses, MIRV is negotiable."

It is evident, though, that despite public statements to the contrary, MIRV is not a negotiable item to military planners. It was not conceived originally as an anti-ABM device, and the Air Force is not prepared to give it up solely because a Russian ABM system has not appeared. The initial decision to develop MIRV was linked to the desire to increase the U.S. counterforce capability. The MIRV program was launched in the early 1960s, long before there was any need to penetrate a Soviet ABM. Defense research head John S. Foster, Jr., explains: "The MIRV concept was originally generated to increase our targeting capability rather than to penetrate ABM defenses." In 1961–62, the Air Force found that the number of aim points on its target list exceeded the number of Minuteman launchers they were being allowed by Secretary McNamara. (He had cut their request from three thousand to one thousand.) Their planning, which centered on attacks on missile sites along with other military targets, required more independent warheads, and a natural solution was to adapt each missile so it could carry several individually targetable warheads. In 1964, trade journals reported that the Air Force had several study contracts dealing with multiple warheads having separate propulsion systems to direct them in "patterned bursts" to destroy hard targets such as missile sites. The following year, this had evolved into the present "bus" concept, in which a single propulsion system directs the individual warheads to their separate targets.

While assured destruction is a second-strike doctrine, this attempt to knock out the enemy's missile sites—that is, to achieve a damage-limiting or counterforce capability—requires a first-strike strategy. And an accurate MIRV, which would permit one of our missiles to destroy several of theirs, would be ideal for such a pre-emptive posture. Most assured-destruction proponents have been civilians; most proponents of a damage-limiting capability have been military leaders. As General Wheeler stated: "Secretary McNamara, I believe, has stressed the assured destruction as a deterrent perhaps more than the Joint Chiefs of Staff have."

While official statements deny that the United States is seeking a first-strike capability, it is clear that elements within the military deem it imperative to have a first-strike option. Typical is the position of former Air Force Chief of Staff Thomas White that ". . . a purely anti-city strategy would be an extremely dangerous approach because it would preclude the possibility of limiting damage to the United States." Even Secretary McNamara was equivocal on this; although he spoke of "riding out" a Soviet first strike, he also warned that this would not necessarily be the military's operational tactic, and his Congressional testimony made clear that a pre-emptive strike was one of the "options" for which we were preparing.

While MIRV will certainly not give us confidence that we can launch a first strike with impunity—nothing can do that, in an age when one warhead can destroy a city—it must be seen by the Soviet Union as a clear threat to their deterrent. The extent to which it will multiply our offensive capability was illustrated in 1967 by Defense Department figures that compare the damage inflicted by a hypothetical MIRV package of ten fifty-kiloton warheads, with that from a single ten-metagon warhead. The MIRVs would destroy:

–10 times the number of airfields, soft missile sites, or other soft military targets;
–1.2–1.7 times the number of hardened missile silos;
–3.5 times as many cities of a hundred thousand population.

And the Department also stated that "each new MIRV warhead will be aimed individually and will be far more accurate than any previous or existing warhead. They will be far better suited for destruction of hardened enemy missile sites than any existing missile warheads." Even several years ago, then, MIRV was seen as an increase in our counterforce potential. However, improvements in MIRV accuracy will bring the United States closer than ever before to a true counterforce capability.

. . . Unto the Third and Fourth Generation Thereof

Even as MIRV enters the final phases of its flight testing and the beginning of operational deployment, the Air Force is working on the next generation of missile refinements. As one journal comments, "MIRV technology is in its infancy."

The most significant advance will be in warhead accuracy. The accuracies of our present missile systems are approaching a quarter of a mile (in more-precise technical terms, the circular error probable, or CEP, the radius of a circle within which half the missiles are expected to fall, is approaching that distance). The Air Force, through its ABRES (Advanced Ballistic Re-entry Systems) Program, is carrying on an extensive development effort aimed at providing a MIRV system with substantially greater accuracy and, more specifically, with the ability to home in directly on preselected targets. Like the original MIRV program, this work is usually justified publicly by the presumed need to penetrate any ABM defense the Russians might deploy, but the techniques will be ideally suited for attacking hardened missile sites. As Air Force Chief of Staff John D. Ryan testified in 1969, "We have a program we are pushing to increase the yield of our warheads and decrease the circular error probable so that we have what we call a hard-target killer, which we do not have in the inventory at the present time."

Herbert F. York, former Defense Department research chief, has noted that missile accuracies have improved tenfold since the beginning of the ICBM program and that "an improvement of somewhat less than a factor of two in our guidance accuracy would almost certainly give our planned forces the capability to destroy virtually all their silo-based missiles in a surprise attack." And Harold Brown, his successor and later Secretary of the Air Force, has testified very bluntly on the program's objectives: "The principal value for a very accurate ICBM, or very accurate MIRV, is actually in the destruction of hard military targets, which, of course, is connected with damage limitation. And so, to the extent that we work on very small CEPs, if we do, it is a sign we have not abandoned completely damage limitation as a role of our forces." Foreseeable developments, using guidance units contained within each warhead and operating all the way to the target, can bring that accuracy to the neighborhood of fifty to a hundred feet. With such accuracies, there would be no such thing as a "hardened" missile site; all sites would be vulnerable to destruction by nuclear attack.

The Air Force has for several years been sponsoring a

series of studies of small, maneuverable re-entry vehicles called ARV (Advanced Re-entry Vehicle). Unlike the present MIRV warheads, these would carry individual propulsion systems, in order to guide themselves along separate glide paths after being ejected by the final stage of the MIRV system. With their internal guidance systems, they would correct for errors in the earlier part of the trajectory and for wind effects encountered on the way down. There are multimillion-dollar contracts with General Electric and McDonnell-Douglas to design such maneuverable vehicles, and Singer-General Precision Systems, Inc., is developing miniaturized guidance packages for such vehicles.

At the same time, the Air Force is developing terminal guidance systems that can home on preset targets. Such devices use radar map-matchers, in which a radar system carried in the warhead generates a picture of the terrain below and compares it with a pattern stored in the vehicle. Using such a device, a maneuverable vehicle can guide itself directly to a previously selected site. Such work has been underway for some years at the Raytheon Corporation, Ling-Temco-Vought, and Goodyear Corporation. A "hard point decoy" is also being developed; this would be carried by each warhead to enable it to destroy a missile site protected by an ABM system.

Programs to improve the accuracy of existing guidance systems are also continuing with heavy funding. MIT's Instrumentation Laboratory, where most of the pioneering work on missile guidance systems, including the MIRV system, was performed, is developing these new, high-accuracy guidance devices. The SABRE (Self-Aligning Ballistic Re-entry) System, originally developed by MIT for installation in maneuverable re-entry vehicles, is being upgraded in a $5 million SABRE-2 program. Professor C. Stark Draper, who headed this program for many years, believes that accuracies of less than one hundred feet can eventually be achieved in this program.

The Air Force has now classified all information on these programs, including even the existence of most of the development contracts. Like the original MIRV program, this next stage in missile development will be well underway before the public and its Congressional representatives become aware of it and of its probable impact on the arms race. With the Soviet Union depending today almost completely on its land-based missile force, these efforts will surely produce an acceleration in their program (if we are not already witnessing that acceleration today) and a reluctance to consider halting their build-up of land- and sea-based forces while we continue with this growing threat to their deterrent.

At the same time that we are working hard to make the Soviet force vulnerable to attack, we are realizing that our own force is becoming increasingly susceptible to Soviet attack. Their accuracies are undoubtedly also improving, and there are signs that they are also following our lead in developing a MIRV warhead for their ICBMs.

As the Minuteman force becomes increasingly vulnerable, through improving Soviet missile accuracy, ABM and MIRV can be seen to be only expensive last-ditch efforts to salvage what is clearly an obsolete system. The best solution would clearly lie in unilaterally abandoning this increasingly costly land-based program and relying on an invulnerable submarine-based missile force.

The Air Force, of course, is not following this tack. To meet this challenge to the future of Minuteman, it has been developing a variety of new "basing" techniques intended to reduce the vulnerability of the land-based force. These are discussed in the following paper, by Marc Kramer.

The aerospace industry seems certain of the inevitability of further developments in the Minuteman missile system. Not unexpectedly, one of the most voluble proponents of Minuteman IV or V is Boeing Aircraft, which has absorbed more than a third of the Minuteman budget, has an annual Minuteman business of about $350 million, and employs fourteen thousand men on the Minuteman project. In 1968, the Minuteman project manager at Boeing told employees that he could see at least eight more years for Minuteman and that "the future of Minuteman appears almost limitless." So long as the counterforce goal remains attractive, and technology advances unfettered, there is little reason to doubt his prediction.

NOTES

Insight into changing attitudes toward nuclear strategy and the role of the ballistic missile can be obtained through the successive Congressional hearings, especially those of the Senate Armed Services Committee (SASC), the House Armed Services Committee (HASC), and the House Defense Appropriations Committee (HDAC). The best source on cost overruns and the mismanagement of military programs is "The Military Budget and National Priorities," *Hearings Before the Subcommittee on Economy in Government of the Joint Economic Committee,* June 1969. Admiral Hyman Rickover's testimony on the submarine program before the Preparedness Subcommittee of the Senate Armed Services Committee, March 1968, provides an interesting inside view of mismanagement.

Information on defense contracts and new-weapons developments appears in the *Defense Marketing Service* (DMS) and in such journals as *Aviation Week and Space Technology, Missiles and Rockets* (now *Technology Week*), *Air Force/Space Digest,* and in the valuable newsletter *Aerospace Daily.*

The Rise of the ICBM

An official Air Force history of the development of the intercontinental missile, prepared by Dr. Ernest G. Schwiebert, the historian of the United States Air Force Systems Command, appears in the May 1964 issue of *Air Force/Space Digest.* It was published separately as *A History of the U. S. Air Force Ballistic Missiles,* by Ernest G. Schwiebert (Praeger, 1965). H. L. Nieburg presents a brilliant analysis of the implication of the new management structure that the Air Force evolved for its missile program in his book *In the Name of Science* (Quadrangle, 1966).

The Search for Certainty

John F. Kennedy's speech on the missile gap, delivered in August 1958, appears in his book *The Strategy of Peace* (Harper, 1960).

Secretary of Defense McNamara's explanation of his early decision to build an unnecessarily large strategic force was made in a speech delivered in September 1967 in San Francisco before the United Press International; it is reprinted in his book *The Essence of Security* (Harper & Row, 1968). Jerome Wiesner described McNamara's justification for the large Minuteman force in a speech delivered at the annual meeting of the American Association for the Advancement of Science on December 26, 1969.

Alain Enthoven's description of the greater than expected threat appeared in HDAC 1961, page 425. The need to respond to a projected greater than expected threat and the description of an assured destruction capability are expressed by former Secretary of Defense Clifford in SASC 1969, pp. 28–30. The statement of John S. Foster, Jr., Director of Defense Research and Engineering, regarding the effects of our uncertain knowledge of Soviet forces appeared in HDAC 1969, Part I, p. 48.

General McConnell's support of ABM as a means of enhancing Soviet uncertainty appears in SASC 1969, p. 931, while General Johnson's views were presented before SASC 1968, p. 359.

A comparison of Soviet and American weapons technology, along with a description of our own R&D program, is presented by the Defense Department's Director of Research and Engineering, John S. Foster, Jr., in SASC 1969, pp. 1770 ff.

Keeping up with the State of the Art—at Any Cost

General Shriever's comment appears on p. 105 of Schwiebert's history of the missile program.

Air Force management specialist A. E. Fitzgerald described the origins of the designations Minuteman I, II, and III in the Military Budget and National Economic Priorities hearings of the Joint Economic Committee, p. 610. An early reference to the MIRV, associating it with Minuteman II, appears in *Aviation Week and Space Technology,* August 22, 1966, p. 19.

The reliability problems of the Minuteman II system were described in the Washington *Post* of June 17, 1969, and the New York *Times* of March 22, 1969.

Ernest Schwiebert's observations on the cost-free environment of the missile program appear on p. 102 of his history. Merton Tyrell of Performance and Technology Corporation testified in the 1969 hearings of the Joint Economic Committee on the difficulty of having cost control taken seriously in the Minuteman program.

MIRV—the Instant Multiplier

The decision to develop and deploy the Poseidon missile is presented in the 1965 and 1966 hearings of the Senate and House Armed Services committees. The first official description and rationale for the MIRV program appears in the Defense Department's Posture Statement of 1968, published in both committee hearings. A great deal of official information was developed during Congressional hearings and debates in 1969; a good source is "Diplomatic and Strategic Impact of Multiple Warhead Missiles," *Hearings Before the Subcommittee on National Security Policy and Scientific Developments of the House Committee on Foreign Affairs,* 1969. The current estimated cost of the MIRV program appears in the *Congressional Record* of December 15, 1969, p. S16766. The Pentagon's assertion that it considers the MIRV negotiable appears in the Washington *Post* of June 22, 1969.

Research Chief Foster's explanation of the origin of MIRV may be found in HDAC, 1968, Part IV, p. 2310. Early references to MIRV development contracts appear in *Missiles and Rockets* of April 27, 1964, p. 15, and *Aviation Week and Space Technology* of March 9, 1965, p. 15, and July 12, 1965, p. 28. There was little public discussion of MIRV until late 1967, since even the acronym was considered classified until then.

General Wheeler's comparison of the Joint Chiefs' attitude toward deterrence with that of Secretary McNamara appears in the hearings of the Preparedness Committee of the Senate Armed Services Committee, 1968, p. 38. General White's views on an anti-city strategy were recorded in the Washington *Post* of July 18, 1968.

The Defense Department's comparison of relative effectiveness of MIRV and a single warhead appears in HASC, 1968, p. 8504, and in DOD Press Release No. 1074-67, November 8, 1967. Its statement regarding the increased destructive power of a MIRV warhead against hardened missile sites was published in the Washington *Post* of January 16, 1968.

. . . Unto the Third and Fourth Generation Thereof

The Air Force program to develop new re-entry vehicles and improved guidance is described in *Aviation Week and Space Technology* of March 17, 1969, p. 23, and September 1, 1969, p. 16; in the Washington *Post* of August 7, 1969; and more extensively, in reports of the *Defense Marketing Service.* General Ryan's reference to the program appears in HDAC, 1969, Part 7, p. 47.

Herbert York's projection of the effect of improved guidance appears in "Strategic and Foreign Policy Implications of ABM System," *Hearings Before the Senate Foreign Relations Committee,* 1969, Part III, p. 659. Harold Brown's comments were given in *Hearings on Status of U. S. Strategic Power Before the Preparedness Investigating Subcommittee of the Senate Armed Services Committee,* 1968, p. 219. D. G. Brennan, in the House Foreign Affairs Committee hearings on MIRV, p. 113, describes the potential improvements in delivery accuracy.

The Boeing Minuteman project manager's description of the future of his program was reported in *Aerospace Daily,* May 10, 1968.

BUCK ROGERS IS ALIVE AND WELL—AND DOING R&D FOR THE PENTAGON

by Marc Kramer

UNTIL recently, much of the public, and many members of the Congress, were under the illusion that the arms race had reached some permanent plateau–an impression undoubtedly created by the relatively static quality of the strategic arms race of the 1960s and the absence of publicity on new developments. A lax and uninformed Congress had lost sight of the deadly new technology being developed in defense laboratories and test ranges. As a consequence, when the destabilizing implications of ABM and MIRV were discovered, many laymen were taken by surprise. Congress had willfully or ignorantly allowed the military technocrats to lead us into a new arms race in the mid-1970s. It is the hope of this paper to forewarn those who are complacent concerning the developments that will be upon us by 1980 if we fail to act.

Offensive Weapons

Intercontinental missiles are being given a dogfighting and evasive capacity similar to that of manned aircraft in the past. The new aim with missiles is to penetrate anti-ballistic-missile defenses, and the advanced research focuses on how to make the missile as flexible as possible. The Minuteman III, with its MIRV warheads and greater payload capacity to enable it to carry decoys and chaff, is the first to emphasize this kind of evasive action. But much attention is being given in the hundred-million-dollar Advanced Ballistic Re-entry System (ABRES) Program to guidance and re-entry physics. For instance, Project ARP studies the best geometric configuration of a warhead to avoid enemy radar detection, while Projects SLAM and WAKE study stress waves created by a warhead as it enters the atmosphere, to make detection of the warhead harder for the enemy.

Several new types of warhead are under development in the ABRES Program, for use on the Minuteman III and future ICBMs. One is the BGRV (boost-glide re-entry vehicle), which can descend several hundred miles before reaching a target, and then glide in at a low altitude to achieve a kill. An observer on the ground would be fooled into thinking that the warhead had missed its target, and, by gliding at a low altitude, it could slip under a radar undetected. Another vehicle that is already tested is the MBRV (Maneuverable Ballistic Re-entry Vehicle), which has aerodynamic surfaces that allow it to pull out of its descent, much like a dive bomber, as it enters the atmosphere. This deceptive little warhead can fake hitting one target and attack another.

The ultimate in re-entry vehicles is the MRV (Maneuverable Re-entry Vehicle), which uses small jets to make evasive action as it attempts to make a kill, using a terminal guidance system to home in upon the desired target. Techniques are under development for communicating with the missile during the entire course of its flight. It could then be directed toward targets that might have been missed in earlier waves of the attack. As Gordon MacDonald, a Pentagon science adviser, described it, "Beyond MIRV lies the missile which delivers large numbers of warheads, each one of which is guided to its target in real time [that is, while the "battle" is underway] with a target selected by a real-time analysis of the battle." And, of course, to further confuse the enemy, ABRES has developed chaff to black out the radar, radar-jamming systems, and decoys that look like warheads to an enemy radar.

Advances such as these, combined with terminal guidance, will soon render land-based missiles obsolete. Some would move to rely on our Polaris force as the primary deterrent, and abandon the land-based missiles altogether. However, the Air Force and the aerospace companies have other plans which will keep them both in business for a long time to come.

One approach under intensive development involves placing the missiles in superhard silos designed to withstand between ten and fifteen times the blast pressure of current missile silos. In 1969, $38 million was spent on this project, and it is estimated that research and development alone would require an additional $250–300 million.

A new ICBM, known as the Advanced ICBM, or ICBM-X, is also in the development stage. This vehicle would be larger than Minuteman III, with a greater range and payload, so that it could carry more MIRVs or penetration aids and, in larger numbers, be a more potent threat than even the Minuteman III force. The superhard silo is intended to accommodate either Minuteman III or a completely new ICBM, should it be deployed. Since the lead time for construction and installation of the silo is between three and five years, it will not be available until two or three years after Minuteman III has been fielded. The silo will thus stand invitingly open for a whole new generation of Minuteman or advanced ICBMs.

However, even a superhard silo will become "soft" when accuracies become of the order of one hundred feet or less. Further, the Air Force is finding that the hard-rock sites necessary for these silos are not available in sufficiently abundant or convenient locations to make this avenue seem feasible. In an attempt to save the Minuteman, current interest has turned to the possibility of making the Minuteman mobile.

A truly mobile missile, moving across the country by rail or truck, could not be targeted by an opponent, who would not be able to know its location at the time when his missile might impact. An approach using railroad flatcars to carry the missiles was considered during the early sixties, but it was canceled when it was found to be too expensive and to pose very serious "command and control" problems–that is, who is in charge of the missile, who can give the order to fire, and who can prevent a hijacking?

Secretary Laird has expressed skepticism that a mobile Minuteman, whether moving by rail or on large trucks, would be feasible in the United States. As he noted, "We have enough trouble moving some mustard gas." Wouldn't citizens react with even more hostility to nuclear weapons traveling down their main streets?

One idea involves the use of a huge van–125 feet long and thirty feet high–moving either along special roads in the Great Plains or, as described in an Air Force Association journal, in "a circuitous tunnel, many miles in length, in the base of a mountain, from which the mobile system need not emerge, launching its missile through one of a number of vertical shafts." However, even bad ideas cannot be dropped without multimillion dollar studies, and the Air Force has contracted for studies of transportation schemes and for guidance systems that would continuously update the position and targeting of the missile as it moved. Boeing has received a $1.5 million contract to design, develop and test a plan to place Minuteman missiles atop trucks located in garages at various spots throughout the country. According to this concept, there would be more garages than Minuteman trucks, and the missiles would be moved around on a random basis, in a kind of nuclear shell game. North American is studying guidance systems to be used with this scheme, and there is even a General Electric contract for a re-entry system for the Garage Mobile Minuteman. A new gravy train—or better, convoy—seems to have arrived.

The "flying officers" of the Air Force are also interested in the mobility idea. One suggestion is that the huge C-5A transport aircraft be used as an airborne launching platform for the missile. The plane could fly part of the way toward its target and launch its missile during mid-course—if the showdown hadn't already come.

The Navy sees the chance to become the chief custodian of the nation's deterrent, and is as interested as the Air Force in the continuing procurement of new systems. Even as the first submarine enters drydock for conversion to carry the new Poseidon missile, the Navy is looking toward its successor, the ULMS—Undersea Long-Range Missile System. This large missile would be carried either on the outside of the present submarines or in new, larger submarines especially designed for it. With its long range, any target would be within range as soon as the submarine left port, and all the world's oceans would be available as cruising space. It could even be launched from the deep sea—either fixed to the ocean bottom or able to crawl along it.

Defensive Weapons

In a similar fashion, the Services are perfecting a series of defensive measures that might be deployed in an attempt to prevent an enemy's missiles and bombers from descending on this country. Without reviewing the great ABM debate of this past year, it is clear that such efforts could present grave new obstacles to the achievement of a stable strategic balance between the nuclear powers.

Besides the Army's Safeguard missile defense, approved by the Congress this past year, the Air Force is seeking approval for a new bomber defense intended to surmount the great vulnerability of the present system. (Long before any Russian bombers had reached our shores, the present ground-based system would have been knocked out by a few ICBMs aimed at the warning radars.)

Also, with conventional radar, planes can fly low and can slip beneath it, as in the recent incident in which a Cuban pilot flew into Florida undetected. AWACS–Airborne Warning and Control System–is the Air Force's solution to this problem. The building blocks for AWACS are a long-endurance airplane carrying an advanced surveillance and tracking radar with the capacity of looking downward at low-flying planes, and a data-processing display and communications center located in the aircraft. The command aircraft would direct a fleet of F-106X or YF-12A interceptors toward enemy bombers approaching the mainland. They would be directed to the general area of enemy action and would take over the tracking and kill mission with their own "look-down" radars.

Seeing already the many weaknesses of the Safeguard ABM system, and sensing the opportunity it provides for follow-on systems that would improve on it, the Air Force, Army, and Navy are studying a variety of ABM concepts that go far beyond the Safeguard approach. As an aerospace journal recently commented, ". . . the present Safeguard deployment is thus sure to be an interim step as a Minuteman defense."

One of the most active programs involves a new low-altitude interceptor, the Upstage-Hibex combination. Hibex (High-acceleration Booster Experiment) utilizes a new, very fast booster, permitting accelerations up to

1000 g, ten times greater than the acceleration of the Sprint missile used in the Safeguard system. Upstage is a highly maneuverable anti-missile warhead which would seek out incoming warheads and follow them if they change course. If their warheads, like the ones we ourselves are now developing, are capable of maneuvering, the result would be computer-controlled dogfights in space!

For the defense of cities, the Army is investigating a new concept called RUDI (Regional Urban Defense Intercept), in which high-explosive warheads would shower gravel over a wide area in the path of incoming warheads, eroding them as they pass through this screen. (Perhaps, if air pollution over our cities becomes much worse, this won't even be necessary!)

To date, most ABM research has focused on the reentry stage of the enemy missile's flight, but active research is also being pursued toward the goal of intercepting in the boost and mid-course stages. The Air Force's SORTI (Satellite Orbital Track and Intercept) system would place "detection" and "kill" satellites in stable, synchronous orbits, standing continuously over the Soviet Union. When the Soviets launched their ICBMs, detection satellites would feed tracking information back to ground and to kill-satellites. On direction from the ground, the kill-satellites would either launch space-borne anti-missile missiles or use a laser beam to destroy the Soviets' missiles almost immediately after take-off.

Such a system is likely, of course, to be extremely complex and costly. It will also be very provocative to any country subjected to such a "space blockade." According to an aerospace trade publication, the State Department has been opposing the deployment of such a system since the early 1960s. Nevertheless, the technology is being developed so that, as one expert put it, "at least it will be available when Safeguard falls on its face."

The detection satellite would use a sensitive infrared detector that would sense the heat from the missile exhaust immediately after launch. Such detectors were first tested in the MIDAS (Missile Detection and Surveillance) system during the early sixties, but infrared detectors were not sufficiently sensitive at that time. Since then there have been significant improvements in these devices, and their advocates are pushing for their deployment. The satellite will also carry a low-resolution television picture of the launch area, providing additional information on Soviet missile activities.

The use of laser beams to destroy missile warheads has long been thought to be impractical because of the enormous power requirements of such devices. However, recent advances with gas and chemical lasers have caused some experts to believe that a satellite-borne laser beam may be feasible within the next decade. (Already, a drone aircraft has been disabled with a laser beam, but that is a long way from disabling a "hardened" warhead at distances of thousands of miles.) Such a beam would deposit a large burst of energy upon the enemy warhead, evaporating its heat shield and disabling its nuclear bomb. Unlike a conventional interceptor, using either nuclear or high-explosive warheads, it would not run out of ammunition, and, from space, could track the warhead until it achieved a "kill"; and, of course, the beam—being simply high-intensity light waves—travels with the speed of light.

Mid-course ABMs are also receiving some attention. The Navy's SABMIS (Sea-based Anti-Ballistic-Missile Intercept System) program is one of the most ambitious projects, and has been touted by the Navy as a supplement to the Army's Safeguard system and as a means of protecting our allies in time of crisis. It would use Poseidon missiles in a defensive role by placing them on surface ships and deploying them off the Soviet and Chinese coasts. While it could knock out multiple warheads before they separated, thereby making Safeguard more effective, SABMIS would have too few interceptors to be effective against a major nuclear attack, and its ships would be vulnerable to destruction even before the attack began. (The Navy counters that the system would then serve as a good early-warning network!)

The Air Force is also working on mid-course ABMs. ABMIS (Airborne Ballistic Missile Intercept System) is its version of SABMIS, utilizing an anti-missile-carrying version of the C-5A transport plane to circle over the Arctic on a round-the-clock patrol. With its own radar and associated ground radar, it could track and fire anti-missile missiles at the enemy warhead in mid-course.

The Army's entry is FABMIS (Forward Area Ballistic Missile Intercept System), with radars and interceptors based on Texas-Tower-like launch platforms in the North Sea and elsewhere around the borders of the Soviet Union.

The Air Force is also studying new ways to utilize obsolete Minuteman I missiles in a defensive role. Known as the Minutemaid project, its aim is the conversion of Minuteman I into a long-range interceptor missile that could be launched so as to intercept an incoming missile before it reached mainland America. Minutemaid would be radio guided so that it could change course easily in mid-flight.

Although the orbiting of nuclear weapons in space is prohibited by treaty, plans are being undertaken to engage in warfare against reconnaissance satellites and orbiting bombs by other means. Navy Program 922 focuses on firing hypervelocity steel pellets into the path of a hostile satellite to deorbit it or set it off course. The Navy has suggested that the first ten Polaris submarines, which are approaching obsolescence, could be used in an anti-satellite or anti-ballistic-missile role. Air Force programs

706 and 437 are investigating other techniques for satellite detection and kill. By placing a "buddy" satellite in orbit close to an enemy satellite, it could be rendered useless by either blinding its optical sensors with flashing lights or laser beams, overloading its infrared sensors with heat generated by the buddy satellite, or by the "lamprey" concept: A buddy satellite would attach a small bomb to the side of an enemy satellite. The "lamprey" would remain on the enemy satellite for an indefinite period of time, detonating only if the satellite began to deorbit over the United States. Conversely, if the satellite were deemed non-military, the lamprey could be detached from the enemy satellite with a signal from the ground.

As a former high-ranking Pentagon official once explained to a visitor, "Welcome to the magic military land where we make weapons that won't work for threats that don't exist." So it goes on and on and on . . .

NOTES

Offensive Weapons

The ABRES Program is described in *Aviation Week and Space Technology* of September 1, 1969, and in reports of the *Defense Marketing Service*. Gordon MacDonald's description of a missile battle of the future was presented in hearings on the Strategic and Foreign Policy Implications of ABM Systems, Part III, before the Senate Foreign Relations Committee, 1969, p. 655.

The hard-rock silo program was described in *Air Force/Space Digest* of June 1968 and in HDAC, 1969, Part IV, pp. 730–53. The reasons for its likely demise are reviewed in *Aerospace Daily* of January 5, 1970. The new mobile Minuteman program is described in *Aerospace Daily* of January 9, 13, and 15, 1970. "Missile in a Mountain" was described in *Air Force/Space Digest* of June 1968.

ULMS is described in SASC, 1969.

Defensive Weapons

The AWACS system is described in *Space/Aeronautics Magazine* of February 1968 and in SASC, 1969. Advances in ABM technology are described in *Space/Aeronautics* of November 1969, pp. 48–55. Space-borne ABM systems are discussed in *Aerospace Daily* of January 7, 1970, while the recent advances in laser technology are described in *Aviation Week and Space Technology,* January 12, 1970.

The Navy SABMIS is discussed in *Data* of February 1968 and in SASC, 1969. The potential dual role for Minuteman is described in *Aviation Week and Space Technology,* March 31, 1969.

Satellite interception techniques are discussed in *Space/Aeronautics* of June 1969, p. 45. *Air Force/Space Digest* and *Space/Aeronautics* provide continuing surveys of the latest weapons technology.

THE COMING ARMS RACE UNDER THE SEA

by Sam Baker and Kerry Gruson

IT IS in the middle of the Atlantic Ocean, inside a glass sphere resting at the top of a mountain. The mountain rises ten thousand feet from the surrounding plain, but there is still a mile of ocean above. Ahead, also resting on the mountain, is a huge, barge-like vessel with sixteen fat tubes attached. Swarming around the craft like insects are various small craft, some manned, some remote-controlled, and also divers able to breathe fluids other than air (thanks to a special operation). The barge is mated to a concrete structure in the seabed that forms the entrance to a supply depot bored deep into the mountain rock. The barge bears a legend on its side. It reads UNITED STATES NAVY, and the sixteen tubes contain missiles.

Today this is science fiction. But if Navy programs now underway continue on schedule, this piece of fiction could become reality within ten years.

In the fall of 1969, the Navy received from its contractor the first of a series of vessels capable of transferring men or supplies from one submerged installation or craft to another. Once this vessel is proven, manned bases embedded in the sea floor will be feasible.

Three years ago, in 1967, a progress report for the Navy Ocean Engineering Program outlined the Navy's plans. "Prototype underwater manned installations are planned to develop construction techniques, equipment, and methods. Submerged military support bases have application with submersibles requiring replenishment and exchange of personnel. . . . Other potential uses of submerged military manned installations are as command centers, weapon sites, and surveillance-network headquarters."

The Defense Department's excursion into the deeps is not limited to developing new weapons systems: It has taken responsibility for much of the nation's basic scientific work under the seas. Of the $528 million requested annually for the marine sciences in a report by President Johnson's National Council on Marine Resources and Engineering Development, the military would spend over half—$297.9 million. In the fiscal year 1970 budget, only $143 million of the military appropriation for marine sciences was intended for projects identified as directly related to "the national security."

Undersea Mobility

Total Navy expenditures are $287.2 million of the $297.9 million allocated to the Department of Defense. How does the Navy spend this money? Its underwater effort is broken down into three categories: Ocean Science, with $62.6 million budgeted for 1969; Ocean Engineering and Development, with $113.5 million; and Oceanographic Operations, with $111.1 million.

The relative importance of these categories has changed over the past six years, marking the program's success. Six years ago, the bulk of the money went to Ocean Science for basic research. Now, says Oceanographer of the Navy O. D. Waters, "basic research has paid off so well that the results are being translated into expanded operations and engineering efforts," that is, into hardware for experimental and operational use.

The most important projects are lumped together in two offices—the Deep Submergence Systems Program (DSSP) and the Deep Ocean Technology Program (DOT). These two programs account for the single largest appropriation in the Navy oceanographic program, with $81.5 million in fiscal year 1969. Projects underway in these offices are concrete indications of the directions the Navy is mapping out for itself.

The Deep Submergence Systems Program is headed by the energetic, brilliant Dr. John P. Craven. Despite the Vietnam War, he has managed to secure more money for his program each year. He states its public goal as "giving us the capability for submarine search and rescue, the rapid recovery of small objects such as the nuclear bomb off Palomares, the salvage of large objects, and the development of a life sciences technology."

The highest-priority project within the DSSP is the Deep Submergence Rescue Vehicle (DSRV). Billed as the answer to the *Scorpion* and *Thresher* disasters, in which these submarines sank at sea with loss of their crews, the rescue vehicle will be the first submarine capable of transferring men and cargo to another vehicle without surfacing, as well as the first capable of investigative work along the ocean floor.

These technological innovations have important military significance far beyond the possibility of aiding submarines in trouble, though public discussion of the program is almost always limited to the submersible's use as a rescue ship. In fact, as Dr. Craven admitted in an interview, the new ship's capabilities as a submarine rescue vehicle are a thin cover. "The DSRV isn't worth its cost as a rescue ship. Submarines just don't sink that often. But that was the only way we could sell it," Craven said.

Only two submarines have been lost in the past ten years; and even in these cases, the DSRV would have been of little help. Unless the damaged sub is located very near a port with a rescue vehicle handy, it would take, on the average, two days to load the rescue ship into a plane, fly it to the port nearest the distressed sub, provide a support submarine to piggy-back it to the wreck, and then to shuttle the trapped men back, twenty-four at a time, to the attending sub. This scenario rests on the assumption that at least portions of the sub would remain relatively undamaged. Of course, once a sub sinks below its crush depth, nothing can save it. Only on the continental shelf is the water shallow enough so that a disabled submarine will not quickly fall below its crush depth. The *Thresher* in 1963 and the *Scorpion* in 1968 were both lost in the deep sea.

The real significance of the rescue vehicle is that it will make the nation's submarine fleet almost completely independent of the surface for long periods of time. The great advantage of the Polaris fleet is that it is very hard to trace a sub once it is at sea; the United States is assured that it will never be caught without a retaliatory capability. Submarines are most vulnerable when they surface—even on the high seas, they can be spotted by anti-submarine reconaissance planes or satellites—and when they dock. With a larger, developed rescue vehicle, a sub could be resupplied almost anywhere underwater, giving it a much longer underwater cruising time and a much larger area in which to operate. The sub would be difficult, if not impossible, to track.

It also becomes feasible to deploy underwater forces far from home without resorting to support bases in unreliable allied territories—an important consideration in distributing the nation's strategic forces or, for instance, in planning an amphibious attack.

The rescue vehicle's potential and the objectives of the DSSP are clearly stated in an article by a Navy officer for a 1968 issue of *Naval Ships Technical News*. "[They will] provide a capability for supporting rescue and recovery operations, maintaining bottom-mounted equipment, exploring and exploiting the continental shelf, and possibly assisting in covert military operations associated, for example, with mine defense and amphibious assaults."

The ship is an important step toward developing the technology for undersea bases, and there seems to be little doubt that this is the direction in which the Navy is moving. In a report by the President's Scientific Advisory Panel on Oceanography, formed to make recommendations for a national program on the use of the oceans, the following are considered: "Missiles of Polaris' size or even considerably larger, placed on relatively shallow underwater barge systems on the Continental Shelf in a way which conceals their location and requires the system to move infrequently, so that the potential of its being tracked by motion-generated noise is minimized. In addition, one might consider a slightly mobile, ocean-bottom system which creeps along. . . . Such systems can involve much larger missiles, might require underwater maintenance by personnel also located underwater, might entail development of new kinds of implacement gear for positioning missiles, might necessitate new kinds of detection and survival equipment to prevent attacks on the implacement, and so on."

An underwater arsenal makes good sense, from the Navy's point of view. With the development of anti-ship missiles, flotillas of giant ships are becoming obsolete. Without submarine and ocean-floor warfare, the only other direction the Navy could move would be toward hovercraft and hydrofoils.

The invulnerability of underwater weapons systems and the fact that the United States would no longer be dependent on sometimes-unreliable allies, are used over and over again by the Navy in discussing proposed weapons systems such as the SABMIS—the Navy's version of a sea-based anti-ballistic-missile system. Navy officials have predicted that these arguments will become increasingly relevant as the U.S. military presence abroad becomes less popular.

The rescue vehicle is not the Navy's first venture into the deeps. In 1960, it sent the bathyscaphe *Trieste* down 35,800 feet to the ocean floor off the Philippines, at the ocean's deepest point. The "landing" of the *Trieste* with two aquanauts on board—they performed a few simple mechanical experiments but were not able to leave the bathyscaphe—was, in some ways, the underwater equivalent of landing on the moon. The feat showed that man could get there—that he was able to make observations and to work.

The *Trieste,* like the astronauts' *Eagle,* was inadequate for any real exploration. A bathyscaphe is much like an elevator, raised and lowered by cables from a surface craft. Because of the difficulties of co-ordinating the movements of the bathyscaphe with the surface craft, even in the calmest seas, the *Trieste* has almost no horizontal maneuverability. Because of the great pressures under the sea, which would collapse a Polaris submarine, and the corrosive effects of sea water, constructing a maneuverable submersible is not just a matter of adapting a submarine or fixing engines to a *Trieste*-style craft. The Navy needed a new kind of vessel, but until 1963 it found it impossible to generate interest in a deep-submergence program.

What the Navy needed was something to dramatize the need for expenditures in a deep-sea program—a Russian "threat," to justify moving into this new area. In 1957, the Air Force was blessed with *Sputnik*. The Navy had to make do with the *Thresher* disaster and the hydrogen bomb lost for three embarrassing months off Spain.

On April 10, 1963, the nuclear submarine *Thresher* was lost in 8400 feet of water off the New England coast. Public attention focused on the fact that submarine rescue technology, developed in the 1930s, had not kept up with modern submarines. In answer, the Deep Submergence Systems Review Group was set up to study the Navy's ability to locate and recover objects from the sea floor. The DSRG report went to the Chief of Naval Operations with the following recommendations: The Navy should develop a new rescue system, a search capability for depths down to twenty thousand feet, methods to salvage submarines and other large wrecks from the continental shelf, and a system allowing man to work as a free diver without bulky equipment in ever-deeper water. The report was accepted in May 1964 by then Secretary of the Navy Paul H. Nitze, and the new Deep Submergence Systems Project was set up to carry out the objectives outlined in the DSRG report.

On January 17, 1966, a United States B-52 carrying four nuclear bombs collided with a jet refueler and fell into the sea off Spain. Three of the bombs were recovered immediately. The fourth was found only after a three-month search using almost every operational American military or civilian deep-diving submersible. Two months later, the Deep Submergence Systems Program, then under the Special Projects (Polaris) Office, was made autonomous and designated an official Navy field activity under the Chief of Naval Material. This organizational upgrading gave the program more visibility and attention from top Navy officials. Spread over the six years from 1966 to 1972, the office will receive about $300 million, and today has chief responsibility for developing a technology for underwater warfare in the 1980s. As Admiral Waters put it, ". . . the grand objective of the DSSP is to make it possible to operate deep-diving vehicles, both manned and unmanned at any depth, at any time, and at any location in the ocean. Nothing so ambitious and imaginative has been undertaken since the inauguration of the space program."

Beyond the rescue vehicle, the program office is

also working on the Deep Submergence Search Vehicle (DSSV), which will go to depths of twenty thousand feet and cruise at three knots, with a maximum speed of five knots. Although the first of these craft will probably be able to remain on the bottom for only thirty hours when cruising at three knots, operational capabilities at that depth will give the search vehicle access to 98 per cent of the ocean, making it virtually impossible for an enemy to locate it. This program has been slowed due to fund cutbacks as well as key technological problems such as developing an efficient power source and material strong enough to withstand the pressure at such depths. The first model was expected in 1973, but has now been delayed to 1975.

One possible source of power now being considered is an electric fuel cell, which could revolutionize submarine design by providing a long-lived source of power without the expense involved in a nuclear-propelled sub. Another important advantage of such a cell is that it makes very little noise, again making it harder to track the sub.

The search vehicle has been talked of in connection with the development of an underwater station as a base for sea-floor construction efforts, under the auspices of the Naval Civil Engineering Laboratory. It would function as the supply ship and emergency rescue vehicle for the station, which is to be located at six thousand feet.

A third project in the Deep Submergence Systems Program is the Man-in-the-Sea effort, which has received more publicity than any other work in this area. Sealab I, the first experiment, began in the summer of 1964, when a group of aquanauts lived for eleven days in a dry "habitat" 193 feet under the sea off the Bermuda coast. The pressure inside the habitat was maintained at the same level as the pressure outside, so the men could enter and leave the underwater cabin as they pleased, undergoing decompression only at the end of the experiment.

Sealab III, the most recent phase of the project, was slowed by the death of one aquanaut in early 1969. This experiment was to test man's ability to live and work six hundred feet below the surface for sixty days. Eventually, Man-in-the-Sea will make it possible for man to work effectively for long periods of time at depths up to eight hundred and fifty feet, resting in a transportable "habitat." Present plans restrict the project to the continental shelf, though a blueprint for work in the deep ocean has been drawn up.

Again, the military implications of such technological developments are clear. John Craven, head of the DSSP, points out that, with man as a free agent working in water of great depths for extended periods, it is an easy conceptual leap to underwater armies, operating under the sea as soldiers do on land. The importance of such forces becomes clearer, should a nation deploy underwater bases for military or economic reasons.

Another project in the DSSP is the NR-1 nuclear-powered research and ocean engineering submarine. Launched in February 1969, the NR-1 uses instrumentation designed for the rescue vehicle, and a nuclear reactor developed jointly with the Atomic Energy Commission, to make it the first deep submersible with an underwater cruising time limited only by the amount of water and food it can store.

Underwater Weapons

The second program under Craven's direction is the Deep Ocean Technology Program (DOT), which concentrates on new weapons systems. According to a 1968 DOT status report, the program represents "a major new Navy initiative" that will give the Navy the technological base to "provide technical options for potential weapons systems, and will permit the Navy to operate in the total ocean." The report continues: "The Chief of Naval Operations on 4 January 1968 requested advanced development in deep ocean systems for the post-1970 era. The objective is to define and assess the technical feasibility, military usefulness, and financial acceptability of undersea weapons and other system concepts."

Unlike the Deep Submergence Systems Program, the DOT is explicitly oriented toward developing future weapons. Its short-range role is to fill any technological gaps in other Navy projects. The middle-range goal, according to the report cited above, is to make possible an ocean-bottom manned installation at six thousand feet, a manned surveillance vehicle operable at twenty thousand feet, and a system-support platform at three hundred feet.

To fulfill these objectives, the DOT program has several projects underway. The office is working on a quiet electric drive system for deep-surveillance craft. It is developing sea-floor engineering techniques, designing new propulsion systems, and studying new materials, such as glass and plastic, resistant to high pressures. A clear plastic sphere that could carry a man to six hundred feet was tested in 1969. The office is planning eventually for a series of unmanned vehicles that would search the bottom using television and sonar, and repair, maintain, and recover sea-bottom objects. A few of these vehicles are already operational.

Budgeted at only $4 million in its first year, Navy officials stress they expect this seed money to lead to "bigger things," as O. D. Waters told a group in San Diego, a town heavily dependent on Navy oceanographic work: "I suggest that industrialists with an interest in future developments in oceanography keep an eye on it [the DOT program]," Waters said. "Past endeavors have been fragmented, but the future success of the DOT program can be realized by allying private industry and Navy resources in a manner similar to that displayed in the Polaris Program, where the technological advances became a true measure of foresight and creativity," Waters continued.

The 1968 DOT status report points out that, while "budgeted funds for fiscal 1969 cannot be considered abundant for such a broad and advanced project as this, it is noteworthy that in this time of shrinking funds for non-weapons-systems projects, funds budgeted to DOT have doubled over those for fiscal 1968."

Undersea Bases

How serious is the Navy about underwater bases? One indication came in a New York *Times* article (August 1, 1968) describing a survey for the Environmental Science Services Administration by a team of oceanographers scouting out the feasibility of a manned research and engineering station on the ocean bed. The *Times* reported that while Navy spokesmen "were cautious about discussing the military implications of the surveys, it is known that the Navy is interested in the data that has been obtained." The oceanographers concluded that there was no depth limitation on underwater stations, though costs could go very high. "Defense theorists as well as the Office of Naval Research have long toyed with the idea of underwater stations," the report said.

A classified Navy study of ocean engineering and deep submergence for 1970 to 1982 urges the Navy to develop a manned underwater habitat. The Navy will need the sea-bed station in the next ten years, the study says. Conducted by a small group of specialists from key Navy commands, the study recommends as a starter an underwater laboratory housing forty to one hundred scientists, to go into operation in the mid-seventies. The report suggests a number of projects, with five options ranging in cost from $2.9 billion to $3.8 billion for the next twelve years.

This first comprehensive plan for a twelve-year deep-ocean program was considered at the highest levels, and in March 1969, the $3.8 billion option was approved by the Department of Defense. The first appropriations for the new program should appear in the 1971 budget.

One of the central proposals in the report is a plan for two new submersible support systems named Argonaut. The Argonaut would launch, recover, and maintain two search vehicles without surfacing, support free divers, control unmanned vehicles, and deploy and recover underwater television, sonar, and communications devices.

According to the March-April 1969 issue of *Military Engineering,* the Navy has already signed contracts with General Dynamics, Westinghouse, and Southwest Research Institute to develop design specifications for a bottom-tethered, single-atmosphere station, housing a five-man crew for thirty days at six thousand feet. The Navy requires that the structure be independent of the surface, as versatile as possible, easily placed in any desired location, and reasonably priced. Final design of the station does not yet have Navy approval.

Meanwhile, the Navy Bureau of Yards and Docks is preparing to build underwater stations for such diverse uses as fuel caches, supply depots, refueling stations, submarine-repair facilities, nuclear-weapon shelters, and power generators. The bureau is presently conducting a series of experiments in California to test materials, components, and submersible devices, exposing them to corrosive sea water for periods ranging from six months to four years. This program is being conducted under the auspices of the Naval Civil Engineering Laboratory, and has been mentioned as one user of the search vehicle.

The Naval Undersea Research Center in San Diego has been studying another approach—an alternate to the

Sealab-style habitat. The project, known as Rocksite, would bury the underwater station in the ocean rock. The project began with a 1966 inspection tour of conventional sea mines. The idea is by no means new; records make note of undersea coal mines off England as early as 1575. However, all present-day subsea mines are tied to the land by an "air umbilical," or tunnel.

In 1967, Carl F. Austin, who had made the initial inspection tour, wrote, "A major goal of the Rocksite program is cutting this 'air umbilical' and achieving completely submerged and isolated undersea operations wherever valuable and geologically possible." The only limit Austin sees is the amount of rock available; he estimates that at least 20 per cent of the deep-ocean floor is bare rock and that another 40 per cent has bare rock within drillable distance of the sea floor. Surveying current mining technology and anticipating the development of the rescue vehicle with its dry-transfer capabilities, Austin concluded that "using only the tools and techniques of today's raw-materials industry, manned installations of a large size containing a one-atmosphere, shirt-sleeve environment can be built today on much of the world's continental slope, the deep ocean, and on seamounts and ridges."

"Some day, and a not too distant day at that," he predicts, "we will see men and their families living and working beneath the oceans. The tools and technologies exist today. How soon these possibilities become realities will depend on the vision and courage of both government and industry."

The idea was elaborated on in an issue of *Ocean Science News,* a newsletter given to some speculation:

> The Navy is thinking specifically in terms of subseafloor military bases, surveillance gear, manned missile stations, and providing logistic support and staging areas for military forces of the future. It is talking only secondarily about such forces

on the continental shelves. It is far more interested in the deep ocean–and the "deep ocean" in this context ballparks out to about six thousand feet, which not at all coincidentally is the depth of the higher peaks of the Mid-Atlantic ridge and of the guyots of the Pacific Ocean top. This is the kind of program which, if carried to its ultimate conclusion, would turn the federal ocean market into a major market indeed. . . . It's only a matter of time before the Polaris/Poseidon Fleet Ballistic Missile loses some of the security it enjoys in the black and briny depths. And, when Polaris subs can be found and tracked by the enemy, structures rising from the ocean floor will not enjoy a great deal of security either. But, an eight-foot diameter shaft into the deep ocean floor would be almost impossible to find–except, of course, by trailing the submarines that supplied it. Even in this instance, they might be very difficult to destroy, since the main facilities would probably be many hundreds of feet down into the seabed. And once ensconced in the seabed, there's no telling how far one might bore–right up into Red Square, or Peking, perhaps?

One project that does not, at this writing, have any government money is a joint proposal by the University of Miami and the Chrysler Corporation to build a series of undersea bases at depths of one thousand feet off the Florida coast. Entitled Project Atlantis, it has been shelved, at least temporarily. The project proposal, which states that these bases would eventually be built at depths up to twelve thousand feet, says the bases could serve as command and control centers for anti-submarine warfare operations, describing a string of manned stations along the Mid-Atlantic Ridge extending from Iceland to the tip of Africa. The project was billed as an opportunity for the Navy and private industry to collaborate in advancing technology. It could be of vital importance, as "the ability to occupy and control areas of the sea floor may eventually have political implications as significant as the military implications—the sea floor may become national property," the project proposal states.

According to an official with the Marine Sciences Council, everyone in government with money to spend on such projects has looked at Atlantis. Secretary of the Navy John Chaffee is reported to have been interested in the program, but found, according to one Navy spokesman, that there are simply no funds available for work of this kind. Nevertheless, Navy technical assistance in reviewing the initial design was promised. The Navy reportedly plans to pass Atlantis on to the Marine Sciences Council with the recommendation that it be adopted as a "national project." The current schedule for Atlantis—it has already slipped by six months—would see one habitat completed by the end of 1972, and experiments at one thousand feet beginning in 1973.

The most ambitious interdepartmental project is Tektite I, sponsored by the Navy, the National Aeronautics and Space Administration, the Department of the Interior, the Coast Guard, and General Electric. This is an experiment to test man's ability to live under the sea for long periods of time under saturated diving conditions—that is, where pressure inside the habitat and in the surrounding waters is the same. Four scientists spent sixty days in fifty feet of water off St. John, in the Virgin Islands, in the spring of 1969, marking the first undersea venture by a group of federal agencies with industry collaboration. There is speculation that Tektite II could involve a mobile habitat. The $2.5 million price tag on Tektite I was split evenly among the four participants.

General Electric has been working on the Tektite concept since 1966. The company initially financed the work, with the hope of attracting government money. Quoted in a September 1968 issue of *Data* magazine, G.E. systems engineer Ed Kronowski explained: "Our approach is from a generic technological point of view. Whatever markets open up, either defense or commercial, we will be ready where the market manifests itself. . . . Naturally things will center on the military first because that has always been the flow of events."

General Electric has been trying to assure itself a share of the DOT Program money. Kronowski suggests one argument to the military in the same article. "Why not use the rationale that money is needed now for a set of defensive stations—across the mid-Atlantic Ridge—to look up at the waters with sophisticated sonar? . . . A plan like this could get quantities of money pumped into it."

Describing business opportunities in the ocean, the *Harvard Business Review* recently suggested, ". . . the overall position of the United States in the field of oceanography appears quite similar to our position in the guided missile development in the early 1950's." This statement may be even more appropriate a description of the military scene. Expenditures in the engineering and development area, that is, spending for hardware, is a little over one hundred million dollars. Plans for the military use of the deep oceans go almost unpublicized. And while the general public may have no real idea of the potential in this area, the Navy is developing programs that will make a fourth front in the armaments race of the only true "wilderness" still left on Earth.

Summarizing Navy plans, John Craven has pointed out (in the April 1969 issue of *Astronautics and Aeronautics*) that only two factors are needed for weapons systems to become completely independent of the surface. The first is the ability to transfer cargo and personnel from one sub to another underwater. The second is the ability to transfer cargo and personnel to submerged terminals. The former is within grasp—the top-priority project in his office, the rescue vehicle, will have that capability. The latter will come more slowly. These technological developments will redefine the conditions for great powers, in effect making

U.S. forces supreme for the foreseeable future as "cost and total technical resources in a true submersible system are such that to date only the U.S. has been able to avail itself of this new capability in significant quantities."

Science for Whom?

The Navy's concern with the oceans is not limited to military activities. In 1969, a little more than half the Navy's oceanographic budget—$173.7 million—went for ocean science. As former Undersecretary of the Navy Robert H. B. Baldwin explained, ". . . the plain truth is, of course, that modern oceanography is absolutely essential to national security." More directly, an issue of *Nav-News,* published by the Navy Office of Information, explained the importance of oceanography for the Navy in the following terms: "Since 1952 virtually every weapons system or technique has required extensive oceanographic data to aid in its developmental stages." Or again, from Admiral David L. MacDonald, Chief of Naval Operations, "Since the free oceans of the world comprise our operating medium, every advance in understanding and predicting both physical and biological oceanography will be reflected immediately in improved naval warfare capability. For instance, at the operating depth of today's subs, each one hundred feet deeper a sub can dive adds nearly 2½ million cubic miles to the volume of water in which he can operate."

In 1966, a conscious decision was made to expand the Navy's involvement in ocean research. An issue of the official magazine of the Navy League led off with a statement by then Secretary of the Navy Paul H. Nitze, summarizing the Navy's rationale and intentions:

> In our year-long review of the Navy's programs, it was

obvious that while pursuing military objectives, the Navy has an obligation to the national interest in ocean technology; that since so many of our defense interests are identical with those other aspects of the national interest, we will—within the restraints imposed by cost—accept the responsibility for helping develop the national technology needed for mastery of the sea. . . . We must make certain that the United States, through both public and private enterprise, leads the world in working toward understanding and harnessing the ocean depths.

In August 1966, Secretary Nitze established the Office of the Oceanographer under the command of the Chief of Naval Operations and responsible to the Assistant Secretary for Research and Development. Headed by the capable Rear Admiral O. D. Waters, Jr., the office was to direct the Navy oceanographic program, comprising the following three offices: 1) The Assistant Oceanographer for Ocean Science, responsible for supporting academic and institutional scientists and engineers in private as well as Navy laboratories. 2) The Assistant Oceanographer for Oceanographic Operations, responsible for oceanographic survey work. 3) The Assistant Oceanographer for Engineering and Development, in charge of new projects which will shape the Navy of the 1980s and 1990s.

The trend toward involvement in basic science continues. In May 1967, John S. Foster, Jr., Director of Defense Research and Engineering, issued a policy statement indicating that defense agencies need not justify all their oceanology programs in purely military terms. He promised that the Department of Defense would provide funds for marine technology projects that were only partly military. In September 1967, a progress report on the Navy Engineering Program concluded: "It is obvious that while pursuing national defense objectives, the Navy would like to see its dollars do double duty in supporting the civilian sector as well as the military. The Navy has accepted the responsibility for helping to develop the undersea technology needed for effective use of the sea in the military, economic, social, and political sense. This must be a corporate venture: a science-industry-Navy team."

To what extent should the military take on responsibility for non-military research? Navy work in non-military oceanography is now so important that its marine sciences budget would be halved if the Navy were to restrict itself to projects that the Marine Sciences Council defines as national security projects. This development is largely due to the fact that the Navy has been the only agency able to wangle funds from Congress.

The Navy's dominant role in ocean studies is not a new one. In 1842, Lieutenant Matthew Fontaine Maury, considered the world's first true oceanographer, took charge of the Navy Depot of Charts and Instruments, soon renamed the U. S. Naval Observatory and Hydrographic Office. Using information laboriously compiled from old ships' logs and from a worldwide reporting system he set up, Maury drew a set of wind and current charts that helped the clipper ships of the nineteenth century set their speed records. Maury also published the first chart of the Atlantic Ocean floor, a chart that proved its worth when the first trans-Atlantic cable was laid. From this modest start—in 1849, three ships were assigned to deep-ocean survey duty—the Navy role has grown to the point where it now employs over one thousand civilian scientists and engineers at over one hundred universities and private institutions and at a dozen Navy laboratories. Although only one per cent of the Navy's budget is spent on oceanographic research, the Navy is still the nation's largest employer of oceanographers; the Office of Naval Research is the oldest (1946) and the largest ($20 million annually) government agency supporting research by scientists.

Some of the most important work in oceanography involves research on sonar equipment, the oceanographer's only tool for "seeing" into the ocean for significant distances. Light, radar, and other electromagnetic waves can penetrate only a few hundred feet. Sonar (Sound Navigation and Ranging) was invented by a civilian scientist at the U. S. Naval Academy in 1921.

Satellites are also used for oceanographic work, to observe, for instance, cloud patterns related to water temperatures, or to find large concentrations of marine life. Potential military applications are enthusiastically mentioned in several technical journals, citing the possibility of detecting submarines from satellites by photographing the "scars," that is, the wake, with infrared light, although many Navy officials indicate that the system is not very effective.

A review by Admiral Waters of the Navy's activities on ocean science demonstrates the extent of Navy interests. Waters lists the following areas:

1. Exploring and charting the oceans
2. Exploring and charting the ocean floor and sub-bottom
3. Examining sea water and its properties
4. Examining sound propagation and the effect of air-sea and bottom-sea interfaces in propagation
5. The effect of certain classes of marine life on men and equipment
6. The interaction between the ocean and the atmosphere
7. Ice formation and movement
8. The ocean's dynamics, the tides, and the currents
9. Testing and developing equipment to resist corrosion in the ocean water, as well as material capable of withstanding great pressures, for use in the ocean deep.

The Navy's wide range of interests and its dominant

role in ocean science have had a number of effects and brought along a score of problems. In a study initiated by the Navy to examine its role in oceanography, the Navy concedes with no little pride that most of the outstanding oceanographers' work is for the Navy. It stresses that the "fall-out" or non-military benefits from the work of these scientists are many, including new drugs, improved recreation facilities, unlimited fresh water, better weather-prediction services, and an increased food supply by tapping the sea's resources. Nevertheless, critics are beginning to claim that not only is the Navy doing too much work not immediately related to defense interests, but also that the concentration of oceanographic resources and manpower in the Defense Department has distorted the direction of scientific inquiry to meet military needs alone.

There is considerable evidence to support these criticisms. Project Bluewater, Phase I, the 1968 Navy study of its oceanographic program, identifies the issues very openly. Canvassing other federal agencies with responsibilities in oceanography, it finds a mixed reaction to the Navy's non-military research. For instance, despite a widely quoted statement by Oceanographer Waters that 90 per cent of ocean science research is unclassified and easily available, the Bluewater report admitted, ". . . there is considerable feeling that a considerable proportion of data is classified and therefore of very limited availability." Private industry nurses much the same feelings. Testifying before the Senate Foreign Relations Committee on July 2, John Crawford, of Crawford Marine Specialists, Inc., a small firm that engages in ocean mining, made the same charge. In an interview after the hearing, Crawford said, "Very little basic science research of any use undertaken by the Navy is available, though they stay legal by making it available in due time. But it takes forever. They [the Navy] believe the ocean belongs to them." (The National Academy of Sciences' Committee on Oceanography fought a hard campaign through the House Committee on Merchant Marine and Fisheries to force the Navy to declassify its soundings of the ocean floor and other oceanographic research. The Navy eventually approved the request, which had been pushed since World War II.)

The Bluewater study acknowledges that there are still problems. "Impediments to data exchange owing to slowness in processing, and unwillingness of investigators to release data until they have completed their reports, are under study by a committee."

Another criticism of the Navy oceanographic program stresses the military's relative neglect of marine biology. Marine biologists claim that their field has suffered seriously because the Navy, which controls how most of the money for oceanography is spent, has been uninterested in this field. "Biological oceanographers as a group are vehement in their belief that 'their' portion of oceanography has been discriminated against. They tended, more often than not, to blame the Navy for 'diverting' money into areas of more immediate interest to the Navy," the report says. The study's answer for the problem is that the Navy should begin to move into this field.

On balance, the Bluewater report's conclusions are, not surprisingly, flattering to the Navy. Although ambivalent about the Navy's preponderant role in oceanography, the report says that other federal agencies have a high regard for the quality of the work the Navy produces. One reason for this favorable opinion, the report speculates, may be the high number of ex-Navy officials dispersed throughout these agencies. It recommends that both the Navy and the National Science Foundation (which now funds 40 per cent of federal oceanographic work) should continue to sponsor research, with the Navy playing the major role. Bluewater cites agency officials outside the Navy to explain why the Navy must continue to lead the oceanographic effort. These officials, the study reports, stated their belief that the "national security" label carried by naval research allows the Navy consistently to obtain funds from Congress that would not be forthcoming if other agencies requested them.

Again, there is proof of similar attitudes outside the government. The Navy, which channels funds to approximately one hundred ten private labs for oceanographic work, is the main source of funds for non-government oceanography. Scientists with projects that other agencies have turned down for lack of funds, end up submitting their proposals to the Navy, altering only a few words in the original write-ups to suggest that their work will satisfy some military need.

Bluewater warns the Navy that no government agency considers the situation ideal, but accepts Navy dominance as "a concession to 'realism.'" Researchers for the study reported the following attitudes prevalent in rival agencies: The belief that times are changing, that while national security aspects of the ocean are most important today, technological change will make civilian uses of the ocean of far greater importance, and, therefore, that relative priorities should be changed; the belief that "science" would result if the Navy played a smaller role in setting priorities for ocean-science work; and a belief that current Navy funding of oceanography has already distorted the science by an overemphasis of the physical and underemphasis of the biological side.

In one attempt to solve these problems, the President's Commission on Marine Sciences, Engineering, and Development, in a report issued January 1969, urged the executive to set up an independent civilian agency responsible for the government's oceanographic programs. The report was held up until after the elections in an attempt to disassociate its recommendations from the outgoing President and make it politically acceptable to Nixon, who had promised "a grand strategy of the oceans" in his platform. So far, Nixon's only action has been to send the commission's recommendations back to the Marine Sciences Council, for further study.

Navy officials do not hide the fact that they are delighted that reorganization schemes have been put on ice. The plan to give all responsibility for non-defense-related research to an independent civilian agency was "insane," Navy Ocean Science Director J. Brackett Hersey said in an interview. "It makes no sense to divide up the research effort," he added.

Since the commission's recommendations have been tagged as a Democratic effort, there will be at least another year's delay before any comprehensive program is ready. "Essentially what that means for me," said John Craven, a member of a panel studying the Man-in-the-Sea effort, "is that we will resubmit our original recommendations, worded slightly differently, and then they'll be able to call it a Republican program." (President Johnson's plan for an International Decade of Ocean Exploration to begin in 1970 also has been set aside in Nixon's economy drive.)

There is little question that any successful move to reorganize the national oceanographic effort will have to come from the executive rather than through the Congress, where pressure from rival agencies would be too great. As Congressman Bob Wilson (D-Calif) explained before an oceanography subcommittee in 1969, his 1964 attempt to introduce a bill to reorganize the oceanography community brought him "fifteen of the saddest letters you ever saw in your life. . . . They would rather fight than switch." As one veteran observer of the oceanographic scene described it, ". . . the ocean-oriented and would-be ocean-oriented agencies of the federal government are engaged in an orgy of grabism and empire building such as has seldom afflicted this town."

Navy opposition to reorganization is long-standing. Their central argument is that there is no way of telling when basic research will prove vital in warfare. Had the Navy known of the existence of thermal layers in the ocean—layers of warm water—and their effect on sonar beams, many submarines could have been saved by using these layers to conceal their positions. Admiral Waters makes his position clear: "We have to do with a large amount of all the various disciplines that involve oceanography for national defense. We have to do these things, and a great deal of what we do is useful to other people. We hope that the machinery set up will recognize this and that there will be an easy way of giving our useful information to the people who need it. . . . The worst thing that could happen would be for someone to say, 'All right, Navy, you stay in your corner and do military oceanography, and let another, civilian agency over here do it for the civilians. . . .' The Navy doesn't want to be in the fishing business or the oil business . . . but the things we are doing will help them." This statement points out some of the difficulties in the Navy's position. It seeks to show at the same time that its work in oceanography is related to defense, yet is also useful to civilians; but could not be more effectively carried out by a civilian agency whose express purpose would be to serve civilian needs.

Finally, Bluewater's complaint that the oceanography needs of the Navy are not clearly defined presents some interesting insights on the haphazard nature of long-range Navy planning and the important role technological "progress" assumes in dictating military strategy.

Enter Private Industry

The most active commercial interests in the seas, and the Navy's chief rivals for the use of ocean space, are the fishing and oil industries. Navy statements tend to play down the competitive aspects of their relationship. "Government and industry must make common cause to assure American leadership in the whole field of oceanography, for the sake of our political and economic survival," Admiral Waters has written.

This is not quite how it has worked out. The fishing industry is generally equipped with World War II-vintage sonar for locating fish. The U.S. fishing fleet is considered greatly inferior to the new, highly efficient Japanese fleet, as well as to the Russian trawlers. And the fishing industry has not been overeager to establish close connections with the Navy. In an attempt to enlist the industry's help in accumulating oceanographic information, the Navy a few years ago launched Project Neptune, requesting fishing boats to take Navy instruments on board. The program had very limited appeal, with only four out of forty-three U.S.-flag companies contacted favorable to the scheme.

While there is little love lost for the Navy among fishermen, the oil industry's attitude toward the military is probably better described as a love-hate relationship. The industry obviously welcomes Navy investment and the resulting advances in deep-ocean technology, though again there are complaints about the unavailability of information. This time the grudge is reciprocal. The Navy complains that oil companies refuse to release the oceanographic data they accumulate surveying an area for oil. The Navy has also benefited from discoveries intended for the oil industry, such as saturated diving techniques, and more recently, the semi-submerged fuel-storage systems.

The real conflict between industry and the Navy is over the use of ocean space. As the oil industry moves into ever deeper water, first crisscrossing offshore areas with survey ships, then installing floating platforms, rigs, and bottom installations, congestion is becoming a serious problem. Navy surface maneuvers have been interrupted by industry activities. In a number of places, the industry moved into Navy testing ranges and confused anti-submarine listening devices by drilling in the area. The most publicized case has been the struggle over the Pacific Missile Testing Range, off Santa Barbara. To the Navy's great annoyance, the Department of the Interior leased out the area to an oil company. The Navy has also accused the Interior Department of leasing areas beyond the continental shelf. (The Geneva Conventions ratified by the United States in 1964 limit a nation's right to exploitation of the seabed to the continental shelf.) In California, the Navy claims, the oil industry has asserted title to stretches of sea floor beyond several deep trenches that should mark the edge of the shelf.

The Navy's problem with Interior's leasing arrangements is due, in part, to the fact that there is no way of settling conflicting claims between agencies or between industry and an agency. Project Bluewater, which also includes a case study of the Pacific Missile Testing Range controversy, predicts that such conflicts with the oil industry and with other commercial users will become more frequent. The offshore-oil industry is a fast-growing enterprise, with the oil industry investing another $4 million offshore each day. Sixteen per cent of known world oil reserves are now at sea, with these reserves expected to more than double by 1980. There are over twelve thousand wells off the United States now, with new ones being drilled at the rate of fourteen hundred a year. An easy resolution of conflicts between the industry and Navy is thought unlikely, with the Navy firmly rejecting any system that would award an area to the highest bidder.

Navy relations with defense industries are obviously much easier. The major contractors ardently woo the Navy for funds, and invest heavily in the hope of attracting Navy interest. This is the story of the General Electric Tektite Program. It is also the story of many of the independently funded deep-ocean submersibles that the major defense contractors are building. Some firms, such as Grumman, which developed its submersible, the Ben Franklin, under contract to the Navy for research on the Gulf Stream, work very closely with the Navy in designing crafts. They hope to recoup their investment by leasing out the crafts for fees ranging from twenty-five hundred dollars to six thousand dollars a day, and by landing future contracts. Also, a number of aerospace firms have contractual agreements with oil companies to develop underwater production systems. One example is a joint effort by North American Rockwell and Mobile Oil to develop a system for work at one thousand feet by early 1971.

Cooperation between industry and the Navy has been institutionalized in the National Security Industry Association and the American Ordnance Association, both of which have underwater divisions to do consulting work for the Navy. The American Ordnance Association, for instance, provides free advice from the defense industries. In return, they find out what programs and problems the Navy is interested in. "They never come to us with project specifications all laid down. The way we play it, you have two people who know the problem working *with* each other," an Ordnance official explained.

Ocean research and engineering in the United States keeps some one thousand firms occupied; a study by Arthur D. Little, Inc., of Cambridge, Massachusetts, shows that three hundred companies did 90 per cent of the work, and yet two thirds of them had contracts amounting to less than $1 million annually. The giants of the industry are the same firms that are involved in the aerospace defense market: General Dynamics, Westinghouse, Lockheed, General Electric, Grumman, Sperry Rand, General Motors, Honeywell, etc. The reason is simple. By the mid-1960s, the prospects for a deep-submersible market were looking bright, just as aerospace seemed to hit a ceiling. At a 1966 meeting in Orlando, Florida, the aero industries were told quite bluntly by NASA and Air Force officials that there was not enough space business to go around. A report of that meeting in the *Navy Magazine* noted: "The oceans, it was suggested, offer the best opportunity for future business." Until that time, the Navy had farmed very little of its oceanographic engineering projects out to industry, preferring to work through the Office of Naval Research. The aerospace industries were confident that this pattern would change as work proceeded on the Deep Submergence Systems Program and related programs, and foresaw that the extractive industries would need deep-sea vehicles.

Whose Ocean? Whose Seabed?

Perhaps the most serious differences between the Navy and industry revolve around legal questions. They have conflicting ideas of the law they would like to see enacted to regulate the use of the ocean. With a treaty to ban undersea weapon installations now under discussion at the Geneva Disarmament Conference, and technological advances testing the vague Geneva Conventions which limit jurisdiction over the sea floor to a nation's continental shelf, legal issues are becoming the focus for dispute.

Domestically, the oil industry is anxious for a quick resolution of the problem. It would like to feel secure about its right to recover oil, before assuming the risks of investing in an area. The oil industry is pushing for an agreement that would extend the definition of the continental shelf—and thus a nation's right to exploit ocean resources—to the base of the shelf, to the point where it reaches the ocean floor. The Geneva Conventions do not specify where the shelf ends, since oceanographic experts at the time the agreements were drawn up in 1958 did not expect that man would be able to penetrate the ocean depths. If the industry's position is adopted, large areas off the U.S. Atlantic coast where the continental shelf extends into the ocean could be claimed by this country.

Suspicious of international agencies, the oil industry has resisted any suggestions to internationalize the ocean floor and establish an international licensing agency. In 1968, the United States delegation to the United Nations abstained from voting on a proposal by the Secretary-General to study international machinery to regulate the ocean floors. Commenting on the U. S. Government's reluctance to back any form of internationalization, Senator Claiborne Pell has remarked: "I think it is quite evident that the petroleum industry has been able to block the Administration's acceptance of any other position than the industry's."

The importance of this dispute can hardly be overestimated. As John Craven has written, "The problem is a key one, because even a marginal exploitation of ocean resources will give the controlling institution a probable majority of the world's wealth."

Craven is not the first to notice this. Peru has staked its claim to the sea area up to two hundred miles from its coast, and other developing nations are expected to follow suit in what may turn into a hectic scramble to control the oceans. President Johnson warned of this in a 1966 speech. "Under no circumstances, we believe, must we ever allow the prospects of rich harvest and mineral wealth to create a new form of colonial competition among the maritime nations. We must be careful to avoid a race to grab and to hold the lands under the sea. We must insure that the deep seas and the ocean bottoms are, and remain, the legacy of all human beings."

The Navy is in complete agreement. Traditionally, the Department has maintained that the seas must be kept free to allow all ships passage, with the territorial waters as narrow as possible. The United States claims only three miles from its shores, whereas many other nations, including the Soviet Union, favor a twelve-mile limit. The reasons are simple. The U. S. Navy is easily the most powerful maritime force in and on the oceans. The more room it has to operate, the farther it can extend this power. Navy officers fear that once a nation lays claim to the ocean floor off its coast, it will automatically extend its jurisdiction to the water column above, thus excluding warships.

The Navy's views on the territorial sea are national policy at present. The prevailing attitude in the Navy and the government at large regarding the continental shelf now is to leave the present situation unchanged. A report, by a special subcommittee of the Senate Foreign Relations Committee, on the United Nations study group looking into an international licensing agency, urges the government to consider the idea with extreme caution and not to rush into the area. The report admits that, in doing this, the United States will be aligning itself against the underdeveloped nations, who favor an international agency as the only way they are likely to benefit from ocean exploitation.

Who may claim the ocean floor and how much of it are not the only important questions. In 1969, the nineteen-nation Geneva Disarmament Conference discussed an agreement limiting weapons systems to be allowed on the ocean bed. The Soviet version of such a treaty proposed that "the use for military purposes of the seabed and the ocean floor and the subsoil thereof beyond the 12 mile maritime zone of coastal states is prohibited. It is prohibited to place on the seabed and the ocean floor and the subsoil thereof objects with nuclear weapons or any other types of weapons of mass destruction, and to set up military bases, structures, installations, fortifications, and other objects of a military nature."

The United States dismissed the proposal as a publicity stunt. "It is simply unworkable and probably harmful," said Gerard C. Smith, director of the Arms Control and Disarmament Agency. In effect, the clause "and other objects of a military nature" ruled out use of the ocean bottom for military purposes including listening posts and surveillance. Arguing that the Soviet treaty was much too broad and therefore unenforceable, the United States rushed out its own version a month later. The key clause in the U.S. treaty reads: "Each state party to this treaty undertakes not to emplant or emplace fixed nuclear weapons or other weapons of mass destruction or associated fixed launching platforms on, within, or beneath the seabed and ocean floor beyond a narrow band as defined in Article II [three miles] adjacent to the coast of any state."

The U.S. position that "the freedom of the seas is vital for the defense of the nation" and that "the Defense Department and the Navy are in agreement with the U.S. treaty" provide some clues to U.S. intentions. Over and over, in interviews, Navy officials emphasized that they are profoundly uninterested in bottom-fixed "weapons of mass destruction." They explained that fixed installations are easily detectable and thus more vulnerable. "You have to figure the Soviets know where an installation is twenty minutes after we start building it." John Craven summed it up in an interview: "The U.S. treaty is an exercise in sophistry. It bans systems no one would build anyway. There is no point in fixing things to the bottom, since it's just as easy to make them movable."

The weaknesses in the seabed treaty were further brought out in a series of exchanges before the Senate Foreign Relations Committee in July 1969. Questioning witness William Hancock of the State Department, Senator Clifford Case asked whether the U.S. treaty covered weapons capable of destroying communications systems. (Such a weapon could neutralize an entire navy.) Hancock finally admitted it did not. Senator Pell went on to ask for a definition of "mobile." Would a craft that was designed to move, but in fact did not, be considered mobile? Again, Hancock was nonplused. He finally said that a treaty including mobile weapons could not be negotiated at this time and that the problem of definition was too complex.

How does the Navy justify its undersea plans? Why does it believe these weapons systems are needed? One answer by Robert Frosch, is, ". . . as civilian activities increase in the ocean, the Navy will have to move and take advantage of the technology to protect U.S. nationals. The movement of American extractive enterprises out to the deep sea and the ocean floor has produced pressure for a deep-sea Coast Guard." A 1967 progress report on the Ocean Engineering Program states that "international confrontation" as nations turn to the sea to fill their needs is almost inevitable. The same report makes another telling point in justifying the need for advanced undersea military technology: "Major changes may be sought in the scope and interpretation of current laws and conventions pertaining to the oceans and their resources. Historically, the presence of effective military power at strategic locations in oceans has exerted a significant influence on the negotiations to effect such changes." In other words, a sophisticated deep-ocean weapons technology is needed to give the United States a decisive voice in deciding how political and economic control of the oceans will be distributed.

There is little question in the military of how such a distribution should work out. "Perhaps it is an oversimplification, but in my mind these programs can best be described as the development of a technology leading toward the occupation and the exploitation of the ocean bottom and the deep ocean," former Navy Undersecretary H. B. Baldwin said at a Symposium on Man's Extension into the Sea. Baldwin went on to urge "mastery [of the sea] in the military, economic, social, and political sense." Edward Wenk, executive secretary of the National Council on Marine Resources and Engineering Development, made the point even more explicitly: "The ocean could become a fifty-first state."

The Navy also argues that a land war is now so frightful that it makes more sense to move weapons into the sea and away from population centers. One scientist states, ". . . the Navy has devoted considerable attention recently to the idea of a limited war at sea," while the *Armed Forces Journal* (March 1969) says, "Navy-minded people contend that the nation should base more and more of its military strength at sea." This argument might be dismissed as a Navy puff job, but with the capabilities and the invulnerability of land forces under increasingly critical questioning, the case to be made for Polaris and other sea-based systems looks more attractive.

With the evident U.S. dominance in the sea, references to the Soviet threat in order to justify expanding the underwater program are rare. Discussion of Soviet capabilities deals almost exclusively with their oceanographic program. They are thought to be ahead in aspects of oceanography neglected by the United States, especially in some aspects of basic research and in fishing. The Soviet oceanographic fleet is larger, and the government also makes greater use of merchant and shipping vessels for research purposes. One observer summarized the Russian effort: "The Russians are not to be laughed at. They may be driving Model T's, but there are a lot of them, and they are good mechanics."

However, the Soviet Union is far behind in deep-sea technology. The U.S.S.R. offered to buy a General Dynamics Star III for a generous $2.5 million, but the U. S. Government turned thumbs down on the deal. They performed one Sealab-style experiment in 1968 in thirty-three feet of water and were expected to try for sixty-six feet during the summer of 1969. The Soviet Union did send a bathyscaphe to a deep point in the Marianas Trench some months before the *Trieste* descent, but the Soviet *Vityaz* was unmanned. The United States is the only nation doing spacecraft oceanography, and its anti-submarine detection system is far in advance of anything the Russians have developed. "There are at present no areas where we know Soviet technology to be significantly ahead of U.S. work," John S. Foster, Jr., Director of Defense Research and Engineering, has stated to the Senate Armed Services Committee.

Unless it is stopped, the U. S. Navy will extend the arms race to the ocean depths and extend the American military presence into the farthest reaches of nature's watery realm.

NOTES

The sources of most quotes are identified in the body of the text.

Chief Oceanographer Waters' speech, delivered in San Diego, June 5, 1967, and other speeches, are available from the Office of Naval Information, the Pentagon.

Information on the DSSP is available in an article by Gene Mayhall in *Data* magazine, Sept. 1968.

An article by R. Ramsey in *Naval Ships Technical News,* Oct. 1968, shows a chart which breaks down the DOT Program into the purely military missions, military missions with commercial spin-off, and purely commercial missions. Ramsey is a Navy officer with the Submarine and Special Types Design Branch, Naval Ship Engineering Center.

Armed Forces Management, Nov. 1968, discusses the Deep Ocean Technology Status Report. The existence of this study is also noted in the Oct. 1968 issue of the *Oceanology Newsletter.*

Project Bluewater, the Navy study of its oceanography program, can be obtained from the Office of Naval Information, the Pentagon.

"20,000 Guns Under the Sea," by Seymour Hersh, *Ramparts,* Aug. 1969, deals with many of the issues raised in this paper and draws similar conclusions.

APPENDIX

There are a handful of groups around the country that are researching various aspects of the national security establishment and American foreign policy. A list of these groups, with brief descriptions of their activities, follows. Also included is a guide to research on the defense establishment, compiled by the North American Congress on Latin America. Lastly, there is an outline of course readings, which proved valuable in organizing a seminar around the questions of national security, foreign policy, and the military-industrial complex.

RESEARCH/ACTION GROUPS RELATED TO MILITARY AND FOREIGN AFFAIRS

1. National Action/Research on the Military-Industrial Complex (NARMIC)

A project of the American Friends Service Committee, designed to aid community groups in taking action against the military-industrial complex. Provides information on defense contracts, military installations, weapons systems, etc., and publishes guides to help local groups.
160 North 15th Street, Philadelphia, Pa. 19102. 215-LO3-9372

2. New Mobilization Committee to End the War in Vietnam (NEW MOBE)

Provides information on the Vietnam War, taxes, and the draft, and is conducting research on the military activities of major American corporations.
1029 Vermont Avenue, N.W., Washington, D.C.

3. North American Congress on Latin America (NACLA)

Publishes a regular newsletter as well as separate pamphlets about American imperialism in Latin America. NACLA has also published excellent guides to military research conducted by American universities, and a research methodology guide.
P.O. Box 57, Cathedral Station, New York, N.Y. 10025. 212-749-6513

4. Pacific Studies Center

Publishes a regular newsletter on American penetration into the Pacific area.
1963 University Avenue, Palo Alto, Calif.

5. Union of Radical Political Economists (URPE)

Aims at organizing radical economists to research various aspects of the American economic system, with a view toward change. URPE organizes conferences and publishes a regular bulletin.
P.O. Box 287, Cambridge, Mass. 02138

6. Committee of Concerned Asian Scholars (CCAS)

Publishes a regular journal dealing with events in Asia, and holds annual and regional conferences.
1737 Cambridge Street, Room 305, Cambridge, Mass.

7. Student Action Co-ordinating Committee (SACC)

Group of young scientists that organized the March 4 research-stoppage day on campuses. Publishes a regular newspaper and pamphlets on weapons research.
SACC Office, Massachusetts Institute of Technology, Cambridge, Mass.

HOW TO RESEARCH THE MILITARY*

A. DEPARTMENT OF DEFENSE AGENCIES AND BASES

1. AGENCIES

All major Department of Defense (DOD) agencies are identified and described briefly in the *United States Government Organization Manual,* published annually. The manual also identifies the principal military and civilian officers in charge of the various agencies. DOD libraries, laboratories, and information centers are described in the *Directory of Information Resources in the United States: Federal Government.* Organizational charts of major DOD agencies and commands, providing names of key officers, are available on a subscription basis from the *U. S. Organization Chart Service.* DOD agencies concerned with research, development, and procurement are described in the *DMS Market Intelligence Report on Agencies, Facilities, and Laboratories.* Telephone numbers of all DOD agencies and key personnel are listed in the *Department of Defense Telephone Directory.*

Most military agencies distribute brochures describing their major activities and functions, intended for use by military recruiters, vocational guidance counselors, college placement offices, etc. These are usually available upon request from the DOD agency itself, or from military recruiting offices (these can be located by looking in the telephone book under United States Government and then the particular service). Most libraries have a vocational or career section, where such documents are stored.

Descriptions of individual DOD agencies frequently appear

* Copyright reserved, North American Congress on Latin America. The complete NACLA Research Methodology guide is available from NACLA, P. O. Box 57, Cathedral Station, New York, N.Y. 10025. $1.25, postpaid.

as feature articles in the military periodicals (see section 4 of category B, Military Posture, for a list of these publications); especially useful in this regard are: *Armed Forces Management, Data,* and *Defense Industry Bulletin.*

2. BASES

All Army bases in the United States are listed in *United States Army Installations and Major Activities in the Continental United States.* All Air Force bases and agencies in the United States are listed and described briefly in the annual Almanac Issue of *Air Force and Space Digest,* usually published in the fall. A list of Navy and Marine Corps bases, "Navy and Marine Corps Activities in the United States," is available upon request from the Office of the Chief of Naval Operations, Department of the Navy, Washington, D.C. 20350. All Army, Navy, and Air Force installations in the United States are listed in the *U. S. Military and Government Installation Directory Service.* DOD bases both within and outside the United States are discussed in the annual hearings on Military Construction Authorizations (see section on Hearings in category B, Defense Posture).

3. BOOKS ON THE MILITARY SERVICES

Among books on the U. S. military, attention should be called to the "Praeger Library of U. S. Government Departments and Agencies," published by Frederick A. Praeger (111 Fourth Avenue, New York, N.Y. 10003). Titles in this series include: *The Department of Defense,* by C. W. Borklund; *The United States Navy,* by Capt. Daniel J. Carrison; *The United States Marine Corps,* by Col. James A. Donovan, Jr.; *The United States Air Force,* by Erig. Gen. Monro MacCloskey; and *The United States Army,* by Lt. Col. Vernon Pizer. Each volume in the series contains a short history of the Service and a general description of its organization. Praeger also publishes *A Guide to National Defense,* by Lt. Col. Patrick W. Powers, which provides an overview of the national security establishment.

B. DEFENSE POSTURE AND STRATEGY

1. DOD ANNUAL REPORTS

A general description of the status of U.S. military forces and planned weapons acquisitions appears in the annual posture statement of the Secretary of Defense, which is usually reproduced in the hearings on Department of Defense Appropriations and Military Procurement Authorizations (see section #2, below). At the beginning of 1969, the then Secretary of Defense, Clark Clifford, issued his posture statement, *The 1970 Defense Budget and Defense Program for Fiscal Years 1970–74,* which describes the strategic world environment from the Pentagon's point of view, and identifies the major weapons systems that the DOD seeks to acquire in the coming five years. The Defense Department also has issued an *Annual Report,* the most recent of which is dated 1966.

2. HEARINGS

A basic source of information on U.S. military strategy and weapons development is the annual series of Congressional hearings on the DOD budget. The hearings are usually held in the spring, and the transcripts published in the fall. These documents are available from the Congressional committees involved, from local congressmen and senators, and from the Government Printing Office; they are also stored in Government Depository Libraries (usually the largest municipal or university library in each state), which are listed in the *Monthly Catalog of United States Government Publications.*

Four sets of budget hearings are held each year: hearings before the Senate and House Armed Services Committee on military authorizations, and hearings before subcommittees of the Senate and House Appropriations Committee on military appropriations. The precise titles are: "Department of Defense Appropriations for Fiscal Year 19**,"

Hearings Before the Department of Defense Subcommittee of the House (Senate) Committee on Appropriations; and "Military Procurement Authorizations for Fiscal Year 19**," *Hearings Before the House (Senate) Armed Services Committee.* Hearings on military construction appropriations are held separately; these are identified as "Military Construction Authorization Fiscal Year 19**," *Hearings Before the Committee on Armed Services and Subcommittee on Military Construction of the Senate (House) Committee on Appropriations.*

The hearings consist of budget statements and testimony by DOD officials, followed by questioning from the committee members. Although these reports contain a cursory index, it is usually necessary to hunt for information on specific weapons or policies. The most valuable reports are the volumes on Procurement and on Research & Development of the House Appropriations Subcommittee hearings.

Debate before the full House and Senate on the DOD budget is recorded in the *Congressional Record;* this is a particularly valuable source of information, since many congressmen insert documentary material on the military to supplement their spoken remarks.

Special hearings on various military matters are sometimes called by Congressional committees, particularly the Senate Foreign Relations Committee and the Senate and House Committees on Government Operations. For a complete list of all such documents, consult the *Monthly Catalog of United States Government Publications.*

3. U. S. MILITARY TREATIES

The complete test of all collective defense treaties to which the United States is a signatory appear in *Collective Defense Treaties,* compiled by the House Committee on Foreign Affairs. In past years, the Senate Foreign Relations Committee, under the chairmanship of Sen. J. W. Fulbright, has held hearings on various aspects of U.S. treaty commitments to foreign powers. For a list of these hearings, consult the *Monthly Catalog of United States Government Publications.*

4. ARTICLES ON MILITARY STRATEGY AND POSTURE

Articles on U.S. military strategy and the status of military forces appear regularly in many newspapers and magazines, particularly the New York *Times*, the Washington *Post*, *The Christian Science Monitor*, and *U. S. News and World Report*. Longer articles, often written by military personnel, frequently appear in the military journals, including: *Air Force and Space Digest*, *Airman*, *Armed Forces Journal*, *Army*, *Army Digest*, *Army Research and Development Newsmagazine*, *Aviation Week and Space Technology*, *Data*, *Defense Industry Bulletin*, *Marine Corps Gazette*, *Navy*, and *Ordnance*.

A number of publications are concerned primarily with questions of tactics and strategy; these include: *Adelphi Papers*, *Air University Review*, *Army Quarterly and Defense Journal*, *Military Review*, *Naval War College Review*, *Royal United Service Journal*, and *U. S. Naval Institute Proceedings*.

5. BOOKS

Several publishing firms specialize in books on military affairs, and will send price lists on request; among the most prominent firms in this field are Frederick A. Praeger (111 Fourth Avenue, New York, N.Y. 10003) and Stackpole Books (Cameron and Kelker Streets, Harrisburg, Pa. 17105).

C. MILITARY THINK-TANKS AND MILITARY ASSOCIATIONS

1. MILITARY THINK-TANKS

Several non-profit research organizations, or "think-tanks," publish reports on U.S. military strategy and related subjects, usually under contract to the Department of Defense. Among the most active organizations of this sort are: The RAND Corporation, the Institute for Defense Analyses (IDA), the Hudson Institute, and the Stanford Research Institute (SRI).

Most of the major military think-tanks are described in NACLA's *The University-Military Complex.*

Non-classified strategic studies commissioned by the U. S. Government are sold through the Clearinghouse for Federal Scientific and Technical Information, and are listed in the *U.S. Government Research and Development Reports.* Classified studies are listed in the *Technical Abstract Bulletin;* RAND memoranda are also listed in *Selected RAND Abstracts,* and can be ordered directly from RAND (1700 Main Street, Santa Monica, Calif. 90406); RAND documents are also stored in selected "depository" libraries (usually the largest municipal and/or university library in each state). IDA and Hudson studies are usually listed in their annual reports, which are available upon request (IDA, 400 Army-Navy Drive, Arlington, Va. 22202; Hudson Institute, Quaker Ridge Road, Croton-on-Hudson, N.Y. 10520). SRI will send upon request a catalog of Stanford Research Institute Publications Available for Distribution (write: Publications Dept., SRI, Menlo Park, Calif. 94025).

2. MILITARY ASSOCIATIONS

There are a number of private, non-profit organizations concerned with military affairs, to which the public may belong. These organizations are pro-military in their orientation, and maintain close ties with the Armed Services. Each of the organizations publishes a journal and holds annual meetings for members. These journals are particularly interesting because they are much more forthright in discussing U.S. military affairs than the public-relations officers of the Services themselves. The annual meetings are equally interesting; usually held in the fall and in the Washington, D.C., area, they often include appearances by leading military officials, and feature briefings by industrial representatives on new weapons systems. The military associations include:

(*a.*) The American Ordnance Association (819 Union Trust Bld. Washington, D.C. 20005), organized in 1909 to promote "military preparedness" (i.e., increased defense spending), is an important lobby for military contractors. The AOA publishes *Ordnance,* a bimonthly journal, and *The*

Common Defense, a monthly Washington newsletter (both publications sent free to members–annual fee: $7.00).

(*b.*) The Association of the United States Army (AUSA, 1529 18th Street, N.W., Washington, D.C. 20006) publishes *Army* (sent free to members–annual fee: $6.00).

(*c.*) The Air Force Association (AFA, 1750 Pennsylvania Avenue, N.W., Washington, D.C. 20006) publishes *Air Force and Space Digest* (sent free to members–annual fee: $7.00).

(*d.*) The Navy League of the United States (818–18th Street, N.W., Washington, D.C. 20006) publishes *NAVY: The Magazine of Seapower* (subscription rate: $3.00 per year).

(*e.*) The Marine Corps Association (Box 115, Marine Corps Base, Quantico, Va. 22134) publishes the *Marine Corps Gazette* (sent free to members–annual fee: $5.00).

D. MILITARY PUBLICATIONS AND TECHNICAL REPORTS

1. DOD PUBLICATIONS

Specialized reports and publications issued by the Defense Department and the four Armed Services, and available to the public, are listed, by subject, in the Price Lists of Government Publications, available free from the Superintendent of Documents, Government Printing Office, Washington, D.C. 20402. The following price lists are of particular interest (order by number): *Army,* #19; *Navy,* #19 (includes Marine Corps publications); *Air Force,* #79; *Defense,* #85.

2. MILITARY PERIODICALS

Military periodicals published by the U. S. Government are listed in the Government Printing Office's Price List #36, Government Periodicals and Subscription Services, available free from the Government Printing Office. Most military periodicals published in the United States are indexed in the Air University Library Index of Military Periodicals, available in large libraries. The Standard Guide to Periodical Literature, available in the reference sections of most libraries, has a list of military periodicals. Most of the important military periodicals are listed in the bibliography which follows these notes on research procedures.

3. MILITARY MANUALS

Technical information on specific weapons systems, military tactics, and military regulations is contained in Army, Navy, Air Force, and Marine Corps field manuals, technical manuals, and training manuals. These manuals, if not classified, are listed in the Monthly Catalog of United States Government Publications and are available from the Government Printing Office or the public information staffs of the respective Services (see: L. Where to Go for More Information, below). These manuals are also stored in the Government Depository Libraries, identified in the Monthly Catalog. One manual that is particularly useful as a reference is the Dictionary of United States Military Terms for Joint Usage.

Among the manuals of particular interest are: Army ROTC Manual ROTCM-145-30, *Individual Weapons and Marksmanship* (September 1966); Army Technical Manual TM 9-1325-200, *Bombs and Bomb Components* (April 1966); Army Matériel Command Pamphlet 700-3-3, *Logistics: Complete Round Charts, Artillery Ammunition* (December 1967); Army Field Manual FM 3-10, *Employment of Chemical and Biological Agents* (March 1966); Army Technical Manual TM 3-215, *Military Chemistry and Chemical Agents* (December 1963); Army Technical Manual FM 3-216, *Military Biology and Biological Agents* (March 1964).

E. WEAPONS SYSTEMS

The annual posture statement of the Secretary of Defense (see above, category B, Defense Posture) contains general descriptions of all the major weapons systems included in the Pentagon's budget request. In 1969, the Democratic Study Group of the House of Representatives published a *Fact Book on the FY 1970 Defense Budget,* which contains a critique of the Pentagon's proposals for weapons acquisition. Descriptions of present and proposed U.S. weapons systems are discussed in the hearings on the DOD budget (see section on Hearings in category B, Defense Posture) and described thoroughly in the various military manuals (see section on Military Manuals, immediately above).

In general, the best sources of information on new weapons systems are the military periodicals (see section 4 of category B above for a list of these publications). The two weekly magazines *Armed Forces Journal* and *Aviation Week and Space Technology* are particularly useful when following debate on the acquisition of new weapons systems. *Aviation Week* publishes an annual Forecast Issue, usually in the spring, which includes a specifications directory of all U.S. aircraft, missiles, and helicopters. *Air Force and Space Digest* publishes an annual Almanac Issue, usually in the fall, which describes most Air Force planes and missiles. Each issue of *Ordnance* contains sections on Air Armament, Missiles and Astronautics, Underwater Ordnance, Chemical-Biological Defense, and Weapons Technology.

Chemical, biological, incendiary, and anti-personnel weapons used by the United States are described in *The Weapons of Counterinsurgency*. Other sources of interest are: *The Military Balance,* which contains an inventory of the strategic weapons possessed by each of the major military powers; and *Jane's Fighting Ships, Jane's Aircraft,* and *Jane's Weapon Systems,* which contain detailed descriptions of all ships and planes in the world.

F. MILITARY CONTRACT AWARDS

1. DAILY ANNOUNCEMENTS

Defense Department contract awards are announced daily in press releases issued by the Office of the Assistant Secretary of Defense for Public Affairs (OASDPA) in the Pentagon, Washington, D.C. 20301 (telephone numbers: for information, 202-OX7-5131; for copies of press releases, 202-OX7-3189). These press releases are usually published in *The*

Wall Street Journal. (The contract awards announced in *The Wall Street Journal* are indexed by company name in the annual Wall Street Journal Index, available in most large libraries.) DOD contracts are also included in the list of government contract awards that appears in *Commerce Business Daily.*

2. MONTHLY ANNOUNCEMENTS

Cumulative monthly lists of all DOD contracts over $1 million appear in *Defense Industry Bulletin.* All Army contracts over $1 million are listed monthly in *Army Research and Development Newsmagazine.*

3. ANNUAL CONTRACT LISTS

An annual cumulative list of all DOD production contracts appears in the Government Contracts Directory. Contract awards for specific weapons systems and those awarded by specific DOD agencies are listed in the *DMS Market Intelligence Reports,* published annually on a subscription basis. The total value of all contracts awarded to the one hundred largest DOD contractors is reported annually in the Pentagon's computation of *100 Companies and Their Subsidiaries Listed According to Net Value of Military Prime Contract Awards* available from the Office of the Assistant Secretary of Defense for Public Affairs (see #1 above) and published in *Defense Industry Bulletin.*

4. OTHER CONTRACT LISTS

For a list of contracts for the production of anti-personnel, incendiary, and chemical weapons, see NARMIC's Local Research/Action Guide No. 1, *Weapons for Counterinsurgency.* For NASA and Atomic Energy Commission contracts, see category K below.

5. THE MILITARY-INDUSTRIAL COMPLEX—GENERAL INFORMATION

A number of recent books and studies are concerned with the economics of military contracting, including: Richard J.

Barnet's *The Economy of Death* (New York: Atheneum, 1969); Ralph E. Lapp's *The Weapons Culture* (New York: W. W. Norton & Co., 1968); Clarence H. Danhof's *Government Contracting and Technological Change* (Washington, D.C.: The Brookings Institution, 1968); and Hitch and McKeen's *The Economics of Defense in the Nuclear Age* (Cambridge, Mass.: The Harvard University Press, 1969). Also useful is *Congressional Quarterly*'s special report *The Military-Industrial Complex.* Among the recent hearings devoted to this subject are *Government Procurement and Contracting,* held by a subcommittee of the House Committee on Government Operations. For a list of publications of the Defense Contract Audit Agency (DCAA), the agency responsible for overseeing all DOD contracts, write for DCAA Index of Publications Available to the Public, DCAA, Cameron Station, Alexandria, Va. 22314.

G. MILITARY RESEARCH CONTRACTS

1. CONTRACT ANNOUNCEMENTS

Research and development (R&D) contracts are included in the sources noted in the preceding section; in addition, the following sources are useful: *R&D Contracts Monthly* contains a monthly cumulative list of R&D contracts; the *R&D Directory* contains an annual cumulative list of R&D contract awards. Both these sources are cross-indexed by company (or non-profit organization) and by the DOD agency monitoring the project. The total value of all DOD contracts awarded to the five hundred largest R&D contractors is provided in *500 Contractors Listed According to Net Value of Military Prime Contract Awards for Research, Development, Test, and Evaluation Work.*

2. PROJECT DESCRIPTIONS

Non-classified Pentagon-financed research projects are described in the *U. S. Government Research and Development Reports,* and classified projects are described in the *Technical*

Abstract Bulletin; these biweekly publications contain abstracts (capsule summaries) of research reports submitted to the Department of Defense. Abstracts of research reports sponsored by the Air Force are published annually in *Air Force Research Résumés.* RAND Corporation reports are described in *Selected RAND Abstracts.*

Pentagon-sponsored research projects are often discussed at length during the hearings on the defense budget, and this testimony is often an excellent source of information (see section on Hearings, under category B, Defense Posture). Most useful is the volume on Research and Development of the hearings before the House Appropriations Committee Subcommittee.

The various *DMS* (Defense Marketing Service) *Market Intelligence Reports,* published by McGraw-Hill, contain much detailed information on military R&D; these reports are sold mainly to corporations, investment firms, and a few universities.

The research agencies of the military Services each publish journals that contain information on the status of current research projects; the Army Research Office publishes *Army Research and Development Newsmagazine,* the Office of Naval Research publishes *Naval Research Review,* and the Office of Aerospace Research (OAR) publishes *OAR Research Review.*

H. IDENTIFYING LOCAL WAR CONTRACTORS

There are a number of procedures that can be used to identify local war contractors. The Records Management Branch of the Office of the Assistant Secretary of Defense for Administration (OASD/A) will supply, for a small charge, a list of all DOD procurement contracts in a given state; the list shows, for each city within the state, the name of the contractor and the total amount of contracts awarded in the current fiscal year. A price list of these tables can be obtained by writing: Records Management Branch, Correspondence and Directives Division, OASD(A), The Pentagon, Washington,

D.C. 20301. Government Data Publications, Inc., sells a Government Production Prime Contractors Directory, which lists DOD contractors by postal ZIP code. The local offices of the Defense Contract Administration Services Region (or District) will provide, upon request, a list of Department of Defense prime contractors in its jurisdiction, identifying the products manufactured by each contractor. These offices, located in most large cities, can be found by looking in the telephone book under United States Government, Department of Defense, Defense Supply Agency.

Firms that specialize in research and development can be identified through a number of sources. Industrial Research Laboratories of the United States and The Research Centers Directory are two library reference books that contain geographic indexes of R&D firms. Many states publish similar directories, which are listed in the Guide to American Directories, found in most libraries; the Commerce Department of New York State, for instance, will supply upon request the Directory of Industrial Research Laboratories in New York State. A number of city and state chambers of commerce have published similar directories.

Most government agencies will be helpful in answering questions concerning defense contracts as long as the intent does not appear too sinister. The offices of Defense Supply Agency and Small Business Administration, located in most large cities, will usually indicate if a specific company in their jurisdiction has received military contracts. The contract-awarding agency *within* the DOD will also answer specific questions upon request; most Army ammunition contracts, for instance, are awarded by the Army Matériel Command, Joliet, Ill.

I. INVESTIGATING MILITARY PROJECTS ON CAMPUS

The sources listed in categories F and G, Military Contract Awards and Military Research Contracts, all include university contracts. Since military work at universities is mostly limited to research, the sources in category G should be consulted first; the R&D Directory is particularly useful in this regard. NACLA's *The University-Military Complex* lists DOD-sponsored university research on chemical and biological warfare and on foreign affairs. For sources on NASA and Atomic Energy Commission contracts, see category K below. Procedures that can be followed in an investigation of military work at universities are described below.

1. RESEARCH CENTERS

Most military contracts awarded to universities are held by semiautonomous research centers and research foundations. A complete list of these centers, cross-indexed by university, can be found in The Research Centers Directory, available in the reference sections of most large libraries. Most university-based research centers are also listed in *Industrial Research Laboratories in the United States.* Both these directories describe the primary field of research of each center, identify the principal officers, and provide other useful information. Research centers primarily devoted to military research are also described in NACLA's *The University-Military Complex.*

Most of the larger research centers publish annual reports and/or publicity newsletters, which describe their current research activities and often indicate sources of financing. These publications are usually supplied on request, but sometimes a good way to get them is to say you're interested in working there upon graduation. Direct contact with members of the staff, or interviews arranged through the campus newspaper, will often elicit useful information on these centers not available from other sources.

2. INDIVIDUAL, GROUP, AND DEPARTMENTAL RESEARCH PROJECTS

Military contracts held by individual professors, research teams, or academic departments are frequently difficult to investigate, because the sums of money involved are relatively small (and thus do not appear in some of the sources noted above) and because university administrations are often uncooperative in providing necessary information. The *U. S. Government Research and Development Reports* and *Technical Abstract Bulletin* are both cross-indexed by university and principal investigator, and thus should be consulted early in an investigation. Most universities publish lists of research contracts held by the faculty, or will permit people to examine such lists on request (these lists are usually kept in the projects-and-grants office of the university, the research office, or an equivalent). Sometimes it is necessary to undertake an anti-secrecy campaign to force the university to make these records public. While such lists usually omit much information, knowledge of any particulars (i.e., faculty name, project title, DOD contract number) can be used to obtain additional information when checked against the data obtained from the R&D Directory, *U. S. Government Research and Development Reports,* and *Technical Abstract Bulletin.*

Projects conducted by a university department are often described in departmental minutes, which can usually be examined by a sympathetic faculty member. Some departments publish annual reports, research progress reports, or similar documents, which should also be examined. Most large universities publish staff newsletters and/or research newsletters, which announce contract awards and describe current research projects; material of this sort is usually available from the university news office or contract-and-grant office. Some university libraries also maintain special collections devoted to the university's history, which often contain useful information (materials such as departmental records, minutes of trustees' meetings, and back issues of newsletters and annual reports). Reporters from the campus newspaper often have access to university records and other materials not available to the public, and should be recruited for investigations of this sort; campus reporters can also arrange interviews with research personnel and thereby obtain information not available in printed sources.

3. INVESTIGATING UNIVERSITY PERSONNEL

It is sometimes important to investigate the background of key individuals in order to establish a pattern of cooperation with the military. Most universities will provide journalists (or campus reporters) with biographies of faculty and administrators; these documents are usually available from the university news office or publicity office. Research centers and academic departments will also provide such information. Who's Who in America and other standard biographical dictionaries are also useful in compiling biographies. Certain specialized "Who's Whos," available in the reference sections of most libraries, are also very useful; in particular, one should consult American Men of Science, Who's Who in Engineering, American Men of Medicine, Who's Who in American Education, Presidents and Deans of American Colleges and Universities, Directory of American Scholars, and Who's Who in Space. Most of these sources will indicate if an individual is a consultant to the government or an officer of a corporation or other organization. Members of the various military advisory committees (Defense Science Board, etc.) are identified in NACLA's *The University-Military Complex.*

4. PROJECT THEMIS

In 1967, the Department of Defense established Project THEMIS to exploit research talents at the smaller universities; for a description of this project, write for *Project THEMIS: A Program to Strengthen the Nation's Academic Institutions* from the Office of Defense Research and Engineering (ODRE), The Pentagon, Washington, D.C. 20301. All THEMIS projects completed through December 1968 are described in DDC Report #587, *Report on THEMIS Project,* available from ODRE. Fiscal year 1969 THEMIS projects are listed in NACLA's *The University-Military Complex.*

5. RESEARCH STATISTICS

The National Science Foundation (NSF) has published a series of statistical surveys on government-sponsored research activities. These include: Dynamics of Academic Science; Federal Support to Universities and Colleges, Fiscal Years 1963–66; and Federal Support to Universities and Colleges, Fiscal Year 1967. The two-volume series on Federal Support to Universities and Colleges contains tables indicating the total amounts of federal spending, by agency, at the one hundred largest university recipients of federal aid. The DOD's table of *500 Contractors Listed According to Net Value of Prime Contract Awards for Research, Development, Test, and Evaluation Work,* published annually, indicates the total value of DOD contracts at universities with substantial military research work. General statistics on the proportion of research funds to general university revenues are provided in *Financial Statistics of Institutions of Higher Education,* compiled by the National Center for Educational Statistics of the U. S. Office of Education.

6. UNIVERSITY-MILITARY RELATIONSHIPS—GENERAL INFORMATION

Several books and studies are worth consulting when organizing a campaign against university-conducted military research. Books on the subject include James Ridgeway's *The Closed Corporation* (New York: Random House, 1968; also in paperback) and two studies published by the Brookings Institution in Washington, D.C.—*The Effects of Federal Programs on Higher Education* (1962), by Harold Orlans, and *The Role of the Federal Government in Financing Higher Education* (1961), by Alice M. Rivlin. NACLA's *The University-Military Complex* also contains valuable background information. A study commissioned by the American Assembly of Columbia University, *The Federal Government and Higher Education,* contains several essays on this subject and includes a description of all federal programs in the area of higher education. The Stanford Research Institute's "R&D Study Series" includes a report on *The Role of the University in Defense R&D,* which contains useful information.

In 1965, a subcommittee of the House Committee on Government Operations held a series of hearings on "Conflicts

Between the Federal Research Programs and the Nation's Goals for Higher Education," which elicited considerable information, in the form of statistics and testimony, from government and university officials.

J. SCIENCE, RESEARCH, AND THE GOVERNMENT

In the past few years, government (especially military) sponsorship of scientific research has become a major issue in the scientific and academic communities. Information sources on this subject are described below.

1. BIBLIOGRAPHIES

The Government Department of the University of Indiana has published Science, Technology, and Public Policy: A Selected and Annotated Bibliography under the sponsorship of the National Science Foundation. The Battelle Memorial Institute, of Columbus, Ohio, publishes a bimonthly journal of bibliographic entries, *Science Policy Bulletin.* The Subcommittee on Government Research of the Senate Committee on Government Operations has published An Inventory of Congressional Concern with Research and Development, which lists Congressional documents issued by the Eighty-eighth and Eighty-ninth Congresses, and the First Session of the Ninetieth Congress.

2. PERIODICALS

A number of scientific periodicals have given special emphasis to this subject, including: *Bulletin of the Atomic Scientists, Science,* and *Scientific Research.*

3. STATISTICS

The National Science Foundation (NSF) has published many volumes of statistics and analysis on government expenditures for research and development; for a complete list, see Government Printing Office Price List #31, Education, available free from the Government Printing Office. Among the most valuable titles are: *Federal Funds for Research, Development, and Other Scientific Activities;* the series on *Research and Development in Industry; Scientific Activities of Nonprofit Institutions;* and *R&D Activities in State Government Agencies.*

4. SRI'S R&D STUDIES SERIES

The Stanford Research Institute (SRI) holds a contract from the Director of Defense Research and Engineering to produce a series of studies on the "structure and dynamics of the R&D industry," known as the R&D Study Series. Publications in this series include: *An Exploratory Study of the Structure and Dynamics of the R&D Industry* (1964); *The Economic Impact of Defense R&D Expenditures: In Terms of Value Added and Employment Generated* (1966); *The Structure and Dynamics of Exploratory Development in Defense R&D Industry* (1966); and *The Role of the University in Defense R&D* (1966).

K. NASA, ATOMIC ENERGY, CIVIL DEFENSE

1. NASA

The National Aeronautics and Space Administration (NASA) publishes a *Semi-Annual Report to Congress* describing major programs. The NASA budget is discussed in hearings before the Senate Committee on Aeronautical and Space Sciences on *NASA Authorization for Fiscal Year 19***. For more information on NASA, contact: Office of Public Affairs, NASA, 600 Maryland Avenue, S.W., Washington, D.C. 20546 (phone 202-963-5302).

NASA's Office of Grants and Research Contracts publishes an annual list of Grants and Research Contracts. Research reports commissioned by NASA are abstracted and indexed in Scientific and Technical Aerospace Reports, available in most university libraries. Other NASA publications are listed in Government Printing Office Price List #79, Space, available from the Government Printing Office.

2. ATOMIC ENERGY AND THE AEC

The Atomic Energy Commission (AEC) publishes an annual report on *Major Activities in the Atomic Energy Programs,* which describes AEC programs and operations, lists AEC costs incurred by universities and industrial contractors, and contains other basic data. The AEC also publishes an annual *Financial Report,* which contains more-detailed information on AEC contracts and expenses. The AEC's budget is discussed in *Hearings Before the Joint Committee on Atomic Energy* on "AEC Authorizing Legislation, Fiscal Year 19**." AEC annual reports and further information are available from: Atomic Energy Commission, Washington, D.C. 20545 (phone: 301-973-1000).

AEC publications are listed in Government Printing Office Price List #84, Atomic Energy and Civil Defense, available free from the Government Printing Office. Other useful publications, including a Directory of Reactors, are issued by the International Atomic Energy Agency of the United Nations. The Committee to End Radiological Hazards, Box 148, 150 Christopher Street, New York, N.Y. 10014, has published a series of reports for the layman on dangers arising from U.S. atomic energy programs (price list available on request).

Information concerning the atomic energy policies of the U. S. Government is contained in: *Atomic Energy Act of 1946 and Amendments; Atomic Energy Legislation Through the 90th Congress, 1st Session; Atomic Energy Commission Rules and Regulations;* and *Atomic Energy Commission Reports: Opinions and Decisions of the Atomic Energy Commission.* For a history of the AEC, see the Pennsylvania State University Press series, which includes: *The New World 1939–1946* and *Atomic Shield 1947/52.*

AEC research programs are described in an annual report on *Fundamental Nuclear Energy Research.* Research reports commissioned by the AEC are abstracted and indexed in *Nuclear Science Abstracts,* available in most university libraries. A number of quarterly journals on nuclear technology are published by the AEC, including: *Isotopes and Radiation Technology, Reactor and Fuel-Processing Technology,* and *Reactor Materials.*

The military uses of atomic energy are described in a number of AEC publications, including: *Effects of Nuclear Weapons, Naval Nuclear Propulsion Program,* and *Principles of Guided Missiles and Nuclear Weapons.*

Industrial applications of atomic energy are described in an annual AEC report on *The Nuclear Industry.* Also useful in this regard are various hearings and reports issued by the Joint Committee on Atomic Energy, including: *Nuclear Power Economics* and *Licensing and Regulation of Nuclear Reactors.* See also *Civilian Nuclear Power.*

3. CIVIL DEFENSE

The Office of Civil Defense publishes an *Annual Report* describing major activities. Publications on Civil Defense are listed in Government Printing Office Price List #84, Atomic Energy and Civil Defense, available free from the Government Printing Office.

L. WHERE TO GO FOR MORE INFORMATION

Listed below are several agencies, military and nonmilitary, that are prepared to answer requests for information from the public. In general, the military services are cooperative in answering such requests. It is helpful to address such questions to the specific military agency concerned (e.g., questions concerning Army research activities should be addressed to the Assistant Secretary of the Army for Research and Development); most military agencies are described in the United States Government Organization Manual, and their telephone numbers are listed in the Department of Defense Telephone Directory. General questions can be addressed to the following:

1. INSIDE THE MILITARY

(*a.*) Department of Defense: Office of the Assistant Secretary of Defense for Public Affairs (OASDPA), The Pentagon, Washington, D.C. 20301 (phone numbers: for information, 202-OX7-5131; for copies of DOD press releases, 202-OX7-3189). Will answer questions pertaining to DOD affairs, and supply copies of DOD press releases.

(*b.*) Department of the Army: Staff Management Division, Office of the Chief of Staff, Department of the Army, The Pentagon, Washington, D.C. 20310 (phone: 202-OX5-6700, extension 78841). Will answer questions pertaining to Department of the Army affairs. The Office of the Chief of Information, Department of the Army, The Pentagon, Washington, D.C. 20310, will also answer questions from the public. The Army also maintains public affairs offices in several large cities, listed in their telephone books under United States Government, Department of the Army.

(*c.*) Air Force: Directorate of Administration, Department of the Air Force, The Pentagon, Washington, D.C. 20330 (phone: 202-OX5-2246), will answer questions pertaining to Air Force affairs. The Office of the Director of Information, The Pentagon, Washington, D.C. 20330, will also answer questions.

(*d.*) Navy: Administrative Office, Navy Department, Main Navy Building, Eighteenth Street and Constitution Avenue, N.W., Washington, D.C. 20360 (phone: 202-OX6-2221), will answer questions pertaining to Navy affairs. The Office of Information, Navy Department, Washington, D.C. 20350, will also answer questions.

(*e.*) Marine Corps: The Commandant of the Marine Corps, Navy Department, Washington, D.C. 20380 (phone: 202-OX4-2500), will answer questions pertaining to Marine Corps affairs.

2. OUTSIDE THE MILITARY

(*a.*) Movement research centers: A number of independent research centers have been set up to assist groups opposing the military-industrial complex, and will answer questions from the public. These include National Action/Research on the Military-Industrial Complex (NARMIC), 160 N. Fifteenth Street, Philadelphia, Pa. 19102 (phone: 215-LO3-9372), and the National Security Research Project, P.O. Box 11004, Washington, D.C. 20008 (phone: 202-234-9382).

(*b.*) Military associations: The various pro-military associations are usually willing to answer questions from their members, usually by directing people to the appropriate military agency. For a list of these associations, with addresses and membership information, see category C, Military Associations.

3. LIBRARIES

(*a.*) The Army Library, located on the first floor of the Pentagon, is open to the public and contains most of the periodicals, directories, manuals, etc., described above. (It is suggested that users of this library dress neatly.)

(*b.*) The Library of Congress, 10 First Street, S.E., Washington, D.C., is open to the public and contains many of the periodicals, directories, etc., described below.

(*c.*) Municipal, state, and university libraries: Most of the larger public libraries store the basic military journals and publications. Often, these will be located in specialized collections–science, engineering, etc. A number of libraries have been designated Government Depository Libraries and receive copies of all non-classified military manuals and Congressional hearings. A list of these libraries appears in the *Monthly Catalog of United States Government Publications.*

BIBLIOGRAPHY

Note: U. S. Government Printing Office (GPO) orders should be sent to: Superintendent of Documents, Government Printing Office, Washington, D.C. 20402. GPO prices are subject to revision; to be sure of price, write for the appropriate GPO Price Lists.

Adelphi Papers. Published irregularly by the Institute for Strategic Studies (18, Adam Street, London W.C.2, United Kingdom). Available from the Institute for $.75 each or on a subscription basis for $6.75 per year (price includes copy of *The Military Balance*). For a list of recent papers in this series, write the Institute.

Aerospace Daily. Valuable source on aerospace industry. $2.50 a year. 1156 Fifteenth Street, N.W., Washington, D.C.

Air Force and Space Digest. Monthly journal of the Air Force Association (1750 Pennsylvania Avenue, N.W., Washington, D.C. 20006). Subscription included with annual membership fee of $7.00.

Air Force Research Résumés. Published annually by the Office of Aerospace Research. Available from the Clearinghouse for Federal Scientific and Technical Information, U. S. Dept. of Commerce, Springfield, Va. 22151.

Airman. Official monthly magazine of the U. S. Air Force. Available from the GPO. Subscription rate: $4.00 per year.

Air University Library Index of Military Periodicals. Published quarterly by the Air University Library, Maxwell Air Force Base, Ala. 36112. Sent to libraries on an exchange basis.

Air University Review. Published bimonthly by the Air University Library. Available for $4.50 per year from Air University Book Department, Maxwell AFB, Ala. 36112.

Armed Forces Journal. Published weekly by Army and Navy

Journal, Inc. (1710 Connecticut Avenue, N.W., Washington, D.C. 20009). Subscription rate: $10 per year.

Armed Forces Management. Published monthly by American Aviation Publications (1156 Fifteenth Street, N.W., Washington, D.C. 20005). Subscription rate: $12 per year.

Army. Monthly journal of the Association of the U. S. Army (1529 Eighteenth Street, N.W., Washington, D.C. 20006). Subscription included with annual membership fee of $6.00.

Army Digest. Published monthly by the Department of the Army. Available from the GPO. Subscription rate: $3.50 per year.

Army Quarterly and Defense Journal. Published monthly by W. Cloves & Sons, Ltd. (Dorland House, 14 & 16, Lower Regent Street, London S.W.1, United Kingdom).

Army Research and Development Newsmagazine. Published monthly by the Army Research Office. Available from the GPO. Subscription rate: $2.25 per year.

Atomic Energy Act of 1946 and Amendments, Aug. 1, 1946–Oct. 13, 1966. Available for $.65 from the GPO.

"AEC Authorizing Legislation, Fiscal Year 1969," *Hearings Before the Joint Committee on Atomic Energy,* 90th Cong., 2d Sess., 1968. In two parts; part 1 available from the GPO for $2.75.

Atomic Energy Commission, Major Activities in Atomic Energy Programs, 1968 Annual Report. Available for $1.75 from the GPO.

Atomic Energy Commission, 1969 Financial Report. Available for $.65 from the GPO.

Atomic Energy Commission Reports; Opinions and Decisions of Atomic Energy Commission with Selected Orders. Available from the GPO. Vol. 1, 1956–61, $3.75; vol. 2, 1962–64, $3.50; vol. 3, 1965–67, $2.50.

Atomic Energy Commission Rules and Regulations. Available on a subscription basis from the GPO for $7.00. Subscription includes accumulated regulations through January 1966, plus all amendments for an indefinite period.

Atomic Energy Legislation Through the 90th Congress, 2d Sess., Dec. 1968. Report issued by the Joint Committee on Atomic Energy. Available for $1.50 from the GPO.

Aviation Week and Space Technology. Published weekly by McGraw-Hill Publications. Subscription rate: $10 per year (address for subscriptions: Aviation Week, P.O. Box 430, Hightstown, N.J. 08520). Subscriptions must be requested on company or organization letterhead.

Bulletin of the Atomic Scientists. Published monthly by the Educational Foundation for Nuclear Science (1100 E. Fifty-eighth Street, Chicago, Ill. 60637). Subscription rate: $6.00 per year.

Civilian Nuclear Power, A Report to the President, 1962. Available for $.45 from the GPO. Appendices ($.55) and 1967 supplement ($.40) also available.

Collective Defense Treaties. Published 1969 by the House Committee on Foreign Affairs. Available for $2.50 from the GPO.

Commerce Business Daily. Published weekdays by the U. S. Department of Commerce. Available from the GPO. Subscription rate: $15 per year.

100 Companies and Their Subsidiaries Listed According to Net Value of Military Prime Contract Awards. Published annually by the Directorate for Statistical Services of the Office of the Secretary of Defense. Available upon request from the Office of the Assistant Secretary of Defense for Public Affairs, The Pentagon, Washington, D.C. 20301.

"Conflicts Between the Federal Research Programs and the Nation's Goals for Higher Education," *Hearings Before the Research and Technical Programs Subcommittee of the House Committee on Government Operations,* 89th Cong., 1st Sess., June 14, 15, and 17, 1965. See also the compendium of "Responses from the Academic and Other Interested Communities" to the Subcommittee's inquiry (Aug. 1965), and the 18th Report of the Committee on Government Operations (Oct. 13, 1965)—both these documents bear the same title as the Hearings.

Congressional Record. Published daily while Congress is in session. Available from the Government Printing Office. Subscription rate: $1.50 per month. A limited number of free subscriptions available from local congressmen.

500 Contractors Listed According to Net Value of Military Prime Contract Awards for Research, Development, Test, and Evaluation Work. Published annually by the Directorate for Statistical Services of the Office of the Secretary of Defense. Available upon request from the Office of the Assistant Secretary of Defense for Public Affairs, The Pentagon, Washington, D.C. 20301.

Data on Defense & Civil Systems. Published monthly by Queensmith Associates, Inc. (West Building, Washington National Airport, Washington, D.C. 20001). Suspended publication, spring, 1970.

Defense Industry Bulletin. Published monthly by the Office of the Assistant Secretary of Defense for Public Affairs (OASDPA). Subscription is free if requested on company or organization letterhead. Address for subscriptions: Editor, Defense Industry Bulletin, OASDPA, The Pentagon, Washington, D.C. 20301.

DMS Market Intelligence Reports. Published by the Defense Marketing Service (DMS), a subscription service of McGraw-Hill Publications (DMS, Inc., 100 Northfield Street, Greenwich, Conn. 06830). Subscription price includes basic directory, monthly revisions, and consultation services. Total DMS service costs $2140 per year; individual services (each $300) include: Missiles and Spacecraft; Military Aircraft; Electronic Systems; Ships/Vehicles/Ordnance; Agencies, Facilities, and Laboratories.

Department of Defense Annual Report. Available from the GPO. Price varies; most recent available, 1966, costs $1.75.

The 1970 Defense Budget and Defense Program for Fiscal Years 1970–74, Statement by Secretary of Defense Clark M. Clifford, Jan. 15, 1969. Available for $1.75 from the GPO.

Department of Defense Telephone Directory. Published quarterly. Available on a subscription basis from the GPO. Subscription rate: $10 per year; single issue, $2.50.

Directory of Industrial Research Laboratories in New York State. Published by the Department of Commerce, State of New York, Albany, N.Y. (available on request)

Directory of Information Resources in the United States: Federal Government. Compiled by the National Referral Center for Science and Technology of the Library of Congress. Available for $2.75 from the GPO.

Directory of Reactors: Power, Research, and Training Reactors Around the World. Published by the International Atomic Energy Agency of the United Nations, New York, N.Y.

Dictionary of United States Military Terms for Joint Usage. Published by the Joint Chiefs of Staff. Available for $2.00 from the GPO.

Dynamics of Academic Science. A Degree Profile of Academic Science and Technology and the Contribution of Federal Funds for Academic Science to Universities and Colleges. Published 1967 by the National Science Foundation (NSF). Available for $.60 from the GPO.

Effects of Nuclear Weapons. Published 1964 by the AEC. Available for $3.00 from the GPO.

Fact Book on the FY 1970 Defense Budget. Published 1969 by the Democratic Study Group, U. S. House of Representatives, Washington, D.C. 20515. (available upon request)

Federal Funds for Research, Development, and Other Scientific Activities. Published by the NSF. Available from the GPO. Vol. 13, FY 1963–65, $1.25; vol. 15, FY 1965–67, $1.25; vol. 16, FY 1966–68, $1.25.

The Federal Government and Higher Education. Prepared by the American Assembly of Columbia University. Published by Prentice-Hall, Inc. (a Spectrum Book, 1960, Englewood Cliffs, N.J.)

Federal Support to Universities and Colleges. Published by the NSF. Available from the GPO. *Fiscal Years 1963–66,* $.70; *Fiscal Year 1967,* $1.00.

Financial Statistics of Institutions of Higher Education, Current Funds, Revenues, and Expenditures, 1965–66. Published by the National Center for Educational Statistics of the Office of Education. Available for $.70 from the GPO.

Fundamental Nuclear Energy Research. Published annually by the AEC. Available from the GPO. Price varies: 1964, $2.00; 1965, $2.25; 1966, $2.50; 1967, $2.50; 1968, $4.25.

Government Contracts Directory. Published by Government Data Publications, Inc. (422 Washington Building, Washington, D.C. 20005). Comprises three volumes: an Awardee Directory (list of contracts held by DOD contractors); an Agency Directory (contracts listed by awarding agency within the government); and a Product Directory (contracts listed by type of product). All three volumes cost $99.50; each volume is also available singly.

"Government Procurement and Contracting," *Hearings Before a Subcommittee of the House Committee on Government Operations,* 91st Cong., 1st Sess., 1969.

Government Production Prime Contractors Directory. Published by Government Data Publications, Inc. (422 Washington Building, Washington, D.C. 20005). List of DOD contractors in Postal ZIP Code order. Price: $15.

History of the Atomic Energy Commission. Published by the Pennsylvania State University Press (University Park, Pa.). Vol. 1, *The New World 1939/1946,* by Oscar E. Anderson, Jr., and Richard G. Hewlett; Vol. 2, *Atomic Shield 1947/1952,* by Richard G. Hewlett and Francis Duncan.

Industrial Research Laboratories of the United States. Edited by William W. Buchanan and published by Bowker Associates, Washington, D.C.

Inventory of Congressional Concern with Research and Development. A Bibliography Prepared for the Subcommittee on Government Research of the Senate Committee on Government Operations. In two volumes: 88th and 89th Congresses (issued Dec. 15, 1966) and 90th Cong., 1st Sess. (issued Sept. 23, 1966).

Isotopes and Radiation Technology. A quarterly technical progress review published by the AEC. Available from the GPO. Subscription rate: $2.50 per year.

Jane's Aircraft. Published in Great Britain; agent in the U.S.: Charles E. Thorp, 175 Greenwich Avenue, Greenwich, Conn. 06830. Price: $49.50.

Jane's Fighting Ships. Availability: same as above.

Jane's Weapon Systems. Availability: same as above.

"Licensing and Regulation of Nuclear Reactors," *Hearings Before the Joint Committee on Atomic Energy*, 90th Cong., 1st Sess., 1967. Available from the GPO. Part 1, $1.75; Part 2, $1.25.

Marine Corps Gazette. Monthly journal of the Marine Corps Association (Box 1775, Marine Corps Base, Quantico, Va. 22134). Subscription included with annual membership fee of $5.00.

The Military Balance. Published annually by the Institute for Strategic Studies (18, Adam Street, London W.C.2, United Kingdom). Sold separately for $2.00, or by subscription with the *Adelphi Papers* for $6.75 per year.

The Military-Industrial Complex. Special report of Congressional Quarterly (1735 K Street, N.W., Washington, D.C. 20006). Price: $2.50.

Military Review. Monthly journal of the U. S. Army Command and General Staff College. Subscription rate: $4.00 per year (address for subscriptions: Book Department, U. S. Army Command and General Staff College, Fort Leavenworth, Kas. 66027).

Monthly Catalog of United States Government Publications. Published and distributed by the GPO. Subscription rate: $4.50 per year.

"NASA Authorization for Fiscal Year 1969," *Hearings Before the Committee on Aeronautical and Space Sciences*, U. S. Senate, 90th Cong., 2d Sess., 1968. Available from the GPO. Part 1, $1.00; Part 2, $1.50; Part 3, $1.25.

National Aeronautics and Space Administration, Semi-Annual Report to Congress. Available from the GPO. Price varies; most-recent available, the fifteenth, is $1.00.

"Naval Nuclear Propulsion Program, 1967–68," *Hearings Before the Joint Committee on Atomic Energy,* 90th Cong., 1st and 2d Sess., Mar. 16, 1967, and Feb. 8, 1968. Available for $1.50 from the GPO.

Naval Research Reviews. Published monthly by the Office of Naval Research. Available from the GPO. Subscription rate: $1.75 per year.

Naval War College Review. Monthly journal of the U. S. Naval War College. Available upon request to authorized persons (address requests to Naval War College, Newport, R.I. 02844).

Navy: The Magazine of Seapower. Monthly journal of the Navy League of the United States (818 Eighteenth Street, N.W., Washington, D.C. 20006). Subscription rate: $3.00 per year.

Nuclear Industry, 1968. Published by the AEC. Available for $2.00 from the GPO.

Nuclear Power Economics, 1962–67. A report of the Joint Committee on Atomic Energy, 1968. Available for $1.00 from the GPO.

Nuclear Science Abstracts. Published semimonthly by the AEC. Available from the GPO. Subscription rate: $42 per year. Quarterly, annual, and cumulative indexes also published.

OAR Research Review. Published monthly by the Office of Aerospace Research. Available from the GPO. Subscription rate: $3.00 per year.

Office of Civil Defense Annual Report. Available from the GPO. Price varies; most-recent available, 1967, $.55.

Ordnance. Bimonthly journal of the American Ordnance Association (616 Transportation Building, Washington, D.C. 20006). Subscription included with annual membership fee of $7.00.

Praeger Library of U. S. Government Departments and Agencies. Published by Frederick A. Praeger (111 Fourth Avenue, New York, N.Y. 10003). Series includes: *The Department of Defense,* by C. W. Borklund; *The United States Navy,* by Capt. Daniel J. Carrison; *The United States Marine Corps,* by Col. James A.

Donovan, Jr.; *The United States Air Force,* by Brig. Gen. Monro MacCloskey; and *The United States Army,* by Lt. Col. Vernon Pizer.

Principles of Guided Missiles and Nuclear Weapons. Available for $2.00 from the GPO.

Reactor and Fuel-Processing Technology. A quarterly technical progress review published by the AEC. Available from the GPO. Subscription rate: $2.50 per year.

Reactor Materials. A quarterly technical progress review published by the AEC. Available from the GPO. Subscription rate: $2.50 per year.

R&D Contracts Monthly. Published by Government Data Publications, Inc. (422 Washington Building, Washington, D.C. 20005). Subscription rate: $24 per year.

R&D Directory. Published annually by Government Data Publications, Inc. (422 Washington Building, Washington, D.C. 20005). Price: $15.

Research and Development Activities in State Government Agencies, Fiscal Years 1964–65. Published by the NSF. Available for $.45 from the GPO.

Research and Development in Industry, 1965; Basic Research, Applied Research, and Development in American Industry, 1965, a Final Report on a Survey of R&D Funds, 1965, and R&D Scientists and Engineers, Jan. 1966. Published 1967 by the NSF. Available for $.65 from the GPO.

Research Centers Directory, 2d ed., 1966. Edited by A. M. Palmer and A. T. Kruzas; published by Gale Research Co., Detroit, Mich. A periodic supplement, *New Research Centers,* is also available.

Resources for Scientific Activities at Universities and Colleges, 1964; A Preliminary Report of a Survey of 1964 Expenditures and Jan. 1965 Employment in the Sciences and Engineering. Published 1966 by the NSF. Available for $.20 from the GPO.

Royal United Service Journal. Published quarterly by the Royal United Service Institution (Whitehall, London S.W.1, United Kingdom).

Science. Published weekly by the American Association for

the Advancement of Science (1515 Massachusetts Avenue, N.W., Washington, D.C. 20005). Subscription included in annual membership fee of $12.

Science Policy Bulletin. Published bimonthly by the Battelle Memorial Institute (505 King Avenue, Columbus, Ohio 43201). Available upon request.

Science, Technology, and Public Policy: A Selected and Annotated Bibliography. Edited by Lynton K. Caldwell and published 1969 by the Department of Government, University of Indiana (Bloomington, Ind.). Available upon request.

Scientific Activities of Non-Profit Institutions, 1964 Expenditures and Jan. 1965 Manpower. Published 1967 by the NSF. Available for $.60 from the GPO.

Scientific and Technical Aerospace Reports. Published semimonthly by NASA. Available from the GPO. Subscription rate: $54 per year. Quarterly and annual cumulative indexes also available.

Scientific Research. Published semimonthly by McGraw-Hill Publications (330 West Forty-second Street, New York, N.Y. 10036). Subscription rate: $20 per year; applications must indicate organizational affiliation and position (limited to scientific fields).

Selected RAND Abstracts. Published quarterly by the RAND Corporation (1700 Main Street, Santa Monica, Calif. 90406). Subscription rate: $15 per year; annual cumulative edition, $5.00.

"Stanford Research Institute R&D Studies Series." Each report available for $5.50 from Publications Department, SRI, Menlo Park, Calif. 94025. Titles include: *An Exploratory Study of the Structure and Dynamics of the R&D Industry* (1964); *The Structure and Dynamics of the Defense R&D Industry: The Los Angeles and Boston Complexes* (1965); *The Economic Impact of Defense R&D Expenditures: In Terms of Value Added and Employment Generated* (1966); *The Structure and Dynamics of Research and Exploratory Development in Defense R&D Industry* (1966); *The Role of the University in Defense R&D* (1966).

Technical Abstract Bulletin. Published semimonthly by the Defense Documentation Center, U. S. Department of Defense, Alexandria, Va. This publication was given a "Confidential" security classification in Sept. 1967 and is now available only to authorized persons. Earlier issues are available in some college libraries.

U. S. Army Installations and Major Activities in the Continental United States. Published by the Department of the Army. Available for $.25 from the GPO.

U. S. Government Organization Manual. Published annually by the General Services Administration. Available for $3.00 from the GPO.

U. S. Government Research and Development Reports. Published semimonthly by the Clearinghouse for Federal Scientific and Technical Information, U. S. Department of Commerce, Springfield, Va. 22151. Available in most libraries.

U. S. Military and Government Installation Directory Service. Published by the U. S. Organization Chart Service (P.O. Box 15175, San Diego, Calif. 92115). Subscription price of $60 per year includes basic directory plus three quarterly revisions.

U. S. Naval Institute Proceedings. Monthly journal of the U. S. Naval Institute (Annapolis, Md. 21402). Subscription rate: $8.50 per year.

U. S. Organization Chart Service. Published by U. S. Organization Chart Service (P.O. Box 15175, San Diego, Calif. 92115). Subscription price of $225 includes basic directory plus three quarterly revisions.

The *University-Military Complex: A Directory and Related Documents.* Published 1969 by NACLA (P.O. Box 57, Cathedral Station, New York, N.Y. 10025). Price: $1.25.

The *Weapons of Counterinsurgency: Chemical, Biological, Anti-Personnel, Incendiary.* Published by National Action/Research on the Military Industrial Complex (160 N. Fifteenth Street, Philadelphia, Pa. 19102). Price: $1.00.

A COURSE OUTLINE

National Security and the Military-Industrial Complex

This reading list is based on a semester course offered at the University of Maryland, spring 1970. The purpose is to provide a critical introduction to the operation of the state and economy as related to national security policy.

I. INTRODUCTION. STATE AND ECONOMY

"Is There a Military-Industrial Complex Which Prevents Peace?" by Tom Hayden and Mark Pilisuk, *Journal of Social Issues,* Vol. XXI, no. 3, reprinted in *The Triple Revolution,* eds. Pilisuk and Penucci (Little, Brown, 1968).

The Military-Industrial Complex–a special report, *Congressional Quarterly,* May 24, 1968, no. 21.

" 'We Must Guard Against Unwarranted Influence by the Military-Industrial Complex,' " by Richard Kaufman, *The New York Times Magazine,* June 22, 1969.

The Economy of Death, by Richard Barnet (Atheneum, 1969).

"National Security in Perspective," address by Rep. L. Mendel Rivers, *Congressional Record,* June 12, 1969.

II. NATIONAL SECURITY POLICY

The Common Defense, by Samuel Huntington (Columbia University Press, 1961).

Containment and Change, by Carl Oglesby and Richard Shaull (Collier, 1967).

The Essence of Security, by Robert McNamara (Harper & Row, 1969).

Global Defense: U. S. Military Commitments Abroad, a Congressional Quarterly publication, September 1969.

Intervention and Revolution, by Richard Barnet (New American Library, 1969).

"National Security: Are We Asking the Right Questions?" by Paul Warnke, *Washington Monthly,* October 1969.

Problems of National Strategy–a reader ed. by Henry Kissinger (Praeger, 1965), Part I.

The Anti-Communist Impulse, by Michael Parenti (Random House, 1969).

III. FORTIFYING THE STATE

The Forrestal Diaries, ed. by Walter Millis (Viking Press, 1951).

The Warfare State, by Fred J. Cook (Collier, 1966), ch. 2 and 3.

The Military Establishment, by John Swomley (Beacon Press, 1964), ch. 1–8.

The Roots of American Foreign Policy, by Gabriel Kolko (Beacon Press, 1969).

Present at the Creation, by Dean Acheson (Norton, 1969).

Corporations and the Cold War, ed. by David Horowitz (Monthly Review Press, 1970), papers by Domhoff, Gardner, Williams, and Eakins.

The Politics of Military Unification, by Demetrios Carley (Columbia University Press, 1966).

IV. THE ARMS RACE

The Weapons Culture, by Ralph Lapp (Penguin, 1969).

"The Dynamics of the Arms Race," by George Rathjens, *Scientific American,* April 1969.

"Military Technology and National Security," by Herbert F. York, *Scientific American,* August 1969.

"Nixon and the Arms Race: The Bomber Boondoggle," by I. F. Stone, *New York Review of Books,* January 2, 1969.

"How Much Is Enough?" by I. F. Stone, *New York Review of Books,* March 27, 1969.

"The Usury of War," by Richard Kaufman, *The Nation,* May 26, 1969.

"Our First-Strike Capability," by Morton Kondrake, *Washington Monthly,* June 1969.

V. COUNTERINSURGENCY

The Guerrilla and How to Fight Him, ed. by Lt. Col. T. N. Green (Praeger, 1962), section I on Theory and the Threat.

The Weapons of World War III, by John Tompkins (Doubleday, 1966).

The Green Berets, by Robin Moore (Dell, 1965).

"Confessions of a Green Beret," by William Pfaff, *Commentary,* January 1970.

"Air War: Laos," by Peter Scott, *Ramparts,* Feb. 1970.

The Invisible Government, by David Wise and Thomas Ross (Random House, 1964).

Weapons for Counterinsurgency, by NARMIC, a project of the American Friends Service Committee, copies $1.00, 160 N. Fifteenth Street, Philadelphia, Pa.

"Green Berets and the CIA," by Fletcher Prouty, *New Republic,* August 30, 1969.

VI. THE DEFENSE ECONOMY

The Economics of Military Procurement–report of the Subcommittee on Economy in Government of the Joint Economic Committee, May 1969.

"Billion-Dollar Grab Bag," by Richard Kaufman, *The Nation,* March 17, 1969.

"Arms and the American Economy: A Domestic Convergence Hypothesis," by Murray Weidenbaum, *American Economic Review,* vol. 58, May 1968.

"Concentration and Competition in the Military Market," by Murray Weidenbaum, *Quarterly Review of Economics and Business,* Vol. 8, spring 1968.

Pentagon Capitalism, by Seymour Melman (McGraw-Hill, 1970).

The Pentagon, by C. L. Mollenhoff (Putnam, 1967), Ch. 25.

"American Arms Abroad," by George Thayer, *Washington Monthly,* January 1970.

"The U.S.: Supplier of Weapons to the World," by Eugene J. McCarthy, *Saturday Review,* July 9, 1966.

The Economics of Defense in the Nuclear Age, by C. Hitch and R. McKean (Harvard University Press, 1960).

VII. SCIENCE AND THE UNIVERSITIES

In the Name of Science, by H. L. Nieburg (Quadrangle Books, 1966).

The Politics of Science, ed. by W. R. Nelson (Oxford University Press, 1968).

The University-Military Complex, by Mike Klare (North American Congress on Latin America, Box 57, Cathedral Station, New York, N.Y. 10025).

VIII. CONGRESS

"The Military Committees," by Seymour Hersh, *Washington Monthly,* April 1969.

"Why the Pentagon Pays Homage to John Cornelius Stennis," by James K. Batten, *The New York Times Magazine,* Nov. 23, 1969.

"Rivers Delivers," by Don Oberdorfer, *The New York Times Magazine,* August 29, 1965.

"Military Mountain," by Robert Sherrill, *The Nation,* Feb. 9, 1970.

"Who Won the Debate?" by Richard Kaufman, *The Nation,* Feb. 17, 1970.

"The Supineness of the Senate," by I. F. Stone, *New York Review of Books,* Feb. 13, 1969.

"U. S. Security Agreements and Commitments Abroad," *Hearings Before a Special Subcommittee of the Senate Foreign Relations Committee,* Part I, Sept. 20, Oct. 1, 1969.

The Case Against Congress, by Drew Pearson and Jack Anderson (Pocket Books, 1969).

Congress and Foreign Policy-Making, by James A. Robinson (Dorsey Press, 1962).

"Congressional-Executive Relations and the Foreign Policy Consensus," by Roger Hilsman, *American Political Science Review,* Sept. 1958.

IX. CBW

Chemical and Biological Warfare: America's Hidden Arsenal, by Seymour Hersh (Doubleday-Anchor, 1969).

The Ultimate Folly, by Richard McCarthy (Vintage Books, 1969).

X. THE COSTS OF NATIONAL SECURITY

"The Monetary and Real Costs of Defense," by E. Benoit, *American Economic Review,* 1968.

"The Price of War," by Bruce Russet, *Trans-Action,* October 1969.

"Vietnam: The 200-Year Mortgage," by James Clayton, *The Nation,* May 26, 1969.

"CONUS Intelligence: The Army Watches Civilian Politics," by Christopher Pyle, *Washington Monthly,* January 1970.

"The Militarization of the American Economy," by Charles Nathanson, printed in *Corporations and the Cold War,* ed. by D. Horowitz (Monthly Review Press, 1970).

"The Military Budget and National Priorities," *Hearings Before the Subcommittee on Economy in Government of the Joint Economic Committee,* June 1969.

Our Depleted Society, by Seymour Melman (Delta, 1966).

XI. CONVERSION OR CHAOS?

How to Control the Military, by John K. Galbraith (Signet, 1969).

"The Case for Cutting Defense Spending," by Juan Cameron, *Fortune,* August 1969.

"The Authoritarian Prescription," by William D. Phelan, *The Nation,* November 3, 1969.

"Decade Ready for a Dustbin," by Carl Oglesby, *Liberation,* July–Aug. 1969.

The Age of Imperalism, by Harry Magdoff (Monthly Review Press, 1969).

"Conversion of Industry from a Military to a Civilian Economy," series edited by Seymour Melman (Praeger, 1970).